The Enigma of the Gift

The Enigma of the Gift

MAURICE GODELIER

Translated by Nora Scott

The University of Chicago Press

First published in English in 1999 by the
University of Chicago Press and by Polity Press
in association with Blackwell Publishers Ltd.

Published with the assistance of the French Ministry of Culture.

Printed in Great Britain

08 07 06 05 04 03 02 01 00 99   12345

ISBN 0-226-30044-7 (cloth)
ISBN 0-226-30045-5 (paperback)

Library of Congress Cataloging-in-Publication Data

Godelier, Maurice.
   [L'énigme du don.   English]
   The enigma of the gift / Maurice Godelier : translated by Nora
Scott
      p.   cm
   Includes bibliographical reference and index.
   ISBN 0-226-30044-7 (alk. paper). — ISBN 0-226-30045-5 (pbk.
alk. paper)
      1. Ceremonial exchange. 2. Gifts. 3. Economic anthropology.
   4. Mauss, Marcel. 1872–1950. Essai sur le don. English.
   I. Title.
   GN449,8,G63   1998
   394 — dc21   98-34500
                                                        CIP

This book is printed on acid-free paper.

Contents

Acknowledgements

The author and publishers wish to thank the following for permission to use copyright material:

Cambridge University Press and Librairie Arthème Fayard for material from Maurice Godelier, *The Making of Great Men: Male Domination and Power Among the New Guinea Baruya*, trans. Robert Swyer (1986). Copyright © 1982 Librairie Arthème Fayard, translation copyright © 1986 Cambridge University Press and Maison Des Sciences De L'Homme.

Routledge for material from Marcel Mauss, *The Gift: The Form and Reasons for Exchange in Archaic Societies*, trans. W. D. Halls (1990); and Claude Lévi-Strauss, *Introduction to the Work of Marcel Mauss*, trans. Felicity Baker (1987) Routledge and Kegan Paul.

Felicity Baker for the use of her translation of Lévi-Strauss' *Introduction to the Work of Marcel Mauss*.

Every effort has been made to trace the copyright holders but if any have been inadvertently overlooked the publishers will be pleased to make the necessary arrangements at the first opportunity.

Introduction
Concerning Things that are Given, Things that are Sold and Things that must not be Given or Sold, but Kept

∾

Why this book? Why yet another analysis of gift-exchange, of its role in the production and reproduction of social ties, of its changing place and importance in the diverse forms of society that coexist on the face of this earth or which have come and gone over the course of time? Because gift-giving exists everywhere, even if it is not the same everywhere. But kinship also exists everywhere, and religion and politics. So why gift-giving? Why this book?

The present work grew out of the encounter between and the converging pressures from two contexts: one sociological, the present state of the Western society to which I belong; and the other, which is personal in another way and which is the occupation I chose to exercise, a professional context, a state of the theoretical problems today debated by the anthropological community, of which I am a member.

The sociological context is not peculiar to me. It is there for everyone to see, it surrounds us all, and, like many, while I am part of it, I did not choose it. I am talking about our Western society, which is in the process of excluding more and more people, an economic system which, in order to remain dynamic and competitive, has to "downsize" its firms, reduce costs, increase productivity, and therefore must decrease the work-force through massive lay-offs and unemployment. It is hoped that this is a temporary solution, but for many it is turning out to be permanent. And lined up at the door of a saturated job market, there are young job-seekers: many are in for a long wait, and a small number will wait forever. For them, this is the start of a strange social existence, a lifetime of welfare of one kind or other, unless of course they find some way to earn money without working. Then there are those who do not wait to be dismissed, and who simply disappear into the shadow-zones of society, the underground zones where there is work, and money to be had without declaring it, or money to be had without having either to work or to declare it. For this is the way our society functions.

While in other parts of the world you must belong to a group in order to live – to a clan, a village or a tribal community – and it is this group which helps you live, in our society, the family does not provide each member with lifelong conditions of existence, however strong the solidarity may be. Everyone must have money to live, and most people have to work for it, but one earns a living as a separate individual. Furthermore, for the majority in our society, working also means working for someone else, for the owners of the companies which have hired them.

Without money, without income, there is no social existence, no existence at all in fact, material or physical. Hence the problems. People's *social* existence depends on the economy, and they lose much more than employment when they lose their job or when they cannot find one. The paradox of capitalist societies is that the economy is the main source of exclusion, but that this exclusion not only excludes people from the economy, it excludes or threatens ultimately to exclude them from society itself. And for those excluded from the economy, the chances of being included once more are increasingly slim.

The economy of a capitalist country does not stand alone. It is part of what has become a worldwide system which exerts constant pressure and constraints on all of its sectors and firms, every one of which is obliged to maximize profits by fighting its way to the top of competitive national and international markets.

The paradox is that this economy which excludes massive numbers of people also charges society with reintegrating them, not into the economy – except for a small percentage – but into society. This is our present situation. We live in societies whose "social fabric," as they say, has been "rent," societies that are breaking down into increasingly watertight compartments.

And given the role of the state in many Western capitalist societies, it is the state that is called upon to recompose society, to bridge the gaps, to reduce the "social fractures." And yet the state cannot do this alone. This is the bundle of contradictions and incapacities that constitutes the context in which, increasingly and from all directions, we are hearing the call to give. It is a "forced" gift when the state passes new so-called "solidarity taxes," compelling the majority of taxpayers to share with the most needy in an attempt to stop up some of the breaches the economy is constantly opening in society. This is an economy from which the state has chosen to withdraw, as it has chosen to retire bit by bit from other areas of social life. But the state is not an abstraction, an institution from another planet. The state governs, and it is what those who govern make it.

This is the context in which first hundreds and then thousands of people have taken to begging in the streets, many of them homeless; this is the context in which the call has been formulated and then gone out to give, to share. The request for gifts was first an appeal to suppliers, and then it began to organize the resources. Countless "charitable" organizations sprang up, from soup kitchens to supermarket collection boxes where potential donors were asked to be generous and to share, not their money directly, but a part of what they had bought with this money for their own consumption.

Charity is back, that virtue which Marcel Mauss, in his major 1925 article, "Essai sur le don," described as being, after centuries of Christianity and religious charitable institutions, "still wounding for him who has accepted it."[1] Today, for many of those in need, it is still humiliating to beg, to accost passers-by, passengers on the subway. These people prefer the pretense of earning a living by selling papers in the street, newspapers which are printed for the purpose and rarely read.

But our society has become secularized, and although charity may be back in fashion, it is no longer seen as a theological virtue, a religious act. For the majority of believers or non-believers, it is a gesture of solidarity between human beings. The need had diminished when the number of the socially excluded fell and social justice increased; it surfaces again and becomes necessary when the excluded populations increase and the state can no longer singlehandedly reduce the injustices, the isolation and the neglect.

And yet it was only a few years ago, with the fall of the Berlin Wall and the sudden collapse of the "socialist" regimes spawned by the revolution early in the twentieth century, which had maintained that the people would manage its own destiny, that the economy would be harnessed to serve the needs of humankind, but which subsequently developed into an insufferable combination of planned economy and dictatorship masquerading as "popular democracy," that some prophesied that the "end of history" was nigh, that at last we were going to see extending, from one end of the earth to the other, the Western social system, the product of what is actually a recent marriage, even in Europe, between laissez-faire capitalism in the economic sphere and parliamentary democracy in the political domain.

To reasonable people and those with a realistic outlook, this system seemed, not the best of all possible worlds to be sure, but the least bad, and therefore the most likely to expand to the far reaches of Africa, Oceania and tomorrow to China, and the most likely to endure. This would be the "end of history": if the market economy was left to its own devices and the state withdrew as much as possible from the greatest possible number of areas, leaving individuals, groups, and firms to come to some arrangement among themselves, everything would work better, not least of all the world's societies. With the failure of those societies whose planning had been in the hands not only of the state but of a caste that had appropriated the state for its own ends, the old myth of laissez-faire capitalism with its belief in a hidden god, an invisible hand guiding the market in the best interests of society towards the best distribution of goods among all of its members, gained a new lease of life and a seeming victory. Since then it has been invoked to urge patience and the courage to wait, to let the economy work itself out. Some day all will get their reward. In the meantime, however, life must go on, and for life to go on, people must give.

This is a far cry from Marcel Mauss and the "Essai sur le don," in which we see a man, a socialist who has just lost half his friends in the First World War, take a stand at the same time against Bolshevism, contending that the market must be maintained, and against laissez-faire capitalism, asking the state to intervene and expressing the hope that the rich might rediscover the generosity of the ancient Celtic or German noblemen, so that society might not fall prisoner to the "cold reasoning of the merchant, the banker, and the capitalist."[2] Mauss was outlining a "social-democratic" program before its time, which France would adopt at the time of the Popular Front and which, following the Second World War, would be taken up by Great Britain, Sweden, and others. Mauss based his conclusion not only on his own experience of French and European society, but on years of scouring the literature concerning the role of gift-exchange in present-day non-Western societies and in Western societies of the past, Germanic, Celtic, and so on.

Here is where our paths converged, producing the second, professional context which incited me to re-examine the phenomenon of gift-exchange. But before going into what moved me to this decision, I would like to say a few more words about the pressure everyone feels to "give," about the call "to give."

This call has been "modernized." Whether sent out by a secular or a religious source, it is now "mediatized" and "bureaucratized." It uses the media to heighten "awareness," to move, to touch, to appeal to people's generosity, to the idealized solidarity reigning in an abstract humankind located somewhere beyond all differences of culture, class, or caste, language or identity. Appeals are made to be ever more generous in the fight against AIDS or cancer, appeals for the victims of Sarajevo. In short, appeals on behalf of all victims of disease or human conflicts. The West is in a sense constantly present in the front lines of every war on evil. Through the media, everyone is exposed to the spectacle of exclusion, of individuals and nations crushed by catastrophes, poverty, civil war, genocide. In a word, it is not only the suffering of friends and relatives, it is the suffering of the world at large that cries out for our gifts, our generosity.

Of course in this new context, it is no longer possible to give to someone you know, and even less so to expect anything other than impersonal gratitude. The giving of gifts has become an act that creates a bond between abstract subjects: a donor who loves humankind and a recipient who, for a few months, the duration of a charity drive, embodies the world in distress. This is a far cry from the situation in our industrial and urban societies only recently.

At that time gift-giving was caught between two powerful agents: the market and the state. The market – job market, goods and services market – is the site of self-interested relations, of accountancy and calculation. The state is the space of impersonal relations of obedience and respect for the law. Presents used to be made between close friends and relatives, both as a consequence of and a testimony to the links binding them together; these imposed reciprocal relations on the participants, expressed by the exchange of gifts, given without "counting," and above all without expecting anything in return. For the mark of the gift between close friends and relatives, then as now, is not the absence of obligations, it is the absence of "calculation."

I read the "Essai sur le don" for the first time in 1957, together with Lévi-Strauss' "Introduction à l'œuvre de Mauss," which preceded the essay. I was not yet a convert to anthropology but still a philosopher, having spent more time reading Aristotle, Marx, Kant, and Husserl than Durkheim and Mauss, even though the latter were regarded as the fathers of French sociology. But already Paris was talking about a new, more rigorous approach to social phenomena, called "structuralism," which claimed to go beyond Marxism and the British functionalist school. This "structuralism" was the approach used by Lévi-Strauss in his first major work, published in 1949, *Les Structures élémentaires de la parenté*; the following year he wrote his preface to Mauss as a case for the superiority of structural analysis as a method of dealing with social phenomena. The notes I made in 1957 reflect the enthusiasm that gripped me as I read these two pieces.

With the "Essai sur le don," I felt as though I had suddenly emerged onto the bank of an immense tranquil river bearing along a mass of facts and customs plucked from a multitude of societies stretching from the Pacific islands to India, from British Columbia to China, and springing from the most varied epochs, from archaic Roman antiquity to the present that Mauss knew, that of Boas' Kwakiutl fieldwork before the First World War or Malinowski's stay with the Trobrianders during it. Even more references to more facts were piled at the foot of each page, as though the author had placed them there as a reminder and planned to come back for them at a later time. All this material dealt with the various forms and complexities of gift-giving, and were carried by a strong current that had torn them from their numerous shores and swept them along. This current was the impetus of a two-pronged question that Mauss had formulated in an attempt to decipher the enigma of gift-giving: "What rule *of law and of interest*, in societies of a backward or archaic type, compels the gift that has been received to be obligatorily reciprocated. What power resides in *the object* given that causes its recipient to give it back?"[3]

An odd question, given that Mauss would go on to show that the act of giving is actually a concatenation of three obligations: giving, receiving (i.e. accepting), and making a return gift once one has accepted. This was a simple, powerful hypothesis which, by postulating the interlinking nature of these three acts, seemed to forbid considering them separately. However both of Mauss' questions focused on only one of the three obligations, that of reciprocating the gift, as though the other two were self-evident. Furthermore, the formulation of the second question seems already to contain the answer to the first: Mauss was obviously evoking the existence of a spirit in the thing which compelled the recipient to return it. In short, it is as if he did not regard the existence of a rule of law or of interest as a sufficient reason and felt the need to add a "religious" dimension.

Lévi-Strauss saw the hole in the reasoning and headed for it, castigating Mauss for having strayed from his analysis and having failed to apply the same method to all three steps, which form a whole: this was a methodological error a structuralist would never have committed, and which stemmed from the fact that Mauss had let down his guard, had momentarily forgotten to think as a scientist, and let himself be "mystified" by an "indigenous" theory.[4] At this point, Lévi-Strauss proposed a global explanation of social phenomena which made the entire social domain a combination of forms of exchange, the origins of which were to be sought in the deep-seated unconscious structures of the mind, in its capacity for symbolization. Instead of being presented with a sociological study on the origin of symbols, the reader was offered the sweeping vision of a "symbolic origin of society." It is not hard to understand my enthusiasm at such critical vigilance, such brilliant thinking, such visionary perspectives on gift-giving, exchanges, the unconscious, the origin of society.

Since this first reading of the "Essai sur le don," I have become an anthropologist and have spent many years doing fieldwork in Melanesia, an area of the world that provided Mauss with some of his richest and most eloquent material through the works of Seligman, Thurnwald, and many others, foremost among them Malinowski, who worked in New Guinea, in the Trobriand Islands. I myself later spent many years in a highland valley in the interior of New Guinea working among the Baruya.

It was there that I encountered non-Western forms of gift-exchange, a new context which was to make me reopen the case of gift-exchange and reassess the legacies of both Mauss and Lévi-Strauss on this as well as other matters. For I had set out for New Guinea with two ideas. The first was that, while gifts are exchanged the world over, this is not simply a means of sharing what one has but also of fighting with what one has; this was the idea – which I attributed to Mauss – that the logic of gift and counter-gift culminated in the potlatch. The second idea, inspired by Lévi-Strauss, was that society is founded on exchange and exists only through the combination of all sorts of exchange – women (kinship), goods (economy), representations and words (culture). And I was laboring under the influence of yet a third conviction, also from Lévi-Strauss, which was that the symbolic dominated the imaginary as well as something else tentatively called the "real." For Lévi-Strauss, the symbol was in some cases more real than the "reality" it signified.

These self-evident truths soon began to unravel, but the entire process was a slow one. In the field, among the Baruya, I observed the giving of gifts and counter-gifts on the occasion of the exchange of women, but no sign of potlatch. On the contrary, everything in the logic of this society precluded the possibility of acquiring power through gifts and counter-gifts of wealth. Power did not go to Big Men, who amassed women and wealth, but to Great Men, who held the inherited powers present in the sacred objects and secret knowledge given to their ancestors by non-human divinities – the Sun, the forest spirits, and others. In sum, these objects are things the Baruya could neither sell nor give but which they must keep. But the Baruya knew about selling since they produced a kind of "money." I analyzed all this in *La Production des Grands Hommes*[5] and then went on to a more theoretical area, the analysis of kinship systems and relations. Once again, it gradually appeared to me that explaining these systems by the various ways in which men exchanged women was too reductive; it left many facts unexplained and it mutilated reality.

It was then that my sociological and theoretical contexts fit together; what made it all click and spurred me to write a book on gift-exchange was my reading, in 1994, of Annette Weiner's *Inalienable Possessions: The Paradox of Keeping-while-Giving*.[6] I had read this author's earlier publications, but here she took her ideas much further. As a Trobriand specialist returning to the same phenomenon, the kula, fifty years after Malinowski's initial study, Annette Weiner had uncovered new facts which shed light on some problems that had been left unresolved by Malinowski and Mauss. In particular she showed how it was possible to keep an object while at the same time giving it. One part of the enigma of the gift was thus solved. In addition, I shared Annette Weiner's interest in objects that cannot be given, things that are sacred. At this point a light dawned, and I decided to re-examine gift-exchange with respect to this basic fact: there are some things which must not be given and which must not be sold either.

It was from this angle that I reread Mauss, Lévi-Strauss, and many others. When I had finished, the following hypothesis seemed self-evident: no society, no identity can survive over time and provide a foundation for the individuals or groups that make up a society if there are no fixed points, realities that are exempted (provisionally but lastingly) from the exchange of gifts or from trade. What are these realities? Are they merely the sacred objects found in every religion? Is there not some general relationship between political power and something called "the sacred," even in secular societies in which power is not conferred by the gods but comes from humans who have founded it on a constitution they have *given* themselves? But what is contained in a sacred object? By whom was it "given"? In a word, the entire burden of analysis had shifted from things that are given to things that are kept, and this shift illuminated the nature of that universally familiar thing which seems to endanger the practice of gift-exchange and to penetrate the sacred only to profane and destroy it: money. Such is the strange itinerary which enabled me to work back to those things that are repressed and whose repression is perhaps the condition of life in society. It has been a long, hard journey. Let us therefore begin with Mauss and attempt to assess his legacy.

1

The Legacy of Mauss

~∞~

A masterwork in chiaroscuro

The simple reason behind a reputation: a powerful global vision of gift-exchange as a concatenation of three obligations

In what terms or from what angle did Mauss broach the question of gift-exchange? The following formulation sums up his approach: Why is it that, in so many societies, at so many periods and in such different contexts, individuals and/or groups feel obliged not only to give, or when someone gives to them to receive, but also feel obliged, when they have received, to reciprocate what has been given and to reciprocate either the same thing (or its equivalent), or something more or better?

It was in seeking to answer this question that he amassed the material contained in his book and that, under the impact of his question, these details quickened with new meaning. Like most readers of the "Essai sur le don," what made the greatest impression on me was seeing Mauss demonstrate the existence, within the most varied forms of exchanges and services, of a single power embodied in three separate but interlinking obligations which drew persons and things into a movement that sooner or later brought the things back around to the persons, and reconnected the point of arrival of all these gifts and counter-gifts with their original point of departure.

Mauss described this power as laying hold of both persons and things; he was speaking of course of societies where there seemed to be no absolute boundary between the two, and therefore no radical separation. Things were an extension of persons, and people identified with the things they possessed and exchanged. Mauss described worlds where everything passes and repasses "as if there were a constant exchange of a spiritual matter, including things and men, between clans and individuals, distributed between social ranks, the sexes, and the generations."[1] We learned that "things create bonds between souls, for the thing itself has a soul, is part of the soul." And we felt as though we understood why, when a thing was given, it carried away something of the person and "wanted" to return sooner or later to the person who had initially ceded it. All seemed clear, providing, of course, the reader shared this type of belief and went so far as to regard it as a "scientific" explanation. That was the rub, and that was to be the focus of Lévi-Strauss' criticism.

We are now going to re-examine the problem step by step, beginning with the fact that, before a gift can be received, it must first be given. Now even if the existence of an in-dwelling spirit in things may seem to explain the obligation to return gifts, it does not, it seems to me, account for the obligation to give them. What then is involved in "giving"?

Gift-giving, a double-edged relationship

In explanation of why people give, Mauss advanced a slightly less "spiritual" hypothesis, which appears explicitly in his explanation of the potlatch. He postulates that *what creates the obligation to give is that giving creates obligations.* To give is voluntarily to transfer something that belongs to you to someone who you think cannot refuse to accept it. The donor can be a group or an individual acting on his own behalf or on that of a group. Likewise, the recipient can be an individual or a group or someone who receives the gift as a representative of a group.

A gift is therefore an individual or collective voluntary act which may or may not have been solicited by the person or persons who receive it. In the West, we place more value on unsolicited gifts. But this is not a universal attitude. In many societies, and in the past in certain of our own social milieux, a suitor was supposed officially to ask the girl's family, and in some cases her clan, for her "hand" in marriage.

I suggest that, at this stage, we set aside the question of specific social contexts which might compel certain individuals or groups to give or receive, and that we assume that both givers and receivers are of *equivalent* social rank before *the gift.* Now what happens *as soon as* the gift passes from one to the other?

The act of giving seems to create simultaneously a twofold relationship between giver and receiver. A relationship of *solidarity* because the giver shares what he has, or what he is, with the receiver; and a relationship of *superiority* because the one who receives the gift and accepts it places himself in the debt of the one who has given it, thereby becoming indebted to the giver and to a certain extent becoming his "dependant," at least for as long as he has not "given back" what he was given.

Giving thus seems to establish a difference and an inequality of status between donor and recipient, which can in certain instances become a hierarchy: if this hierarchy already exists, then the gift expresses and legitimizes it. Two opposite movements are thus contained in a single act. The gift decreases the distance between the protagonists because it is a form of sharing, and it increases the social distance between them because one is now indebted to the other. It is easy to see the formidable array of maneuvers and strategies virtually contained in the practice of gift-giving, and the gamut of contradictory interests that can be served. By its very nature, gift-giving is an ambivalent practice which brings together or is capable of bringing together opposing emotions and forces. It can be, simultaneously or successively, an act of generosity or of violence; in the latter case, however, the violence is disguised as a disinterested gesture, since it is committed by means of and in the form of sharing.

The giving of gifts may ward off direct violence or physical, material, and social subordination, but it may also stand in their stead. And there are countless examples of societies where individuals unable to repay their debts are forced to sell themselves or their children into slavery, ending up as the property, the "possession" of those who had bestowed gifts on them. From this it is clear that, of the two components (sharing and debt), of the two movements contained and combined in gift-giving, it is the second (the distancing) which probably has the greater impact on social life when it is organized around various forms of competition for access to wealth, power, knowledge, or ritual.

It is also clear that the very duality and ambivalence involved in gift-giving create the ideal conditions for it to flourish in societies which operate primarily on the principle of the production and maintenance of personal relationships between the individuals and groups that comprise the society: relations of kinship, production, power, and so forth. From the standpoint of comparative sociology, these conditions can be expected to prevail in societies without castes, ranked classes, or a state to govern them. In such societies, gifts are exchanged between protagonists who enjoyed a potentially or genuinely equivalent social rank before the gift. And that is precisely what we assumed in the "textbook case" we have just analyzed.

Alternatively, in societies based on rank, caste, or class, gift-giving, while widespread, necessarily takes on different forms and meanings, depending on whether it is practiced between persons of equivalent rank or condition (which brings us back to the preceding example) or between persons of radically different status. In the latter case, gifts have a different meaning according to whether the giver is of inferior rank to the receiver or vice versa. Here I would like to note a point to which I will return later: giving to a superior does not necessarily imply that the recipient is a human being. In all societies – whether or not they are divided into ranks, castes, or classes – humans make gifts to beings they regard as their superiors: divinities, nature spirits, spirits of the dead. People pray to them, make offerings, and sometimes even "sacrifice" possessions, or a life. This is the famous "fourth obligation" that constitutes gift-exchange, which Mauss mentioned without going into further detail and which was generally forgotten in subsequent discussions. And yet it is the articulation between his "Essai sur le don" (1925) and his "Essai sur la nature et la fonction du sacrifice" (1899), written and published in collaboration with Henri Hubert. Having made these remarks, I will now argue that, in analyzing a gift, whatever it may be, one needs to consider the relationship that existed between the giver and the receiver *before* the former made a gift to the latter.

Here I would like to dwell for a moment on the fact that the giving of a gift is a "personal" act. This is why, whatever the society, whether ranked or not, gift-giving occurs in all areas of social life in which personal relationships *continue* to play a dominant role. Furthermore, the "personal" character of the gift does not necessarily disappear when the giver and receiver no longer entertain direct personal relations, do not know each other, and are linked by intermediaries. For example, at the end of the twentieth century, the flame of charity once kept alive by various religious institutions of all denominations has now been passed to non-governmental organizations and sometimes to the state itself. National drives are launched to collect funds for cancer or AIDS research, or to send convoys of food and medicine to Bosnia.

Charity has become a secular affair, and once it turned to the media, it became part game-show as well; the telethon has several features in common with the potlatch. As in potlatch, for instance there is the appeal to outgive others, one city more than another, one company more than another, and there is the hope that the total will surpass that of preceding years. As in potlatch, too, it is the practice to announce the names of individuals, towns, and companies who have shown the greatest generosity.

So even in societies where relations between individuals are becoming less and less personal, gift-giving often retains its "personal" character, even if the persons have become fairly abstract; this personal character is associated not only with the donors but also with those who receive the gifts. Virtual representatives of all of the beneficiaries are always shown on the program: children suffering from genetically transmitted diseases or AIDS victims are interviewed, and they arouse compassion and the desire to help, to give. Next to the victims sit the representatives of the agencies appealing to public generosity, who undertake to act on behalf of the many donors, as stand-ins.

Today, then, even in the huge industrial or state-run societies that form the core of the capitalist world, where the individual's personal value is constantly proclaimed, but where just as constantly individuals can be heard voicing regret at being overwhelmed by impersonal relations in all areas, gift-giving has lost nothing of its personal or voluntary nature. We will return to these points, but we may already work from the postulate that, in order for a gift to be genuine, the act of giving must be voluntary and personal; if not it immediately becomes something else, a tax, for example, or extortion.

But our modern capitalist societies stand at the opposite extreme to those Mauss analyzed in the "Essai sur le don." It is no exaggeration to say that our societies are deeply marked by "an economy and a moral code dominated by the market and profit"; and that the societies featured in the "Essai sur le don" appear to Mauss, by contrast, as deeply marked by "an economy and a moral code dominated by gift-giving." This does not mean that gift-giving societies did not know about commercial exchanges or that today's commercial societies have ceased giving gifts. The problem is to see in each case which principle *prevails* in the society and why.

Mauss obviously asked himself why certain societies were characterized by "an economy and a moral code dominated by gift-giving," and his answer was that such societies emerge when several conditions are present: the first is that *personal relations must play an important or even dominant role* in producing the social relations which constitute the framework of a society. However, Mauss saw this as a necessary but not a sufficient condition. These social relations also had to be such that the individuals and groups involved *had every interest, while reproducing themselves and their relationships, in appearing disinterested.* And the interest of giving-while-appearing-disinterested resided ultimately in one fundamental characteristic of gift-giving, which is that, in these societies, what *creates the obligation to give is that giving creates obligations.* Here we have the first three components of Mauss' theoretical reconstruction of the sociological basis of gift-giving.

But paradoxically, while these three conditions were perhaps enough to explain why one gives gifts, they were not sufficient to explain why one reciprocates. There was still something enigmatic about gift-giving, or at least the fact of giving remained an enigma. It was at this point that Mauss set out in search of one more condition, one that was necessary even if it was not sufficient. He thought he had found this condition in the belief that *things given have a soul that compels them to return to their original owner who gave them away.*

The enigma of the gift and Mauss' solution

The enigma was, then, that while it was relatively easy for Mauss to understand why one must give, it was hard for him to see why one must give in return, and more particularly give back the very same thing one was given. Why reciprocate the same? We see that, by his very manner of looking at things, Mauss had altered the status of the three obligations. Instead of each being the equivalent of the others in that each is equally necessary, one, the third, which "obliges one to reciprocate the present received," now appears more important in practice and harder to grasp in theory than the other two. But he seems to have resolved the enigma thus created by positing the existence of a power in things which makes them wish to circulate and to return to their original owner. His solution therefore lies in "spiritual mechanisms," in moral and religious reasons, in beliefs that would endow objects with a soul, a spirit that makes them want to return to their place of birth:

> The most important feature among these spiritual mechanisms is clearly one that obliges a person to reciprocate the present that has been received. Now, the moral and religious reason for this constraint is nowhere more apparent than in Polynesia. Let us study it in greater detail, and we will plainly see what force impels one to reciprocate the thing received.[2]

This explains Mauss' analysis of the Polynesian concepts of *hau* and *mana*, and his gratitude to the Maori sage, Tamati Ranaipiri:

> Concerning the *hau*, the spirit of things ... Tamati Ranaipiri ... gives us, completely by chance, and entirely without prejudice, the *key to the problem* ... What imposes obligation in the present received and exchanged, is the fact that the thing received is not inactive. Even when it has been abandoned by the giver, it still possesses something of him. Through it the giver has a hold over the beneficiary ... In reality, it is the *hau* that *wishes to return to its birthplace*, to the sanctuary of the forest and the clan, and to the owner ... in Maori law, the legal tie, a tie occurring through things, is one between souls, because the thing itself possesses a soul ... Invested with life, often possessing individuality, it seeks to return to its "place of origin", or to produce, on behalf of the clan and the native soil from which it sprang, an equivalent to replace it.[3]

We will not now go into the question of whether or not this is what Tamati Ranaipiri really meant. Raymond Firth (in 1929) and later Marshall Sahlins (in 1976) have long since shown that Mauss quoted Ranaipiri out of context, which was the description of a ritual addressed to the spirit of the forest before the start of bird hunting. In so doing, Mauss may well have changed Ranaipiri's original meaning.

But such is the thread of his interpretation, and in another context, analyzing the potlatch, Mauss returns to the same argument: "One can push the analysis further and demonstrate that in the things exchanged during the potlatch, a power is present that forces gifts to be passed around, to be given and returned."[4]

And writing about the precious copper objects which circulated in Haida and Kwakiutl potlatches, Mauss stresses that these coppers "have a power of attraction that is felt by other copper objects, just as wealth attracts wealth ... They are *alive and move autonomously*, and inspire other coppers to do so."[5] To be sure, Mauss reminds us that this is true only in the framework of a mythological vision of the cosmos and society:

> Often the myth identifies them all, the spirits that have given the copper objects, their owners, and the copper objects themselves. It is impossible to distinguish what makes the strength of spirit in the one and wealth in the other: the copper object speaks, and grumbles. It demands to be given away, to be destroyed; it is covered with blankets to keep it warm, just as the chief is buried under the blankets that he is to share out.[6]

Mauss indeed thought that, with the account of Tamati Ranaipiri, Elsdon Best's Maori informant, he had found the answer to the famous questions that open the "Essai sur le don" and which I recalled in the Introduction. But as I have said, his analysis contained a flaw and it was this flaw that Claude Lévi-Strauss was to seize upon.

Mauss mystified by indigenous theories: Lévi-Strauss' critique

Lévi-Strauss writes:

> Does this property [that forces gifts to circulate] exist objectively, like a physical property of the exchanged goods? Obviously not. ... So this property must be conceived in subjective terms. But then we find ourselves faced with an alternative: either the property is nothing other than the act of exchange itself as represented in indigenous thinking, in which case we are going round in a circle, or else it is a power of a different nature, in which case the act of exchange becomes, in relation to this power, a secondary phenomenon. The only way to avoid the dilemma would have been to perceive that the primary, fundamental phenomenon is exchange itself ... the mistake was to take the discrete operations for the basic phenomenon.[7]

And he goes on, indicating the direction the search might take:

> *Hau* is not the ultimate explanation for exchange; it is the conscious form whereby men of a given society, in which the problem had particular importance, apprehended an unconscious necessity whose explanation lies elsewhere. ... Once the indigenous conception has been isolated, it must be reduced by an objective critique so as to reach the underlying reality. We have very little chance of finding that reality in conscious formulations; a better chance in unconscious mental structures to which institutions give us access, but a better chance yet, in language.[8]

Basically Mauss had failed because he was too empirical and because he, the theoretician of religious beliefs, of magic, had fallen victim to the very beliefs he claimed to be analyzing; somehow in his mind these had suddenly taken on the value of a scientific explanation:

> In the "Essai sur le don", Mauss strives to construct a whole out of parts; and as that is manifestly not possible, he has to add to the mixture an additional quantity which gives him the illusion of

squaring his account. This quantity is *hau*. Are we not dealing with a mystification, an effect quite often produced in the minds of ethnographers by indigenous people?[9]

Mauss mystified! Mauss caught with his methodological guard down! An overly empirical Mauss and facing him a Claude Lévi-Strauss who had spotted the flaw and claimed to explain not only what the indigenous concepts of *hau* and *mana* are not, but what they truly are: signifiers "in [themselves] devoid of meaning and thus susceptible of receiving any meaning at all,"[10] or in the terms that have since become famous, "floating signifiers" or "a symbol in its pure state."[11] And all this closely reasoned to reach a conclusion which reveals a sweeping vision of the "symbolic origin of society," explaining why social life is built on "exchange" and is composed of symbolic systems (marriage rules, economic relations, art, science, religion) articulated by unconscious mental structures.

The reader will understand the enthusiasm that seized me as a young philosopher in the presence of such critical vigilance, seeing the research perspectives thus opened on the origin of society, exchange, the unconscious. One had the impression that Mauss had missed the "decisive turn" that would have made him the "Novum Organum of the twentieth-century social sciences," and that Lévi-Strauss on the other hand had successfully negotiated it. And yet with utmost modesty, the latter did not ascribe any of the merit to himself, but put it down to the "objective evolution which has occurred in the psychological and social sciences in the course of the last thirty years," and even maintained that his conception was "rigorously faithful to Mauss' thinking. In fact it is nothing other than Mauss' conception translated from its original expression in terms of [Aristotelian] class logic into the terms of a symbolic logic which summarises the most general laws of language."[12]

We will not linger over the question of whether, in claiming to be Mauss' faithful successor, Lévi-Strauss was acting in all good faith or whether he was seeking to mask the fact that his theories broke with those of Durkheim and Mauss. What is important is that Lévi-Strauss' text, which it must be said is superb, was at the time rightly regarded as the manifesto of the new "structuralism," whose strengths and limitations, whose successes and failures can be better measured today. With Lévi-Strauss, social life became a movement of constant exchanges in which words, wealth, and women circulated between individuals and groups; and we were invited to seek the origin of this movement beyond conscious thinking and explicitly avowed reasons, within the unconscious part of the human mind.

Re-examining Lévi-Strauss' critique of Marcel Mauss

Let us recall that, at the time of his critique, Lévi-Strauss had just published his first major work, *Les Structures élémentaires de la parenté* (1949), in which, putting to work the postulate that all social life is exchange and that society is better understood in terms of language than from the standpoint of any other paradigm, he developed two theses which began to unsettle a few received ideas. One was that kinship is based on exchange (the exchange of women by men). The other was that, between the two components of kinship – marriage and descent – the former outweighs the latter and provides the keys for understanding the diversity of kinship systems, the most elementary like the most complex.[13] It was during this period that Lévi-Strauss had his sweeping vision of a social anthropology: "by associating more and more closely with linguistics, eventually to make a vast science of communications, social anthropology can hope to benefit from the immense prospects opened up to linguistics itself, through the application of mathematical reasoning to the study of phenomena of communication."[14]

Today it would not occur to anyone to deny the fecundity of the marriage of anthropology with linguistics, mathematics, and communication theory, but the outcome of these encounters does not retroactively validate the general *philosophical* postulates which, in Lévi-Strauss' eyes, made them necessary. It was with these in mind that in 1949 Lévi-Strauss reread Mauss in preparation for introducing his work to the public. Here he performed a two-step maneuver. On the one hand, he privileged and adopted all the formulas Mauss had used to describe in such lyrical terms the importance of gifts and exchanges in social life. Yet he completely disregarded the clear distinction Mauss made between two domains which divided the social sphere between them: the domain of alienable, exchangeable things and the domain of those inalienable things kept out of exchange, each of which corresponds to different types of social relations at different moments of the production and reproduction of society. On the other hand, Lévi-Strauss celebrates Mauss as seeming "rightly to be controlled by a logical certainty, namely, that *exchange* is the common denominator of a large number of apparently heterogeneous social activities,"[15] but criticizes him for having failed to perceive that "the *primary fundamental phenomenon* [of social life] is exchange itself."[16]

The same movement which causes Lévi-Strauss to adopt and to amplify certain of Mauss' claims about exchange also leads him to stress the importance of the symbolic in explaining social phenomena and to substitute it for the imaginary, with the result that he all but evacuates the theory of the sacred elaborated by Durkheim and Mauss at the turn of the century.[17] He does this in several stages, which we will follow. At the outset, there was his criticism of Mauss, which we can only share: "*Hau* is not the ultimate explanation for exchange; it is the conscious form whereby men of a given society, in which the problem had particular importance, apprehended an unconscious necessity whose explanation lies elsewhere."[18] Lévi-Strauss goes on to warn of what might happen were we to follow Mauss' approach:

> We would risk committing sociology to a dangerous path: even a path of destruction, if we then went one step further and reduced social reality to the conception that man – savage man, even – has of it. ... Then ethnography would dissolve into a verbose phenomenology, a falsely naïve mixture in which the apparent obscurities of indigenous thinking would only be brought to the forefront to cover the confusions of the ethnographer, which would otherwise be too obvious.[19]

Sage remarks, accompanied by a definition of scientific knowledge to which we can only adhere and which formulates the tasks of scientific investigation in terms very like those used by Marx a century earlier when he encountered the mystery of "commodity value" and showed that if, in its substance, the value of a commodity is the quantity of labor necessarily expended in its production and congealed in it, it is quite the opposite that appears to be the case. Commodities seem to possess a value in themselves, independent of the labor expended in their production.[20]

Lévi-Strauss writes in fact: "a full explanation of the object should account simultaneously for its own structure and for the representations through which our grasp of its properties is mediated."[21]

In the next section of his text he therefore attempts to define the "unconscious mental structure" at work behind the indigenous representations and the practice of gift-giving. As far as the unconscious goes, it should be noted that Lévi-Strauss singles out the underlying unconscious processes of the mind, refusing to

> go along with [Mauss] when he proceeds to seek the origin of the notion of *mana* in an order of realities different from the relationships that it helps to construct: in the order of feelings, of volitions and of beliefs, which, from the viewpoint of sociological explanation, are epiphenomena, or else mysteries; in any case, they are objects extrinsic to the field of investigation.[22]

Lévi-Strauss is clearly concerned to explain how people think and why they think as they do. He refuses, and rightly so to my mind, to follow Lévy-Bruhl when he claims that people think as they feel, and that primitive people are like little children or like madmen, incapable of distinguishing between the self and the outside world, between subject and object, and so on. What, then, in the unconscious of mental structures (and not in the unconscious of desire) is the source of the notions of *mana*, *hau*, and the like, and explains both their nature and their illusory character?

> [C]onceptions of the *mana* type are so frequent and so widespread that it is appropriate to wonder whether we are not dealing with a universal and permanent form of thought which, far from characterising certain civilisations, or archaic or semi-archaic so-called "stages" in the evolution of the human mind, might be a function of a certain way that the mind situates itself in the presence of things, which must therefore make an appearance whenever that mental situation is given.[23]

Confronted with this situation, the human mind, according to Lévi-Strauss, unconsciously sets about producing categories, following "itineraries traced once and for all in the innate structure of the human mind and in the particular and irreversible history of individuals or groups."[24] His task would therefore be, after Mauss, "to reach a sort of 'fourth dimension' of the mind, a level where the notions of 'unconscious category' and 'category of collective thinking' would be synonymous."[25]

If he were to succeed he would have discovered a part of the human being which not only could be said to be untouched by time but which would void of its content the idea that humankind has *evolved* and continues to do so in the irreversible history of the individual societies that comprise it. All that would remain would be the unconscious mind standing opposite the individual histories of societies and persons. But just what is this situation that confronts the mind and each time compels it to produce unconscious categories, of which the concepts *hau*, *mana*, *orenda*, and so on are merely one expression found in a given collective thought? It is the way a mind situates itself when, faced with an unknown quantity, it sets about producing signifiers that have no corresponding signified and are left "devoid of meaning": "those types of notions [*mana*, *hau*] ... occur to represent an indeterminate value of signification, in itself devoid of meaning and thus susceptible of receiving any meaning at all; their sole function is to fill a gap between the signifier and the signified."[26]

Lévi-Strauss' solution to the enigma: "floating signifiers"

The Polynesian religious concepts are now voided of their meaning and reduced to what the French call a "truc" or a "machin," a "thingamajig." *Mana* is "a simple form, or to be more accurate, a symbol in its pure state, therefore liable to take on any symbolic content whatever ... it would just be a *zero symbolic value.*"[27]

Let us take a closer look at the level of analysis Lévi-Strauss has chosen in order that a notion such as *mana* should be transformed into a "*floating signifier* which is the disability of all finite thought."[28] He has chosen the level of *philosophical thought* and a materialistic, critical variety of philosophy at that. For this school of thought, religious concepts, religious explanations of the world are not erroneous explanations of the world but false explanations. They are not more or less right or more or less wrong, as is the case of those explanations established in the field of experimental science or deduced in the field of mathematics, but lie outside this field. They are not cases of erroneous knowledge; they are false knowledge. Of course, from the standpoint of human practice and the history of humankind, these representations which say nothing right or wrong about the world do *say a lot about the people who think them.* They are always full of significations, and these *cannot be reduced* to the projection onto nature and society of *classifications* drawn from one and applied to the other. But let us stay with philosophical thought and see how these collective representations of the Polynesians, the ancient Germans, the Celts, the Hindus, and so forth appear to the universal gaze of the philosopher, and in the intellectual light inherent in all philosophy because it claims to have come closer to the origin, to the foundations, to the real. All illustrate to various degrees

> a fundamental situation ... which arises out of the human condition: namely, that man has from the start had at his disposition a signifier-totality which he is at a loss to know how to allocate to a signified, given as such, but no less unknown for being given. There is always a non-equivalence or "inadequation" between the two. ... So in man's effort to understand the world, he always disposes of a surplus of signification (which he shares out among things in accordance with the laws of the symbolic thinking which it is the tasks of ethnologists and linguists to study).[29]

It is altogether possible to think, on the philosophical level, that religious concepts are not erroneous knowledge but false knowledge

– which is my opinion as well – without having to espouse the idea
that "man disposes from the start of a signifier-totality." This is a
fine formula and it makes one proud to be human, but it remains
obscure. The key, the underlying thesis is the idea of "a symbolic
origin of society."[30] The term "symbolic" is to be taken in both
senses, as a means of communication, language, and in its etymolog-
ical sense (*symbolon* in Greek), a tangible sign of an agreement and,
by extension, of a contract concluded between parties. In short,
society is, in its essence, exchange, language, because it originates in
a contract. And Lévi-Strauss goes on to expose his philosophical
"vision" of the big bang from which human society sprang:

> Whatever may have been the moment and the circumstances of its
> appearance in the ascent of animal life, language can only have arisen
> all at once. Things cannot have begun to signify gradually. In the
> wake of a transformation which is not a subject of study for the social
> sciences, but for biology and psychology, a shift occurred from a
> stage when nothing had a meaning to another stage when everything
> had meaning ... In other words, at the moment when the entire uni-
> verse all at once became *significant*, it was none the better *known* for
> being so, even if it is true that the emergence of language must have
> hastened the rhythm of the development of knowledge. ... It is as if
> humankind had suddenly acquired an immense domain and the
> detailed plan of that domain, along with a notion of the reciprocal
> relationship of domain and plan; but had spent millennia learning
> which specific symbols of the plan represented the different aspects of
> the domain.[31]

And lastly: "Like language, the social *is* an autonomous reality (the
same one, moreover); symbols are more real than what they symbol-
ise, the signifier precedes and determines the signified."[32]

Language's big bang and the symbolic origin of society

I do not know if Lévi-Strauss still agrees with this analysis, but I
know why I no longer would today. In the first place, coming back
to Polynesia and to the concepts of *hau* and *mana*, because, even if
these indigenous concepts are "false knowledge," their content consists of the practices in which they are involved, those of gift-
exchange and of creating lasting, sacred obligations, that of marking
differences, hierarchies, and so on. In sum, even if it is obvious that
the *capacity* for elaborating symbols and for communicating the
content of an experience using the symbols that express it is *not* the

direct product of the development of society but that of the development of the brain, the material support of the mind, it is always necessary, whatever Lévi-Strauss may say, to "develop a sociological theory of [the] symbolism"[33] used by a given society at a given moment to invent and to give expression to itself.

Although it is legitimate to consider that human-ness cannot be reduced to consciousness and that, beyond consciousness there exist powers and principles that are continuously at work, it would perhaps be wise to take care when invoking unconscious mental structures to explain facts and behaviors that are *not* found in all societies or at all epochs, or which are found but do not have the same meaning or importance. *Something more* than the action of the unconscious structures of the mind is therefore needed to explain the transformations and developments which occur in the conscious productions of humans. Lévi-Strauss himself encountered this difficulty some twenty years later when he invoked the "dormant seed" to explain the emergence in ancient Greece of "scientific and philosophical" forms of thinking that were distinct from religious discourse and ran counter to the mythology of the old cosmogonies. Here (but elsewhere as well, in ancient China and India) was the beginning of a process of accumulation of "knowledge" which did not disappear when the gods and beliefs of the Egyptian, Mesopotamian, Greek, and Roman civilizations were engulfed by the tide of history.

Furthermore, one cannot at the same time maintain that thought goes beyond language and proceed as though it were indistinguishable from language and its unconscious structures. And who can affirm that articulate speech (since that is the kind we are talking about) came about all at once, that before it "nothing" had meaning and after it "everything" did? Articulate speech is composed of abstract sounds that are produced and combined in order to communicate "abstract things," namely the products of a type of thinking which not only thinks relationships but discovers or constructs relationships between relationships. This capacity to imagine relationships between relationships is an active part of the production of all relationships that humans entertain with each other and which they establish with nature. The mind produces social reality by combining two parts of itself, two separate powers which complete each other while remaining distinct: the capacity to represent or imagine and the capacity to symbolize, to communicate both real and imaginary things.

And even had articulate speech appeared all at once in one of our distant ancestors, Neanderthal man or whoever, what our ancestor suddenly possessed was merely the *ability to produce* phonemes. To string them together into morphemes, into words, was to produce a given "natural" language which, like all natural languages, had a limited, finite number of words (between 60,000 and 100,000 on average) with which the individuals of this society strove to communicate what they had to say, words which did not necessarily exhaust the totality of their thinking. Alternatively, no human being, not this ancestor or any one of us, will ever personally possess the signifier-totality, and even less a totality containing a "detailed plan" of itself. Furthermore, a signifier never exists in "a pure state," devoid of any reference to one or more signifieds. The notion of a "symbol" or a "signifier" in a pure state is a contradiction in terms. Lastly, everyone knows that, while a child is *capable* of learning all languages, he will only ever speak a few at best, and his mind will contain not the "signifier-totality," but a greater or smaller portion of the thoughts and the "things signified" and relayed by these languages.

In short, it is not clear who is the more mystified: Mauss, who believes in the explanatory value of Polynesian beliefs, or Lévi-Strauss, who believes in the big-bang theory of the emergence of language and in the symbolic origin of human society. It would of course be interesting to reconstruct the subjective historical context of these visions and beliefs, but what matters at this point is that, with Lévi-Strauss as with Lacan and other thinkers of this period, a general change of perspective occurred in the analysis of social facts, a shift from the real and the imaginary to the symbolic and to the affirmation of the principle that, between the *imaginary and the symbolic* (which cannot exist separately), it is the symbolic which dominates and must therefore be the starting point of any analysis.

Lévi-Strauss' postulate: the primacy of the symbolic over the imaginary

Let us remember that, a few years after the publication of Lévi-Strauss' text, Jacques Lacan, building on the same premises, wrote: "what we call the symbolic dominates the imaginary."[34] From what he knew of structural anthropology and linguistics, he soon constructed a theory in which the paternal function was divided into three orders – the real father, the imaginary father, and the symbolic father, the latter being synonymous with the order of language and the law. In the approach of both Lacan and Lévi-Strauss we see the same tendency to overrate the symbolic with respect to the imaginary, and to reduce thought and society to language and contract.

Of course, such a theoretical shift, emphasizing as it did the systematic analysis of the forms and structures of symbolic thought and language, produced an impressive number of innovative results which, on a certain level, enriched the earlier findings of Mauss and Freud. Among other things, Mauss had not attempted the analysis of myths and Freud had not broached the analysis of the relationship with language. Therefore we can by no means today simply "go back" to Mauss or Freud. The crucial point, however, is not that, but whether the positive findings of Lévi-Strauss and Lacan legitimize (continue to sustain) *a posteriori* the theoretical assumption underlying their research, namely that "it is the symbolic that dominates the imaginary."

I do not think so, and I see proof of this in the two conclusions founded on this premise, both of which lead to veritable theoretical impasses. One is Lévi-Strauss': having come to the end of his analysis of American Indian myths, he concludes from the fact that all of the mythic themes echo and complete each other, from the fact that the world of myths is round, that everything happens as if, as he says literally, "the myths were thinking among themselves or thinking each other."[35] The other is Lacan's claim, which still exerts its hold on the disciples of the master as well as on those who have tried to break away, namely that it is as if the Phallus were not only the *object* of desire, but the *signifier* of desire, for men as well as for women. Here are two famous formulas which affirm the idea that "symbols are more real than what they symbolize," and thus more real than the imaginary and "the real" that they re-present (to the mind).

In spite (or rather because) of the fascination they exercise, such formulas are a veritable *coup de force* that speed the thinking process up a blind alley and block the exit. Lévi-Strauss does away with the active role of the *content* of specific historical relations in the production of mythological thought, relations which shed light on the importance of this form of thought with respect to other forms coexisting in the same society at the same time. Does mythology dominate all forms of thought or is it restricted to certain areas of social practice, playing a secondary role elsewhere? It is difficult to deal with this type of problem using the idea that everything happens as if the myths were thinking among themselves. History, in other words the coexistence, the interlinkage, and the succession of the multiple histories of the individual societies within which a given form of thought or way of organizing social life is reproduced or not, is not simply the unconscious and wholly contingent unfolding of a few of the possibilities "lying dormant" in the deep-seated structures of the human mind, that is to say ultimately our brain. As for Lacan's formula, it does away, albeit less abruptly and more ambiguously than Freud,[36] with the active role of the feminine in the production of figures of desire and in the constitution of a person's intimacy, with a feminine which is inescapable because, in the last analysis, it is cannot be reduced to the Phallus and because we cannot, like Lacan, content ourselves with the assertion that there is something-that-takes-more-pleasure (*de l'avoir-plus-de-plaisir*) in women because they are not "all" subject. Desire cannot be reduced to the simple opposition, prisoner of a single symbol, the Phallus, between those who have one and will become one, and those who do not and will never be.[37]

There is no question of denying the existence of the functions (the imaginary, the symbolic and the "real") of these three orders which combine to make up human *social* existence, human social reality. The problem is whether more adequate representations of this reality are constructed by positing that the symbolic dominates the imaginary or by assuming the converse. To my mind, we must opt for the converse. It is first and foremost the different ways humans imagine their relationships with each other and with what we call nature that distinguish societies and the periods during which some of them exist. But the imaginary cannot transform itself into the social, it cannot manufacture "society" by existing on a purely "mental" level. It must be "materialized" in concrete relations which take on their form and content in *institutions*, and of course in the *symbols* which represent them and cause them to send messages back and forth, to communicate. When the imaginary is "materialized" in social relationships, it becomes a part of social reality.

To return to gift-giving, *mana*, and the spirit of things, we must remember that the imaginary is the birthplace of all beliefs, and at the same time the origin of the distinction between the sacred and the profane, in short the world of religion and magic, a world based on the twin belief that there exist invisible beings and powers which govern the universe and that humans can sway them by prayer and sacrifices, and by adopting a behavior in accordance with what they imagine to be their desires, their will, or their law. But the distinction between these three orders did not wait for the second half of the twentieth century; in a short but incisive article on Lacan, Jean-Joseph Goux[38] reminds us that political economic discourse, from the time of its great founders, "had already produced this distinction with regard to a highly privileged object, the object of exchange *par excellence* in modern society, money," and he quotes this astonishing statement by Marx, concerning gold: "As the standard of value, gold is merely nominal money and nominal gold [elsewhere Marx uses the word "imaginary"]; purely as a medium of circulation it is symbolic money and symbolic gold; but in its simple metallic corporeality gold is money or money is real gold."[39]

This quotation is worth pausing over. Goux's commentary is highly apposite. I will summarize his remarks while indicating one essential point that he did not stress. Goux reminds us that Marx was writing at a time when gold, as a precious metal, fulfilled all three functions of money, serving both as a general equivalent of the value of the commodities circulating in the markets and as the primary form of wealth: in this instance money functions as a measure of the value of the commodities, as the medium of their exchange, and lastly as a reserve of wealth, as a treasury. Marx was also writing at a time when nearly all economists, together with the public, shared the idea that all forms of money other than gold (paper, securities, or other tokens of monetary value, especially bank notes) had value only because they *represented* gold.[40] Confidence in money rested on the fact that, in principle, a person could obtain immediately and without restriction, gold coins in exchange for the bank notes or other monetary signs in circulation. Of course in times of crisis, the application of this principle was suspended, since if everyone changed their bank notes for gold, the system would collapse. But under ordinary circumstances, gold did not need to circulate in order to function as a measure of value. It was enough that the bank kept it in reserve. In the extreme case, as Marx said, it could exist merely in the imagination,[41] unlike money in the form of paper or other monetary signs, which circulate in the actual exchange of commodities and function as a substitute, a symbol.

In fact, Goux points us down a trail which leads back to Mauss and the distinction between alienable and inalienable goods. Here, in the very midst of a market economy, of universal currency, and generalized competition, we discover that something needs to be kept out of circulation, to be voluntarily withheld from the sphere and the movement of exchange in order for the mass of market and bank exchanges to be set in motion, for everything that can be bought or sold to begin circulating.

The paradox is that this thing which must be removed, uncoupled from the exchange sphere, "withdrawn as it were from circulation," is the very instrument of these exchanges, the means of this circulation, money. It must therefore be concluded that it is not enough that some kind of currency exist for commercial exchanges to develop and to flood the sphere of exchange, this money (whatever it may be) must also fulfill two functions, occupy two places at the same time, one at the very heart of the exchange process where it functions as a medium of payment, the other prior to or beyond exchange, where it constitutes a stable reference point for measuring the value of whatever circulates in these exchanges. Money is thus both swept along by the movement of the commodities and immobilized as a point around which all this machinery begins to revolve and whose volume and speed it measures.

We seem to be a long way from Mauss here. And yet, with the discovery of the existence of realities which are in a way withheld from exchange while at the same time enabling exchange to take place, we find ourselves very close to certain passages of Mauss, which have never attracted any particular comment, however, and have consequently gone unnoticed. Who is this forgotten, this non-annotated Mauss?

Forgetting the fourth obligation (men's gifts to the gods and to their representatives)

Having introduced the notion of the "spirit" of the thing given, *hau*, and outlined a preliminary description of the potlatch and the *kula*, Mauss mentions for the first time a "fourth obligation," which plays "a part in this system and moral code relating to presents."[42] This is the obligation to make gifts to the gods and to the men who represent them. He evokes ceremonies in which men bear the names of spirits, gods, animals, and so on, and who exchange wealth in order to incite their homonyms to be generous with humans. He observes that this practice appears in certain potlatches but that it is not restricted to this institution. To illustrate, Mauss points to Eskimo ceremonies in which shamans invite the spirits whose masks they wear to take part in the dancing and gift-giving. Afterwards they announce that the spirits have enjoyed their visit with the humans and that they will send game. At the end of the hunting season, other ceremonies are performed to thank the spirits for having given humans gifts of game. The remains of the feast are thrown into the sea, and "[t]hey return to their land of origin, taking with them the wild animals killed during the year, who will return the next year."[43] Mauss thus includes in the category of gifts offerings presented to the spirits and the gods, sacrifices made to seek favors or to give thanks.[44] Offerings and sacrifices are gifts to the dead, to the spirits, to the gods; but sacrifice, according to Mauss, is capable of compelling the gods, of making them give in return, as in potlatch, more than they were given. "The purpose of destruction by sacrifice is precisely that it is an act of giving that *is necessarily reciprocated.*"[45]

Mauss also states that the spirits of the dead and the gods "are the true owners of the things and possessions of this world. With them it was most necessary to exchange, and with them it was most dangerous not to exchange." And he adds: "yet, conversely, it was with them it was easiest and safest to exchange."[46]

Men make gifts to the gods in the form of offerings and destruction of the things offered. Victims are sacrificed, the aroma of the incense and the smoke of the sacrifices rise up to the gods, and in some cases the flesh of the sacrificed animals is consumed. To sacrifice is to give by destroying what is given, and it is in this sense that sacrifice is a kind of potlatch and that gifts made to the gods, to the spirits of nature and of the dead not only belong to the "same complexus," but, as Mauss writes, "realize to the full" the economy and the spirit of the gift, for these "gods who give and repay are there to give something great in exchange for something small." Mauss clearly indicates here the articulation between gift-giving and the practice of contractual sacrifice to the gods and spirits. Taking his reasoning a step further, we see more clearly why, in these social and mental worlds, men who give more than they have been given, or who give so much that they can never be repaid, raise themselves above other men and are something like gods, or at least they strive to be.

It it is strange that Mauss, who takes seriously the fact that, in all these societies, the gods and the spirits of the dead are the true owners of things, should reduce the giving of gifts to the gods to an act of sacrifice, in other words to the hold that humans claim to have over the gods. He should also have taken into account the fact that the gods are free to give or not, and that the men approaching the gods are already in their debt, since it is from them that they have already received the conditions for their existence. His analysis fails to take into consideration the fact that the gods and the spirits are already superior to humans, and that the human donors are from the outset inferior to the godly receivers.

This, I believe, is the reason why men's indebtedness to the gods, the spirits of nature, and the spirits of the dead was probably the starting point, the imaginary structure which enabled caste and class relations to crystallize, to take shape and to acquire meaning. I will develop this idea later when I show that it is in the context of gift-giving and the debts created by gifts that the process of caste and class formation is illuminated and takes on meaning. After all, for the ancient Egyptians, Pharaoh was not a man, he was a god dwelling among men. Born of the incestuous relationship between the twins, Isis and Osiris, he is the sole source of *kâ*, the breath of life in all living beings, men, birds, beasts of the field, flies, fish and the like. The Egyptians believed they owed their life, fertility, and abundance to the gods, and to Pharaoh in particular. Nothing could repay this debt, not the gift of their labor, not the product of their hands, not their own person nor that of their children, "repayment gifts" for Pharaoh's acts of kindness, which I see as so many forms or aspects of the domination-exploitation of the Egyptian peasants by the priestly and warrior elite surrounding Pharaoh and which bore the names of corvée, tribute, servitude. But this will be my only allusion. I could cite a hundred other examples to illustrate the same reality, the fact that all power contains "kernels of imaginary material" which were necessary to its formation and reproduction. But the imaginary has power only when it becomes a belief, a standard of behavior, a source of morality. We will soon see that it is precisely this power of belief inherent in the imaginary that Lévi-Strauss occults when he affirms that the symbolic dominates the imaginary.

Before finishing with the fourth obligation, we need to recall that, although Mauss had already published another famous essay, in 1899, written with Henri Hubert and entitled "Essai sur la nature et la fondation du sacrifice," he felt unable, in 1925, to do more than suggest the existence of a close connection and a continuity between gift and sacrifice, and he explained himself in terms that deserve to be heard:

> We have not undertaken the general study that would be necessary to bring out its importance [of the gifts made to the gods and to nature]. Moreover, the facts we have available do not all relate to those geographical areas to which we have confined ourselves [Melanesia, Polynesia, North America, India]. Finally, the mythological element that we scarcely yet understand is too strong in them to leave it out of account.[47]

Lévi-Strauss was to devote a part of his life to this very study of mythologies.

A forgotten Mauss

Among the important remarks Mauss made concerning the gifts men make to the gods are several allusions to the fact that *not all kinds of wealth enter into exchange*, that, for example, the Trobrianders have two kinds of valuables, of *vaygu'a* (armshells and necklaces),

"those of the kula and those that Malinowski for the first time calls
the 'permanent *vaygu'a*' [which] are displayed and offered up to the
spirits on a platform identical to that of the chief. This makes their
spirits benevolent. They carry off to the land of the dead the shades
of these precious objects."[48] Here Mauss, having laid so much stress
on exchange and gift-giving, carefully distinguishes the two categories of objects, those that must or may be given or exchanged,
alienable objects, and those that must be neither given nor
exchanged because they are inalienable:

> Among the Kwakiutl a certain number of objects, although they
> appear at the potlatch, cannot be disposed of. In reality these pieces
> of "property" are *sacra* that a family divests itself of only with great
> reluctance, and sometimes never ... The sum total of these precious
> things constitutes the magical dower... all of these things are always,
> and in every tribe, spiritual in origin and of a spiritual nature.[49]

Mauss saw clearly, then, that there are two spheres of wealth, one
comprised of alienable goods and the other, of inalienable goods,
and that the former opens onto the vast, frantic field of gifts,
counter-gifts, and other forms of exchange, while the latter follows
the paths of transmission, of anchorage in time. This is further illustrated in the following passage, again on the Kwakiutl:

> It would seem that among the Kwakiutl there were two kinds of
> copper objects: the more important ones that do not go out of the
> family and that can only be broken to be recast, and others that seem
> to serve as satellites for the first kind. The possession of this secondary
> kind of copper object doubtless corresponds among the Kwakiutl to
> that of the titles of nobility and second-order ranks with whom they
> travel, passing from chief to chief, from family to family, between the
> generations and the sexes. It appears that the great titles and the great
> coppers at the very least remain unchanged within the clans and tribes.
> Moreover, it might be difficult for it to be otherwise.[50]

But if Mauss seems to find it easy to understand that it might be
difficult for it to be otherwise, it became very difficult after Lévi-
Strauss to understand that it had to be the way it was.

Concerning things that can be given and things that must be kept (Annette Weiner and the paradox of the gift)

After a long detour, we now come back to Annette Weiner and
the fundamental question of the nature of the social, of the basic

components of any human society. Using her own direct knowledge of the mechanisms and representations of Trobriand society, Annette Weiner managed to find in Mauss what a half-century of commentaries had overlooked.[51] In a series of publications, the latest of which is entitled *Inalienable Possessions: The Paradox of Keeping-while-Giving* (1992), she developed two essential ideas.

We are already familiar with the first and have explored it in our fashion. This is the thesis according to which the interplay of gift and counter-gift, even in a society with "an economy and a moral code dominated by gift-giving," does not completely dominate the social sphere. Here as elsewhere there are some things which must be kept and not given. These things that are kept – valuables, talismans, knowledge, rites – affirm deep-seated *identities and their continuity* over time. Furthermore they affirm the existence of *differences of identity* between individuals, between the groups which make up a society or which want to situate themselves respectively within a set of neighboring societies linked by various kinds of exchanges.

But such differences of identity are not neutral: they constitute a hierarchy, and it is in this process of the production and the reproduction of hierarchies among individuals, groups, and even societies, that the *strategies of giving and keeping play distinct but complementary roles*. Enlarging on Mauss' comment concerning the Kwakiutl's best coppers, Annette Weiner goes on to suggest that, in an economy based on gift-exchange, it is necessary to withhold from the giving process objects (mats, nephrites, and so on) of the same kind as those that are given, but which are finer, rarer, more valuable. Hence her formula *keeping-while-giving*. I think that it is possible to go further and, keeping in mind the gold that is kept in bank vaults for the purpose of guaranteeing the value of the other monetary signs that circulate, that a more fitting formula might be *keeping-for-giving*. Although Annette Weiner does not make the distinction between the imaginary and the symbolic, I would point out in passing that it is highly likely that the valuables, treasures and talismans which are not given but are kept are those which concentrate the greatest imaginary power and, as a consequence, the greatest symbolic value.

Annette Weiner's second *idée-force* concerns the importance of women and/or the feminine element in the exercise of power, in the mechanisms of legitimation and redistribution of political and religious power among the groups that comprise a society. Taking the bulk of her examples from Polynesia, she demonstrates that a large part of the valuables held as clan treasures, symbols of a rank or title, or circulating in the gifts and counter-gifts associated with birth, marriage, and death rituals are *women's* goods, goods produced by women and over which they have individual rights.

Annette Weiner thus revitalizes the role of women and/or the feminine in the production and exercise of the political power from which they seem to be excluded or in which they seem to occupy an altogether minor place. In Polynesia, the woman as sister enjoys a higher rank than the man as brother, and the sister as woman is supposed to be closer to the ancestors and the gods, to the sacred. If it is the relationship entertained with the sacred which, as a rule, confers the highest degree of legitimacy on a political power, then behind the appearances which dissimulate their importance, women and the feminine are actively present at the heart of Polynesian institutions as well as, to be sure, in intimate relations. Annette Weiner acknowledges her debt for this idea to Mauss, who, with regard to the two categories of valuables in the kingdom of Samoa, *oloa* and *le'tonga*, writes:

> [*tonga*] ... designates the permanent paraphernalia, particularly the mats given at marriage, inherited by the daughters of that marriage, and the decorations and talismans that through the wife come into the newly founded family, with an obligation to return them. In short, they are kinds of fixed property – immovable because of their destination. The *oloa* designate objects, mainly tools, that belong specifically to the husband. These are essentially movable goods. Thus nowadays this term is applied to things passed on by Whites.[52]

Annette Weiner's analyses of the role of women and of the existence of "women's goods" indispensable for producing and legitimizing political power led her to look into the strategic role of brother–sister relations in the constitution of the social sphere and in the establishment of power. Reasoning from the fact that, in the Trobriand Islands, where descent is reckoned matrilineally, the identity and continuity of the clan are transmitted exclusively through women and therefore through women as sisters, she rejects, at least for this case, Lévi-Strauss' formula that kinship is based on the "exchange" of women among men. Instead, she advances an argument which she feels to have a more general critical bearing and goes on to contest that a sister given as a wife can be regarded as the equivalent of a wife received in place of that sister, which ultimately raises the question of brother–sister incest. She recalls that incest between brother and sister, which combines the greatest number of positive and negative forces, the greatest number of sacred powers, was practiced by the important noble and royal families of certain Polynesian societies, thus bearing witness to their supernatural origins.

We will not follow her on all of these grounds. As far as Lévi-Strauss' thesis on kinship is concerned, we have shown elsewhere[53] that the prohibition of incest did not necessarily, as Lévi-Strauss claimed, bring about the exchange of women among men. The prohibition of incest opens up three logically equivalent possibilities. Either men exchange their sisters among themselves, or women exchange their brothers among themselves, or groups exchange men and women. Lévi-Strauss retained only one of these three possibilities when he posited the exchange of women among men as the crux of kinship and therefore as a universal fact. Yet all three possibilities exist sociologically. Women exchange men among the Tetum of Indonesia,[54] the Joraï of Vietnam and in a few other societies.[55] In place of bridewealth, these groups pay groomwealth, a matrimonial compensation for the services of the future bridegroom. The third logical possibility, the exchange of men and women by family groups, is obviously more common: it is practiced by the present-day societies of Europe and by many cognatic societies in Polynesia, Indonesia, the Philippines, and elsewhere. In any event, the exchange of women is not a universal *fact*, as Lévi-Strauss claims. It is merely the most statistically frequent form of matrimonial exchange. (In passing let it be said that the fact that Joraï women exchange their brothers does not prove that male domination does not exist in this society; it is very real, but that is not where it operates.) Not only does Lévi-Strauss' theory suffer from having rejected out of hand two logically possible ways of exchanging marriage partners by declaring that they might exist in the imagination or might be evoked to placate women, but that they would not be found in the real world; it also sins in having "reduced" kinship to exchange, to reciprocity, to the symbolic. In so doing, he has left unmentioned or has diminished everything in kinship which falls outside the area of exchange, which partakes of (imaginary) continuity, which is rooted in time, in the blood, in the soil, and so on.

Whatever approach is taken to the question, the same is always found to be true of the essential nature of the social and thus of the origin of society. Henceforth it seems clear that the social cannot be reduced to the sum of all possible forms of exchange among humans and therefore cannot originate or be grounded solely in exchange, contract or the symbolic. Beyond the sphere of exchanges lie other domains, another sphere constituted of all that humans imagine they must withhold from exchange, reciprocity, and rivalry, which they must conserve, preserve, and increase.

Nor is the social merely the juxtaposition or even the addition of the alienable and the inalienable, for society is brought into existence and sustained only by the union, by the interdependence of these two spheres and by their difference, their relative autonomy. The formula for maintaining the social sphere is therefore not *keeping-while-giving*, but *keeping-for-giving and giving-for-keeping*. I believe that this double viewpoint enables us to take the true measure of man as a social being, and of the preconditions for any society.

Concerning the twin foundations of society

If the social sphere rests on a twin proposition, then society cannot have a simple origin or be underpinned by a single foundation. Human society drew on two sources for its emergence: contractual exchange on the one hand, and non-contractual transmission on the other. And it continues to advance on these two legs, to rest on these two bases, both of which are equally necessary and exist only by means of one another. Thus there are always things in the human social domain which are not governed by contract, which are not negotiable, which are located outside or beyond the domain of reciprocity. Whether in the sphere of kinship or of politics, there is always, in every human activity if it is to become constituted, something that precedes exchange and in which exchange takes root, something that exchange both alters and preserves, extends and renews at the same time. This chronological precedence and this logical priority exist only as *moments* in a continuous movement, which flows from man's original mode of existence as a being that not only lives in society (like other social animals), but which produces society in order to live.

If it were necessary to cite a philosopher in conclusion, why not Aristotle, who on the one hand contends, in his *Ethics*: "If there were no exchange, there would be no social life," but who, in his *Politics*, rejected the idea that human society could have sprung from a contract. The *polis*, he writes, is more than a contract, more than an alliance, a *summachia*. Were it not, he says, "Etruscans and Carthaginians and all peoples between whom there are mutual *sumbola* would be citizens of a single city."[56] It is not a matter of chance then that most of the theoreticians who proclaim the primacy of the symbolic over the imaginary base the origin of society on a contract. Before the symbol there was nothing, afterwards, there was everything. Before the appearance of language, before the prohibition of incest, before the primal social contract, society did not exist, or if it did, it had no signification. Afterwards it sprang up and it began to signify something.

Having come to the question of whether the origin of society is single or multiple, we will go no further than these few suggestions, formulated in the guise of a preliminary approach. But they have enabled us to measure what is at stake in analyzing the place and importance of gift-giving in the functioning and the evolution of human societies. This place can be defined and its importance measured only if we can arrive at a more accurate view of the relations between the sphere of sacred things that are not exchanged and that of valuables or monies which enter into exchanges of gifts or exchanges of commodities.

To this end, I am now going to re-examine the ethnographic material I know best, namely the material on the Baruya of New Guinea. This is a paradoxical endeavor, however: as it is practiced among the Baruya, the gift and counter-gift of women between lineages is an attenuated form of total prestation and, while it is of enormous importance to society, it is not found in the other areas of social life. Political relations, for instance, revolve entirely around the ownership and use of sacred objects treasured by each clan, which it is forbidden to give or exchange. Moreover the Baruya also produce a "quasi-money", salt, which they use to procure a variety of means of subsistence and valuables, but without accumulating these in a power contest. The paradox is that, in order to analyze the logic of potlatch societies, we are going to begin by analyzing a non-potlatch society. But we will see that this method follows Mauss' indications and enables us to determine the differences, the significant discrepancies between non-potlatch gift-giving societies and those which engage in potlatch. Furthermore, beginning with societies in which gift-giving does not give rise to competition may also enable us to clarify the social and historical transformations that allowed the emergence and development of those societies in which gifts are systematically given in a spirit of rivalry and antagonism in order to win power and fame.

A critique of Mauss which completes his theory and takes other approaches as well

The better part of the "Essai sur le don" is devoted to analysis of the potlatch, that is to say to the analysis of agonistic forms of gift-giving. But it is frequently forgotten that, for Mauss, the potlatch was merely an "evolved" form of total prestation in which "the principle of rivalry and hostility dominates."[57] Accordingly, we must look elsewhere for the point of departure of his analysis, as he himself affirmed: "In fact the point of departure lies elsewhere. It is provided in a category of rights that exclude the jurists and economists, who are not interested in it. This is the gift, a complex phenomenon, particularly in its ancient form, that of 'total prestations', with which *we do not deal in this monograph*."[58]

If the potlatch is an evolved, altered form of gift-giving-as-total-prestation, it is obvious that it cannot be thoroughly analyzed without having a clear idea of what Mauss meant by "total prestations." I have therefore selected several passages from the "Essai sur le don" and the *Manuel d'ethnographie* which deal with the subject. The French word *prestation*, as Mauss indicates in his *Manuel*, comes from the Latin *praestare*, "to hand over" and designates "a contract to repay a thing or a service."[59] He makes a distinction between total-prestation "contracts" and "contracts" in which the prestation is only partial. He further distinguishes two categories of total prestations, depending on whether the exchange of gifts and counter-gifts takes an antagonistic form or not. He considers the non-antagonistic category of gifts and counter-gifts to be the oldest, and suggests that over time it evolved into increasingly competitive and individualistic forms, culminating in the potlatch. This overall set of non-antagonistic and antagonistic forms he calls "a system of total prestations."[60] His models for non-antagonistic total prestations are taken from the exchanges occurring in societies divided into complementary moieties like the Australian and North American Indian tribes: "The purest type of such institutions seems to us to be characterized by the alliance of two phratries in Australian or North American tribes in general, where rituals, marriages, inheritance of goods, legal ties and those of interest, the military and religious – in short everything, is complementary and presumes co-operation between the two halves of the tribe."[61] Elsewhere he writes:

> Total prestation is the fact, for two clans, of being in a continual state of contract, each person owes everything to every other person in the clan and to everyone in the opposing clan. The ongoing and collective character of such a contract makes it a veritable treaty involving a necessary display of wealth with regard to the other party.[62]

Mauss adds that this type of prestation can still be found in French society: "Originally much more widespread, total prestation still exists in our society between spouses, unless it has been otherwise stipulated at the time of the marriage contract."[63]

But let us return to the description of the essential characteristics of the total services analyzed in the "Essai sur le don":

First characteristic: "it is not individuals but collectivities that impose obligations of exchange and contract upon each other. The contracting 'persons' are legal entities: clans, tribes, and families who confront and oppose one another either in groups who meet face to face in one spot, or through their chiefs, or in both these ways at once."[64]

Second characteristic: "what they exchange is not solely property and wealth ... things economically useful. In particular, such exchanges are acts of politeness, banquets, rituals, military services, women, children, dances, festivals, and fairs, in which economic transaction is only one element, and in which the passing on of wealth is only one feature of a much more general and enduring contract."[65]

Lastly: "these total prestations and counter-prestations are committed to a somewhat voluntary form by presents and gifts, although in the final analysis they are strictly compulsory, on pain of private or public warfare."[66]

Agonistic total prestations differ in the greater or lesser violence of the rivalry and competition exhibited by the individuals and the groups engaged in the exchange of gifts and counter-gifts. The potlatch style of "Indians from Vancouver to Alaska" appeared to Mauss as a "typical," "evolved and relatively rare" form of agonistic total prestations:

> Yet what is noteworthy about these tribes is the principle of rivalry and hostility that prevails in all these practices ... they even go so far as the purely conspicuous destruction of wealth that has been accumulated in order to outdo the rival chief who is at the same time his associate ... There is total prestation in the sense that it is indeed the whole clan that contracts on behalf of all, for all that it possesses and for all that it does, through the person of its chief. But this prestation, on the part of the chief, takes on an extremely marked agonistic character ... It is a struggle between nobles to establish a hierarchy amongst themselves from which their clan will benefit at a later date.[67]

Mauss observes that this type of agonistic gift and counter-gift is found elsewhere than in North America or Melanesia, but he chooses to use the word "potlatch" to designate the phenomenon, thus transforming a term taken from a particular Indian language into a general sociological category: "We propose to reserve the term potlatch for this kind of institution, that, with less risk and more accuracy, but also at greater length, we might call: total prestations of an agonistic type."[68]

In contrast to the potlatch, he writes, in non-agonistic total prestations, "the elements of rivalry, destruction and combat appear to be lacking."[69]

Such prestations, whether antagonistic or not, are total in the sense that they involve "juridical, religious, mythological, shamanistic, and esthetic" phenomena and aspects of the "social morphology"; in other words, they engage groups which shape the society (families, clans, tribes). The social fact of exchanging gifts is total because in it are combined many aspects of social practice and numerous institutions characteristic of the society. This is the sense Mauss gives to the word "total." But the word has another meaning. Social phenomena can also be considered to be "total," not because they combine many aspects of a society, but because in a way they enable the society to represent itself (to others and to itself) and to reproduce itself as a whole. Mauss rarely uses the concept of "totality" in this sense, although it applies to the functioning of those societies divided into moieties. In such societies, the reproduction of one of the moieties is the immediate condition of the reproduction of the other, while it in turn depends on the other half for its own reproduction; each part is itself while simultaneously including the other and being included in it.

These clarifications having been made, we find ourselves in a paradoxical situation. Mauss indicated a starting point for the understanding of his analysis, but he did not develop this point in his work. There is a piece missing somewhere, and we are going to look for it by analyzing a case of non-agonistic exchanges of gifts and counter-gifts, a case I observed personally when I was doing fieldwork in New Guinea.

In 1967, ten years after having read Mauss and Lévi-Strauss, and having meanwhile decided to become an anthropologist, I arrived among the Baruya, a population living in one of the high mountain valleys in the interior of New Guinea. I did not know at the time that I would observe an institution that has an enormous impact on the functioning of collective and individual life: this was the practice of marriage by direct exchange of two women between two men and two lineages, *ginamare*.

A brief analysis of an example of non-agonistic gift and counter-gift

It took me some time and effort to understand that this reciprocal exchange in no way erases the debt each of the two men contracts with respect to the other when he receives one of the other's sisters as a wife. From that moment onward, as long as they live, the two men, now doubly brothers-in-law, will share part of the product of their hunting, part of their salt, will invite each other to clear new gardens in the forest. Each will need to stand by the other in feuds between villages and of course each will need to protect and show generosity to the children of his brother-in-law, in other words of his sister. Of course it can happen that a man gives a sister without receiving a wife in exchange. In this case, the credit passes to his son, who will have the right to take a wife, without repayment, among the daughters of this woman, his father's sister. The counter-gift is made, but a generation later. This second type of marriage is called *kouremandjinaveu*, an expression designating the shoot of a banana tree, *koure*, that which grows at the base of the tree and, according to the Baruya, replaces it when the plant has finished bearing fruit.

The Baruya also have another type of marriage, called *apmwet-salairaveumatna*, which means to get together (*irata*) salt (*tsala*) in view of taking (*matna*) a wife (*apmweva*). This marriage formula is not based on the direct exchange of women but on the exchange of wealth for women. It is *never practiced between* Baruya, but only with individuals and lineages from tribes with whom they trade. These tribes do not participate in the war–peace cycle that characterizes the Baruya's relations with their neighbors; they are outsiders, but "friends forever." I will return to the problems raised by the coexistence within a single society of two separate types of marriage, the exchange of women for women and the exchange of wealth for women. This is an important point because, as I will show, although the Baruya give gifts and counter-gifts, there is no potlatch, which strongly suggests that the development of the potlatch presupposes that marriage within the society does not rest exclusively or even primarily on the principle of direct exchange of women.

The interest of this example – which is one of several hundreds like it, with the sole difference that I personally observed this one in the field whereas I read about the others in colleagues' books – lies in the sociological fact that the *counter-gift* of a sister *does not cancel* the debt that each man has contracted with respect to the other by receiving a wife from him. The gift and the debt alike concern not only the individuals, in this case the two men and two of their (real or sometimes classificatory) sisters, but their two lineages, which among the Baruya are kin groups organized according to a principle of patrilineal descent reckoning, that is to say groups of men and women claiming to descend from the same ancestors *through the men*. In short, the exchange of women, the gift of one woman followed by the counter-gift of another woman, is a good example of Mauss' non-agonistic total prestations.

But it is also important to note that, at the conclusion of these reciprocal exchanges, the two men and the two lineages find themselves on an equivalent social footing. Each is, with respect to the other, both creditor and debtor. Each is superior to the other as a giver of women and inferior to the other as a taker of women. Each lineage therefore ultimately finds itself in two unequal and opposing relationships with the other. But the addition of these two opposite inequalities in fact re-establishes the equality of their status within society (which supposes that there exists a common code by which all members of the society reckon status). This means that even when exchanges (of gifts or commodities) involve only two individuals or two groups, the presence of a third party is always implied – or rather the presence of others as a third party. Exchange *always involves* a third party.

It also explains why, between two lineages linked with and obligated to each other by their gifts and counter-gifts, a flow of foods and mutual assistance is set up which continues over an entire generation. In this sense gifts and counter-gifts leave a deep imprint on both the economy and the morality of social life. For the Baruya, these reciprocal obligations and solidarities gradually fade over the following generation, since a Baruya boy must not repeat his father's marriage by re-exchanging a sister with the group from which his mother came. It is only after several generations, two at least, that a new marriage may be contracted between the same lineages.

Here we are at the heart of cultural worlds in which all of the kin groups that make up the society are compelled, in order to continue to exist, both to become indebted to others and to make others indebted to themselves. But the essential problem remains, namely *why is the debt created by a gift not cancelled or erased by an identical counter-gift?* The answer may be hard to understand for a mind immersed in the logic of today's commercial relations, but it is basically simple. If the counter-gift does not erase the debt, it is because the "thing" given has not really been separated, completely detached from the giver. The thing has been *given without really being "alienated"* by the giver.

The thing given therefore takes with it something of the person, of the identity of the giver. Moreover, the giver retains some rights over the thing after having given it. This is clear in the example of *ginamare*, sister-exchange among the Baruya. At the conclusion of the exchange, each woman has *taken the place* of the other, but *without having ceased to belong* to the lineage from which she originated, by birth or adoption. To give, in this instance, means to transfer without alienating, or to use the legal language of the West, to give means to cede the right of use without ceding actual ownership. And this is why giving a woman also confers certain rights over the children she will bear; this holds not only for societies where descent is reckoned exclusively through women, matrilineally, where as a consequence children do not belong to their father's lineage but to their mother's.

Two things happen, in fact, when sisters are exchanged. One person takes the place of another, and this *replacement of one person by another* constitutes at the same time the *production of a relationship*, an alliance between two men and two groups. Behind this twin mechanism, a fundamental social constraint is at work, the fact that a man cannot marry his sister, nor a woman her brother. And therefore at the heart of the exchange of women lies, as Claude Lévi-Strauss showed, the compelling action, the permanent mediation of the incest taboo.

This logic of gift-exchange is entirely separate, as Christopher Gregory has shown so strikingly,[70] from the logic of commercial exchange. When bartering for commodities or buying them with money, at the conclusion of the transaction, the partners own what they have bought or traded. Whereas before the exchange, each partner was dependent on others to satisfy his needs, afterwards each party is once more independent and free of obligations to others. Of course it may be that the buyer did not pay and was given credit, but as soon as he has paid his debt (with or without interest) he is free. This presupposes that the things or the services that are bartered, sold or bought are wholly alienable, detachable from the sellers. This is not the case in an "economy and a moral code based on gift-giving," since the thing given is not alienated and the giver retains rights over what he has given, and subsequently benefits from a series of "advantages."

No sooner given than returned (is there such a thing as an absurd gift?)

Nowhere is this logic more evident perhaps than when the gift of a thing is immediately followed by a counter-gift which returns to the initial donor the same thing as he has just given. For a Western observer, this round trip seems senseless since, if the thing is given right back, it seems to have been exchanged "for nothing", and gift-giving once again becomes an "enigma."

In reality, the nearly immediate reciprocation of the object given is perhaps the clearest illustration of the implicit logic of gifts which create debts that are not cancelled a by counter-gift. For the object which returns to its original owner *is not* "*given back*," but is "*given again*." And in the course of this round trip the object has not traveled in vain. Many things have come about as a result of this transfer. Two social relationships, identical but going in opposite directions, have been produced and are linked to each other, thus binding two individuals or two groups into a twin relationship of reciprocal dependence. Gift and counter-gift of an identical object are perhaps the minimum transfer required to set in motion a "total" prestation. At the conclusion of this analysis of an example of non-agonistic gift–counter-gift exchange, which for Mauss is the distant origin of the potlatch, let us compare the results with the two questions that opened the "Essai sur le don."[71]

It is clear now, at least as far as the logic of non-agonistic gift and counter-gift goes, that these questions are ill formulated in part: first of all, because in this type of gift-giving, nothing is really "given back." "Things" and persons take each other's place, and these transfers produce specific social relationships between the individuals and groups involved which give rise to a set of reciprocal rights and obligations; and secondly, there is, properly speaking, nothing "in" the thing which creates an obligation to return the gift except the fact that the giver continues to be present in the gift and through it to bring pressure on the receiver, not to give it back, but to give in turn, to reciprocate. The effect, then, is one of a rule of law; but this does not mean, as Mauss wrote, that those who follow it belong to a "primitive" or even an "archaic" society.[72] We know of many ancient or modern societies where land, for instance, is inalienable, where usage may be ceded, but never ownership. But the rule of law is also a rule of interest, since by giving, receiving, and giving in return, each party accumulates the advantages created by this type of reciprocal dependence.

Coming back to Mauss' second question, if there is some power in the thing, it is essentially that of the relationship which binds it to the person of the giver. This is a twofold relationship since the giver continues to be present in the thing given, which does not become detached from his (physical or legal) person, and this presence is a force, that of the rights he continues to exercise *over the thing given* and through it *over the recipient* who accepts it. In accepting a gift, one accepts more than a thing, one accepts the fact that the giver has rights over the receiver. Now we come to the point that so fascinated Mauss: there is in the thing given a "power" which works on the recipient and compels him to "give in return." We have seen that this power resides in the fact that the thing or person is not alienated when given. It continues to form part of the realities that constitute the identity, the being, the inalienable essence of a human group, of a "moral person." It is what we call common or collective "property," of which the use may be ceded but not the ownership. We must therefore ask ourselves why certain realities appropriated by human groups – land, sacred objects, ritual formulas, and so on – are inalienable.

This is where I part company with Mauss. For Mauss, the reasons for this inalienability and this "obligation to give in return" are essentially "spiritual", they are of a "moral and religious essence." They arise in the world of beliefs, of ideas and ideologies. I do not deny either the existence or the importance of religious representations and beliefs in attributing an inalienable character to clan, family, or tribal lands (inherited from the ancestors; it is there in that ground that they are often buried, and they watch over it and their descendants). But it seems difficult to explain by religious beliefs alone that, over the course of history, human groups have struggled to preserve their conditions of existence (material or not but always real to them), to prevent their dispersal, their division or their fragmentation, by imbuing them with the character of a possession to be kept and transmitted intact, thereby ensuring the survival of the generations to come. Religion is certainly not the ultimate explanation for the obligation under which individuals and groups have placed themselves to not surrender – or at least not completely – certain "things" necessary to the reproduction of one and all. It is not only "moral" reasons that command to not disperse or surrender – without replacing – realities which are presented and experienced as *necessary* to the reproduction of one and all. This necessity can be material or mental, but in any case it is social. The effect of religion is not to endow common property with an inalienable character, but to impose a sacred character on the prohibition of its alienation.

It is here, confronted with the necessity of explaining the presence of a "power" in that which is given, that, in my opinion, Mauss' analysis veers off course, thus laying itself open to Lévi-Strauss' criticisms. Mauss was certainly not unfamiliar with the notion of inalienable goods and collective ownership, but curiously he did not bring them into his explanation of gift-giving. There were perhaps two reasons for this. One is easily understandable: when speaking of inalienable things, such as the important titles and coppers of the Kwakiutl, he states that these "things" are precisely not given. And without further comment, he adds, "it might be difficult for it to be otherwise."[73] It is as though, for Mauss, things could not be given simply because they were inalienable. The other reason is less clear. Several times he mentions, without using it in his analysis, the existence of common rights over land or other clan or family belongings. For instance, alluding in the "Essai sur le don" to Chinese real-estate law, he writes:

> *But we do not place too much reliance on this fact*: definitive sale of land is, in human history and especially in China, something so very recent. It was, right up to Roman law, and then in our ancient German and French legal systems, hedged in with so many restrictions, arising from the domestic form of communism and the deep attachment of the family to the land, and the land to the family, that *the proof would have been too facile*. Since the family is the home and the land, it is normal that the land should be exempt from the law and the economy of capital. ... Actually we will be talking especially about movable goods.[74]

It is interesting to see that Mauss had no difficulty associating *sacra*, family sacred objects, with land as clan property and seeing them as the same type of inalienable reality. But he seems to have taken it for granted that inalienable realities cannot be given. In a way, as soon as persons or things begin to circulate through exchange, Mauss regards them as "movables," thus occulting or thrusting into the background the inalienable character of the things exchanged.

In fact he focused his critical attention primarily on one fundamental aspect of Western law, which has separated things and persons and created two systems, one pertaining to things and the other to persons. In order to understand the way gift-giving functions in contemporary non-Western societies, he felt it necessary to place himself beyond this distinction. Paradoxically, though, he did not analyze the union of thing and person in terms of law but, as I have said, in terms of an almost religious union. To be sure, he began with the fact that the thing given takes with it something of its original owner and giver, but he did not take into account the fact that it is not only a personal presence but also rights that leave with the object in question. Instead of the force of the rights, he saw a spiritual power, that of a soul inhabiting the thing and urging it to return to its original owner. Lastly, as several of Mauss' commentators have remarked,[75] the thing given is not inhabited by a single power but by two: first of all it contains the permanent presence of the giver, but since, in this world of beliefs, the object too is a person, it therefore has a soul, it has its own spiritual power which also urges it to return to its place of origin.

Perhaps Mauss' lack of interest in analyzing the facts from the standpoint of the notion of inalienable property can be explained by a desire to get away from what he regarded as the chaotic discussions that had surrounded the notions of collective and individual ownership since the end of the nineteenth century and which had been rekindled by the Bolshevik victory in Russia. For we must not forget that Mauss was a lifelong staunch anti-Bolshevist. In 1947 he even took care to reaffirm his position:

> The major distinction dominating our law, that between personal law and real law, is an *arbitrary* distinction which other societies largely ignore. After Roman law, we made enormous strides in synthesis and unification; but law, and particularly laws governing ownership, *jus utendi et abutendi*, does not start from a single principle, that is where it finishes ... *The question of whether ownership is collective or individual will not be dealt with here.* The terms we attach to things are of no importance, there are collectively owned properties administered by a single individual, the patriarch, in extended families, etc., etc.[76]

The reasons for his lack of interest are understandable. The notion of common ownership seems to him vague and to cover very different realities. He feels that "wherever we look we are confronted with a plurality of laws governing ownership ... Ownership by the king, the tribe, the clan, the village, the quarter, the joint family may all be superimposed on the same object."[77]

In addition, we saw earlier that the collective ownership of land as an inalienable possession seemed to him to be excluded from exchange and gift-giving by the very fact of its being inalienable:

> Land ... which is non-transmissible, tied to the family, the clan, the tribe more than to the individual ... *cannot leave the family to be ceded to an outsider.* Remnants of this state of affairs can be seen in Norman law, sale with privilege of repurchase and *droit de parage* [rights associated with (high) birth] which are still in force on Jersey.[78]

These passages clearly show that what interested Mauss primarily was not the inalienable character of the thing given, but the fact that it was a person and acted as one. That is the reason for his enthusiasm and for his gratitude to Tamati Ranaipiri, who handed him "completely by chance the key to the problem ... In reality, it is the

hau that wishes to return to its birthplace." The question arose with
the publication of the "Essai sur le don" of whether Mauss had not
made Ranaipiri say something other than what he had actually told
Best when he questioned him about the *hau* of the forest. Before elucidating this point, however, this would be a good time to take stock
of the findings produced by our analysis of non-agonistic gift-giving
which, although he did not analyze it, Mauss designated as the starting point for understanding the potlatch.

In non-agonistic gifts and counter-gifts:

The thing or the person given is not alienated. To give is to transfer
   a person or thing whose "usage" is ceded, but not its ownership.
Because of this, a gift creates a debt that cannot be cancelled by a
   counter-gift.
The debt creates an obligation to give in return, but to give in return
   does not mean to give back, to repay; it means to give in turn.
The giving of gifts and counter-gifts creates a state of mutual
   indebtedness and dependence which presents advantages for all
   parties. To give therefore is to share by creating a debt or, which
   amounts to the same thing, to create a debt by sharing.
Gift-giving in these societies is not simply a mechanism for setting
   possessions and people in circulation, thereby ensuring their
   distribution and redistribution among the groups comprising the
   society. It is also, on a deeper level, the condition for the
   production and reproduction of the social relations which
   constitute the framework of a specific society and characterize the
   bonds that are formed between individuals and groups. While a
   woman must be given in order for a woman to be received, this
   exchange does not merely replace one woman by another, it
   creates an alliance between two groups, a relationship which
   enables each to have descendants and to continue to exist.
If we take the societies that practice this type of gift-exchange on the
   level of their overall functioning as totalities which must
   reproduce themselves as such, then the transfers of persons and
   goods engendered by the succession and sequence of gifts and
   counter-gifts between the groups and the individuals comprising
   the society ensure that, in the end, the available material and
   immaterial resources necessary to their social reproduction, and
   which belong to the category of "things" which may be given, are
   spread in a relatively equal way throughout the society.

Soon we will be entering another world, one of rivalries and
inequalities, when we analyze the potlatch. But let us not forget that,

for Mauss, this new world was a transformed version of the one I have just described, a version which was at the same time an extension of and a break with the former.

Is the hau *really the key to the mystery? (or how Mauss read the lesson of the sage Tamati Ranaipiri, from the Ngati-Raukawa tribe, as collected by the ethnologist Elsdon Best in 1909)*

From the time the "Essai sur le don" was published, Mauss' interpretation of Ranaipiri's account of the *hau* has been contested. As early as 1929, Raymond Firth, in his *Primitive Economics of the New Zealand Maori*,[79] maintained that Mauss' "excessively religious" interpretation of the notion of *hau* was utterly without foundation: "When Mauss sees in the gift exchange an interchange of personalities, a 'bond of souls', he is following not native belief, but his own intellectualized interpretation of it."[80]

Firth recalled that the Maori term for a reciprocal exchange of goods is *utu*, and that the general rule of these exchanges is that a gift must be repaid by a counter-gift of at least equal value. Firth was careful to stress that this rule not only applied to economic exchanges, but extended to all areas of social practice. He did not deny the religious content of the notion of *hau*, but he rejected Mauss' principal hypothesis, namely that it is the *hau* of the object which makes it want to return to its place of origin or demands to be replaced by something equivalent. The debate wore on, but it was the publication in 1970 of an article by Marshall Sahlins, "*The Spirit of the Gift*: une explication de texte", in the *Mélanges* in homage to Claude Lévi-Strauss on the occasion of his sixtieth birthday, that marked a turning point.[81]

Elsdon Best had taken the precaution of publishing Tamati Ranaipiri's account in Maori, accompanied by his own translation and comments. Sahlins first went back to these two texts, placing the French and English versions side by side, followed by a new English translation of the Maori text produced by a linguist and Maori specialist, Bruce Biggs. For purposes of comparison, here is Mauss' own rendering in French, followed by Biggs' English translation of the Maori original.

Mauss:

Je vais vous parler du *hau* ... Le *hau* n'est pas le vent qui souffle. Pas du tout. Supposez que vous possédez un article déterminé (*taonga*) et que vous me donnez cet article; vous me le donnez sans prix fixé.

Nous ne faisons pas de marché à ce propos. Or, je donne cet article à
une troisième personne qui, après qu'un certain temps s'est écoulé,
décide de rendre quelque chose en paiement (*utu*), il me fait présent
de quelque chose (*taonga*). Or, ce *taonga* qu'il me donne est l'esprit
(*hau*) du *taonga* que j'ai reçu de vous et que je lui ai donné à lui. Les
taonga que j'ai reçus pour ces *taonga* (venus de vous), il faut que je
vous les rende. Il ne serait pas juste (*tika*) de ma part de garder ces
taonga pour moi, qu'ils soient désirables (*rawe*) ou désagréables
(*kino*). Je dois vous les donner car ils sont un *hau* du *taonga* que vous
m'avez donné. Si je conservais le deuxième *taonga* pour moi, il pour-
rait m'en venir du mal, sérieusement, même la mort. Tel est le *hau*, le
hau de la propriété personnelle, le *hau* des *taonga*, le *hau* de la forêt.
Kati ena (assez sur ce sujet).[82]

Tamati Ranaipiri's Maori text as translated by Bruce Biggs:

Now, concerning the *hau* of the forest [and of the *whangi hau*
rite]. This *hau* is not the *hau* that blows (the wind). No. I will
explain it carefully to you. Now, you have something valuable
which you give to me. We have no agreement about payment. Now, I
give it to someone else, and, a long time passes, and that man thinks
he has the valuable, he should give some repayment to me, and so he
does so. Now, that valuable which was given to me, that is the *hau* of
the valuable which was given to me before. I must give it to you. It
would not be correct for me to keep it for myself, whether it be something very good, or bad, that valuable must be given to you from me.
Because that valuable is a *hau* of the other valuable. If I should hang
onto that valuable for myself, I will become *mate*. So that is the *hau* –
hau of valuables, *hau* of the forest. So much for that.[83]

Marshall Sahlins immediately noticed and pointed out that, in the
first sentence, Mauss had deleted the reference to the *whangai hau*
rite. Yet this allusion is crucial because it provides the context which
enables us to choose, from among the many meanings of the word
hau, the one that best fits Ranaipiri's explanation.

Just what was this *whangai hau* rite (literally, food-giving *hau*)?
Ranaipiri explains this too, in the following way. The context is that
of fowling. Before the hunt begins, the Maori priests (*tohunga*) go
into the forest and conceal a sacred stone known as *mauri*; then they
pray to the *hau* of the forest, calling it to come and dwell in the
stone. It is this *hau*, this *mauri*, and this ritual performed by the
priests that produce the plentiful game which will be caught by the
fowlers. Here is the text that immediately follows the passage on
gift-giving:

I will explain something to you about the forest *hau*. The *mauri* was placed or implanted in the forest by the *tohunga*. It is the *mauri* that causes birds to be abundant in the forest, that they may be slain and taken by man. These birds are the property of, or belong to, the *mauri*, the *tohunga*, and the forest: that is to say, they are an equivalent for that important item, the *mauri*. Hence it is said that offerings should be made to the *hau* of the forest. The *tohunga* (priests, adepts), eat the offering because the *mauri* is theirs: it was they who located it in the forest, who caused it to be. That is why some of the birds cooked at the sacred fire are set apart to be eaten by the priests only, in order that the *hau* of the forest-products, and the *mauri*, may return again to the forest – that is, to the *mauri*. Enough of these matters.[84]

This text is illuminated by several comments that Best makes on the *mauri* and the *hau* in his book, *Forest Lore of the Maori*, a posthumous publication which brings together a series of writings devoted to Maori hunting and gathering techniques, and to their knowledge of botany, zoology, and cosmology:

We now come to a remarkably interesting institution that illustrates a peculiar phase of Maori mentality, and which is known as the *mauri*. We have already seen that the prosperity and fruitfulness of the forest, of trees, birds, etc., is represented by the life-principle or *mauri* of such forest, which is an immaterial quality, but a material symbol of that quality was also employed, and it was also known by the same name. This material *mauri* was usually a stone, and it was carefully concealed in the forest. It acted really as a shrine or abiding place for the spirit-gods in whose care the forest was placed. ...

... the *mauri* serves as a medium between the charms recited and the forest they are meant to affect. The *mauri* is said to protect and preserve the *mana* of the forest ... when the *mauri* calls for birds to become numerous in a forest, then assuredly they will become so; for ... that stone medium acts as a voice to the spirit beings (*atua*), who control all things. ...

It should here be explained that the life-principle of a forest, etc., termed *mauri* is also defined by the word *hau*. So far as I have grasped the matter the *hau* and the *mauri* of a forest are one and the same thing, but we must certainly distinguish between the *hau* and *mauri* of man.[85]

If I understand these texts correctly, fowlers who have had luck with their hunting owe their success as much to the spirit of the forest as to the priests who placed the sacred stone there and with their magic spells attracted its *hau*, the life-giving spirit which came to dwell in the stone. The *mauri* then is the material presence of the forest's *hau*. So we have three categories of actor: the forest, a supernatural entity, the source of life and plentiful game; the priests, who possess the stone *mauri* and the spells for invoking the spirit of the forest and are the mediators between forest and hunters; the fowlers themselves, who, after the rites performed by the priests, have gone into the forest, killed a great number of birds and are about to share them. It is with reference to this situation that Ranaipiri makes the comparison with one involving three human actors, in which the first, A, has given the second, B, a valuable object which B then gives to a third, C, who later makes B a present in return.

Two ideas are associated in the example of the forest, the priests and the fowlers. The first is that the forest is the source of life and its abundance. Ultimately it is the forest that presents hunters with game. The second idea is that the game taken by the hunters still belongs to the forest and to the priests who own both the sacred object and the charm that goes with it and which enables them to persuade the forest to be generous with men. The game that the hunters give to the priests, who will cook it at a sacred fire before eating it (leaving a portion for the forest), is an offering of thanksgiving in the hope that the forest and the priests will continue acting on behalf of the hunters, will continue to provide them with food. But making these gifts is also a way of returning part of the game given by the forest to its original donor.

Transposed to the world of gift-giving among humans, the example of the fowlers, the priests and the forest illuminates two things at once. First, it underscores the fact that the object given by the first donor, A, and which is thereby put into circulation, does not, even as it circulates, cease being attached to its first owner, does not stop belonging to him. And second, it illuminates why the series of counter-gifts, induced by the circulation of a given object, must return to the original donor because he is still the sole owner. As a consequence, he also has rights over the "good things," the positive effects entailed by the handing on of the object he gave at the outset. Should it happen that one of the people among whom the object is circulating and who has already had it for some time wants to keep it for himself, to side-track the "good things" (in Maori *hau whitia*, side-tracked *hau*) that have come to him from having given in turn, he would become ill (*mate*), or, as Best wrote elsewhere, "the dread terrors of *makutu* [sorcery]" would be unleashed on him.[86]

Marshall Sahlins, who had the merit of comparing these texts and others, concluded as Firth had done long before him, that Mauss was on the wrong track when he interpreted the return gift as the effect of the "spirit of the thing" wanting to return to its owner. He adds, after Firth, that the threat of punishment by sorcery cannot come from the *hau* of the thing itself, but must come from the real persons who have been frustrated by their failure to receive a return gift and who therefore cast a spell on the guilty party. Sahlins thus rejects the hypothesis of action on the part of the spirit of the thing for the following reason:

> To illustrate such a spirit needs only a game of two persons: you give something to me; your spirit (*hau*) in that thing obliges me to reciprocate. Simple enough. The introduction of a third party could only unduly complicate and obscure the point. But if the point is neither spiritual nor reciprocity as such, if it is rather that one man's gift should not be another man's capital and therefore the fruits of a gift ought to be passed back to the original holder, then the introduction of a third party is necessary. It is necessary precisely to show a *turnover*: the gift has had issue; the recipient has used it to advantage.[87]

Finally, having rejected Mauss' "animistic, spiritual" explanation for returning the thing given, Sahlins advances the notions of "profit" and of the initial giver's rights over the benefits induced by his gift. But he does not take a closer look at the bond which allows the donor to claim these "profits." He stops midway, contenting himself with formulas that do not really satisfy him: "The term 'profit' is economically and historically inappropriate to the Maori, but it would have been a better translation than 'spirit' for the hau in question."[88]

Furthermore Sahlins reminds us that, with the Maori, we are dealing with a society where "the freedom to gain at others' expense is not envisioned by the relations and forms of exchange."[89]

In reality, we need to focus once more on the essential idea, which Sahlins mentions but does not dwell on, namely that the original donor does not forfeit his rights over the object he has given, regardless of the number of times it may change hands. Of course the fact that it circulates means that every person who receives it, each recipient, in turn becomes a donor. But none will have the same rights over the object as the original donor. His ownership is inalienable; the others merely enjoy rights of possession and use, which are alienable and temporary and are transferred with the object.

It is this essential fact of the permanence of the original donor's rights over the thing given which is translated on the conceptual level (in other words on the level of the indigenous representations and interpretations of this permanence) by the idea that a part of the original donor is present in the thing given, that he is attached to it and accompanies it as it passes from hand to hand and place to place. But this indelible presence of the giver in the object given does not actually become visible until the object circulates beyond the simple exchange of gifts between two people. Three or more parties are necessary for everything to become clear. To Mauss, who expressed his surprise at Ranaipiri's introducing a third person, Sahlins replies that it was precisely the presence of a third party which showed that we are dealing with something "more than a merely spiritual reciprocity or even reciprocity itself."

But Sahlins is mistaken on this point. We are not dealing with something more than reciprocity. And this is fairly easy to prove. Let us begin with the fact that A owns an object and gives it to B. B does not become the owner, but he nevertheless gives it in turn to C. The chain could go on, with C giving to D, D to E, and so forth, and we could have an unlimited number of persons occupying the equivalent of B's middleman position. But our example needs only three actors and, like Ranaipiri, we will stop at C. Now, what does C do? He gives B an object which he himself owns in exchange for the object coming from A and which A still owns. B can then only give something back to A, to whom he is indebted, and this will be the object received from C, which takes the place of the object received from A. A and C "owned" the objects they gave, but B, as the intermediary, never owned the things that passed through his hands.

Between A and C, the two ends of the chain, there is reciprocity, since the property of one takes the place of the property of the other. B, on the other hand, served as an intermediary and, in passing, also profited from the object that was circulating. Which means that he, too, incurred a debt to the others. This is exactly the logic that is illustrated by the circulation of the *vaygu'a*, the armshells and necklaces which circulate in the *kula* between the populations of the islands off the northeast coast of New Guinea.

Let us see how Mauss construes Ranaipiri's account:

> This text, of capital importance, deserves a few comments. It is purely Maori, permeated by that, as yet, vague theological and juridical spirit of doctrines within the "house of secrets", but at times astonishingly clear, and presenting only one obscure feature: the intervention of a third person. Yet in order to understand this Maori juridical expert, one needs only to say: "The *taonga* and all goods termed strictly personal possess a *hau*, a spiritual power. You give me one of them, and I pass it on to a third party; he gives another one to me, because he is impelled to do so by the *hau* my present possesses. I, for my part, am obliged to give you the thing because I must return to

you what is in reality the effect of the *hau* of your *taonga*. ... In reality, it is the *hau* that wishes to return to its birthplace, to the sanctuary of the forest and the clan, and to the owner.[90]

Here Mauss invokes and combines two reasons to explain the return of the object to the initial donor. Reason one: the object itself possesses a spirit, a soul, and it is this spirit that makes it want to return to its original owner. Reason two: the giver has a hold over the receiver because the object takes something of the giver with it which compels the receiver to give in return. This something is soul, a spiritual presence. Mauss lays the stress on this spiritual presence rather than on the fact that the original donor continues to have permanent rights over the thing he has given. Mauss thus leaves another reality in the background, a social reality this time: the fact that, in these societies, givers retain ownership of what they have given. This social reality is a force present in the object, which controls and pre-defines its use and movement:

What imposes obligation in the present received and exchanged, is the fact that the thing received is not inactive. Even when it has been abandoned by the giver, *it still possesses something of him.* ... This is because the *taonga* is animated by the *hau* of its forest, its native heath and soil. It not only follows after the first recipient, and even, if the occasion arises, a third person, but after any individual to whom the *taonga* is merely passed on. In reality it is the *hau* that wishes to return to its birthplace, to the sanctuary of the forest and the clan, and to the owner. The *taonga* or the *hau* – which itself moreover possesses a kind of individuality – is attached to this chain of users until these give back the equivalent or something of even greater value. This in turn will give the donors authority and power over the first donor, who has become the last recipient.[91]

Mauss adds a note to the effect that "the *taonga* seem to be endowed with individuality even beyond the hau *that is conferred upon them through their relationship with their owner.*"[92] This text confirms our interpretation that, for Mauss, two spiritual principles abide, side by side, in a single thing: one is the presence of the owner in the object; the other, the presence of a spirit peculiar to this object and independent from its owner. It is above all this latter spirit which, according to Mauss, makes the object want to return to its original owner, a part of whose spirit is also present in the object. Mauss' explanation therefore does indeed place the emphasis on beliefs and on "spiritual," ideological reasons.

With this example we have already stepped beyond the world of gift and counter-gift and across the border into the world of the pot-latch.[93]

Potlatch: the gift-exchange that fascinated Mauss

Mauss was fascinated by gift-exchanges featuring rivalry, competition, and antagonism. The potlatches of the Kwakiutl Indians and their neighbors on the northwest coast of North America seemed to him an extreme case; nevertheless after the description Malinowski had just published (1922) of the *kula* practiced by the societies of northeastern New Guinea, which followed Thurnwald's description of analogous events on Buin in the Solomon Islands, and those of other authors, Mauss concluded that this was a human phenomenon widely distributed in space and over time. He therefore made a broad sociological category of the potlatch, and it is by this name that agonistic gift-exchanges have become known and popularized.

The rules of potlatch seem to oppose term for term the principles animating the gift-exchanges we have just analyzed. In potlatch, one gives in order to "flatten" the other. To do this, one gives more than (one thinks) the other can repay or one repays much more than the other has given. As in non-agonistic exchanges of gifts and counter-gifts, the potlatch-gift creates a debt and an obligation for the receiver, but in this case the goal is explicitly to make it difficult or impossible to give back the equivalent: it is to put the other lastingly in debt, to make him lose face publicly, thus affirming for as long as possible one's own superiority.

Arguing from an abundant literature and not only, as has too often been claimed, from the writings of Boas,[94] Mauss stresses that the potlatch is above all "a struggle between nobles to establish a hierarchy amongst themselves from which their clan will benefit at a later date."[95] This rivalry can go as far as "the purely sumptuary destruction of wealth that has been accumulated by the clan in order to outdo the rival chief who is at the same time his associate."[96] For Mauss, the "exacerbated rivalry" of the potlatch leading to the ostentatious destruction of wealth makes it an evolved but relatively rare form of total prestation: "There is total prestation," he writes, "in the sense that it is indeed the whole clan that contracts on behalf of all for all that it possesses and for all that it does, through the person of its chief."[97] But between this exacerbated form and the "more moderate rivalry" encountered in Melanesia, Mauss finds a considerable number of intermediate forms, in Polynesia, Malaysia, South America, and elsewhere, and in antiquity, in Thrace and further afield in the Indo-European world. Keeping to the Kwakiutl potlatch, here is Mauss' reconstruction of the way it works.

The primary aim of these contests is, from a certain standpoint, "political" supremacy:

> The political status of individuals in the brotherhoods and clans, and ranks of all kinds, are gained in a "war of property", just as they are in real war ... everything is conceived of as if it were a "struggle of wealth". Marriages for one's children and places in the brotherhoods are only won during potlatches, exchanged and given back.[98]

And further on: "The potlatch, the distribution of goods, is the basic act of 'recognition', military, juridical, economic, and religious in every sense of the word. One 'recognizes' the chief or his son and becomes 'grateful' to him."[99]

Mauss saw clearly that competition between clans and between chiefs was bound up with the desire either to *validate* the transmission of a title or a rank already acquired, or to acquire or *conquer* a new title or rank. The escalation of the gifts culminates in the ostentatious destruction of wealth and precious objects in front of a large audience:

> In a certain number of cases, it is not even a question of giving and returning gifts, but of destroying ... the most valuable copper objects are broken and thrown into the water, in order to put down and to "flatten" one's rival. In this way one not only promotes oneself, but also one's family, up the social scale. It is therefore a system of law and economics in which considerable wealth is constantly being expended and transferred.[100]

Mauss stresses the fact that, in these societies, there is a direct connection between wealth and power or authority:

> ... the rich man is one who has *mana* in Polynesia, *auctoritas* in Rome, and who, in these American tribes is "open-handed". But strictly speaking we need only point out the relationship between the notion of wealth, that of authority, and the right of commanding those who receive presents, and the potlatch: it is a very clear relationship. ... The chief is said to "swallow the tribes" to whom he distributes his wealth; he "spits forth property", etc.[101]

The obligation *to give* is the *essence* of the potlatch. A chief must give potlatches for himself, his son, his son-in-law, or his daughter and for his dead. He can only preserve his authority over his tribe ... he can only maintain his rank among the chiefs – nationally and internationally – if he can prove he is haunted and favoured both by the spirits and by good fortune, that he is possessed, and also possesses it. But he can only prove his good fortune by spending it and sharing it out, humiliating others by placing them "in the shadow of his name".[102]

In these circumstances, it is easy to understand that, in such a world,

> [t]o refrain from giving, just as to refrain from accepting is to lose rank, as is refraining from reciprocating. The obligation to *reciprocate* constitutes the *essence of the potlatch*, in so far as it does not consist of pure destruction ... One loses face forever if one does not reciprocate, or if one does not carry out destruction of equivalent value.[103]

Reciprocate, to be sure, but, as Mauss states further on, if the potlatch is an imposed strategy for capturing a rank or validating a title, it is the act of *giving* and of *outgiving* that counts (to fall short is to fail):

> Between chiefs and their vassals, between vassals and their tenants, through such gifts a hierarchy is established. To give is to show one's superiority, to be more, to be higher in rank, *magister*. To accept without giving in return, or without giving more back, is to become a client and servant, to become small, to fall lower (*minister*).[104]

Of course, since there are several chiefs competing for each title or each rank and none either wants or can afford to admit defeat at the outset, each must therefore strive to outdo the others in order not to "lose face": his honor and reputation are at stake. In all aspects of this struggle the supreme obligation is to give, but paradoxically this means to give with the intention of *breaking the chain of reciprocity*, of breaking it to one's own advantage, or at least this is the hope of each competitor. Moreover, in one of his footnotes, Mauss says in passing, even though the statement weakens the idea that the obligation to repay is central to the potlatch: "*The ideal would be to give a potlatch that is not returned.*"[105]

Potlatch logic is therefore wholly different from that of non-agonistic exchanges of gifts and counter-gifts, since, at the end of the latter, every lineage has given some of its own resources to the others but has received the equivalent in return, a woman for a woman, for example.

We have seen how Mauss reconstitutes the sociological context of the potlatch. But we have not yet examined what kind of exchanged wealth fuels this war of property. Basically there are precious objects, shells, coppers, carved objects, but also dances, rites, and so on. These were given publicly in the course of ceremonies accompanied by feasts at which enormous quantities of food were distributed. But, Mauss remarks after Boas, the Kwakiutl did not really count these "provisions" as constituting wealth. Just what are these precious objects, the most valuable of which are the famous emblazoned coppers? Again Mauss stresses the spiritual essence of the precious objects that circulate in these exchanges: "One can push the analysis further and demonstrate that in the things exchanged during the potlatch, a power is present that forces gifts to be passed around, to be given, and returned."[106] The emblazoned coppers that are the stars of the potlatch "are the focus of important beliefs and even of a cult. ... Copper, at least among the Haïda and the Kwakiutl, is identified with the salmon, which is itself the object of a cult. [Amongst the Tlingit], because it is red, copper is identified with the sun; a 'fire falling from heaven'."[107]

There is one essential point (at least in my opinion) in Mauss' text that he did not see fit to dwell on and which did not give rise to subsequent comment from Firth, Lévi-Strauss, or Sahlins. This silence went unbroken until Annette Weiner's publications. Here is the point in question. In a note, referring to Boas, Mauss indicates that the Kwakiutl had two kinds of coppers:

> The *most important ones* that *do not go outside* of the family and that can only be broken to be recast, and certain *others* that *circulate* intact, that are of less value, and that seem to serve as *satellites* for the first kind. The possession of this secondary kind of copper object doubtless corresponds among the Kwakiutl to that of the titles of nobility and second-order ranks with whom they travel, passing from chief to chief, from family to family, between the generations and the sexes. It appears that *the great titles and the great copper objects* at the very least *remain unmovable* within the clans and the tribes. Moreover, it might be difficult for it to be otherwise.[108]

In addition to coppers there are other valuables which do not leave the family. "The large abalone shells, the shields that are covered with these shells ... the blankets themselves that also bear emblems, covered with faces, eyes, and animal and human figures that are woven and embroidered on them."[109] Each of these objects and tokens of wealth has, "as in the Trobriand Islands, its individuality, its name, its qualities, its power."[110] Among the precious named objects are also male and female noble titles, privileges, dances, and the like. These sacred items are transmitted from one generatio to the next through marriage and inheritance. They leave the clan to return to it, since the "privileges" are ceded by a father-in-law to his son-in-law, who hands them on in turn to his son. Thus the privilege ceded to the son-in-law returns with the grandson to the original clan. Hence Mauss' comment:

> It is even *incorrect* to speak in these cases of *transfer*. They are loans rather than sales or true abandonment of possessions. Among the Kwakiutl a certain number of objects, although they appear at the potlatch, cannot be disposed of. In reality these pieces of "property" are *sacra* that a family divests itself of only with great reluctance, and sometimes never.[111]

These sacred things, these valuables constitute as a whole a sort of *"magical dower"*[112] for each family. The objects themselves seem to be the direct source of the clan's wealth. Not only do they produce it in abundance, but they attract wealth from outside. "[Coppers] have a power of attraction that is felt by other copper objects, just as wealth attracts wealth, or dignities bring honours in their train, as well as the possession of spirits and fruitful alliances – and vice versa."[113]

Where does this power, this capacity to produce and to attract wealth come from? The answer is simple: from the fact that these things are "divine": they are gifts from spirits or the gods to men, and the spirits or the gods continue to dwell in them and to act on the humans who now own them because they received them from their ancestors or from the clan's founding hero, who received them from a spirit.

Mythology affirms the continuity and the identity of a spiritual presence or essence flowing from the gods or spirits who originally gave these sacred items to the items themselves and to the humans who now own them because they received them from more or less legendary ancestors reputed to have been the first recipients and the first donors. The important coppers

> are "the flat, divine things" of the household. Often the myth identifies them all, the spirits that have given the copper objects, their owners, and the copper objects themselves. It is impossible to distinguish what makes the strength of spirit in one and wealth in the other: the copper object speaks, and grumbles. It demands to be given away, to be destroyed; it is covered with blankets to keep it warm, just as the chief is buried under the blankets that he is to share out.[114]

Of course, Mauss does not personally believe that the big coppers were made by the gods. He refers to Rivet's work on pre-Columbian gold work (published in 1923 in the *Journal des américanistes*), regretting that he left out the northwest American copper industry, which is still not well known.[115] The native copper came from Copper River and was melted down elsewhere. Mauss suggested that the Tsimshian and Kwakiutl aristocracies most probably had something to do with possession of the secret of melting down and extracting copper and the control of the copper trade. But he did not pursue his analysis of the real conditions of copper production and trade. In fact, as a rule, Mauss does not concern himself with the relations men entertain in the course of producing things, only with those formed between men by the circulation of the things they produce. He therefore simply tells us that the most valuable of these coppers were extremely rare and regarded as gifts from the gods to be hoarded. The other, more numerous coppers circulated in potlatches and were regarded, as he so nicely puts it, as "satellites for the first kind."

Finally, the world Mauss describes is a magical or enchanted world (he uses the word *féerique*)[116] in which precious objects continually circulate through series of potlatches and return-potlatches, gravitating around things more valuable still, sacred things which do not move, which remain within the clan where the gods are said to have deposited them. These immovable objects are the embodiments of spirits, spirits which are things, things which are spirits. "They are alive and move *autonomously*, and inspire other coppers to do so."[117]

The effect of religious beliefs and representations is clearly visible. They propose an interpretation of the world and of human institutions in which, when all causes and origins have at last been explained, things have taken the place of humans, the objects have become the subjects, objects manufactured and exchanged by human beings have become objects made by gods and freely given, out of generosity, to a few distant ancestors of the people living today, preserved in memory, raised to the rank of heroes.

We know that religious beliefs not only are part of this world, but in part make this world. They do this in such a way that they efface another part of it, by replacing real humans with imaginary duplicates, stand-ins who act in their stead. But Mauss says nothing of this. Nor does he linger over the distinction he himself made between family treasures, the immovable *sacra*, and the other precious objects which move through the potlatch circuit. The first, he says, are owned in common by clans and families, and as such, it seems obvious to him that they must remain in place, inalienable. For Mauss, then, "inalienable" means "non-exchangeable." But having opposed these two categories of goods, a few pages later he seems to annul this opposition without giving his reasons:

All in all, when one considers both the copper objects and the other permanent forms of wealth that are *likewise an object of hoarding and of alternating potlatches*, masks, talismans, etc. – all are *mingled together* as regards use and effect. ... Everything holds together, everything is mixed up together. Things possess a personality, and personalities are in some way the permanent things of the clan. Titles, talismans, copper objects, and the spirits of the chiefs are both homonyms and synonyms of the same nature and performing the same function.[118]

These are fine, even superb, formulas, but the fact that objects, precious, hoarded, or circulating in potlatches, have personalities or souls, is no license to confound them, and especially not to confound the functions they fulfill in each case. The problem of why certain things are more valuable than others because they are sacred and why, because they are sacred, they do not enter into the potlatch remains unexplained. Even if an object may, over its lifetime, pass from one category to the other, first hoarded and later given in potlatch (or the converse), over and beyond the fate of this object, there remains the question of why, in the production and reproduction of these societies, of society in general, there are two permanently distinct, clearly separate functions to be discharged, two functions which entail the appearance of two categories of precious objects which, as categories, are equally and always distinct. That, over its lifetime, an object can move from one category to the other is a very interesting point which I will analyze later. But the fact that it is immovable or immobilized for a time when in one category, and always on the move once it enters the other category is the best proof that the functions it fulfills at various times in its life cannot be confounded.

It seems that here we are nearing the limits of Mauss to provide a theoretical explanation of the facts he was analyzing. Further on, when dealing with the same problem, the interpretation of the *vaygu'a*, the precious objects circulated in the *kula*, those far-flung intertribal exchange cycles described by Malinowski, we will encounter the same limits. But before attempting to elucidate the nature of these and the reasons for them, I would like to say that the limits of Mauss' theory cannot be explained, as certain Marxist authors would have it, by his having adopted Boas' descriptions without realizing that the latter was describing Kwakiutl society "in the image of his own society, at a time when the capitalist ethic encouraged speculation on the stock market, a society driven by individualism and profit."[119]

More recently, when invited to comment on an article by Marie

Mauzé, which is a solid, well-balanced assessment of Boas' work situating it clearly in its historical context,[120] Meillassoux reoffends and again accuses Mauss of having "rashly endorsed Boas" and in so doing endorsed the liberal economic ideology that animated him and led him to "be so seriously mistaken in his interpretation of the potlatch." He alleges that Mauss, by his lack of rigor and his prejudged ideas, contributed to "derailing economic research in anthropology for a long time."[121]

This depiction of a Mauss mystified by liberal capitalist ideology is deeply flawed and a caricature of what a critical analysis of a complex and powerful work should be; Mauss' work cannot be reduced to a few quotations which provide a cheap confirmation of the critic's pedantic presuppositions. In reality, Mauss' attitude is just the opposite. Despite his admiration for Boas and his even greater respect for Malinowski, because both were field men whose rich works proved the superiority of "descriptive sociology," Mauss greeted with great critical caution the interpretations these authors advanced of the facts they had observed directly. I will cite a few examples.

While the structures of capitalism are complex, its rules are simple and clearly different from (and even contradictory to) those governing the social systems analyzed by Mauss. The capitalist system is presented as the most highly developed system of commodity production of all time. It is based on the principle of private ownership of the means of production and of consumption, on money, and on the selling and buying of the intellectual and/or manual labor involved in the process of the production and circulation of commodities. The mainspring of capitalism, too, is simple: the desire to make money with money,[122] which implies transforming money into capital, which is in turn invested in the process of the production and circulation of commodities. The use-value of a commodity, be it a material or an immaterial one, its usefulness in other words, is important only insofar as it is the indispensable support for its exchange-value and thereby the means, the instrument of enhancing capital.

But how does Mauss feel about capitalism? Let us not forget that the "Essai sur le don" was written only shortly after the end of the First World War and the Bolshevik victory in Russia. Nor should we forget that Mauss was a socialist and politically committed to reforming capitalist society, that he was a regular contributor to the newspaper *L'Humanité*, before it was taken over by the communists. Now the reform he suggests – we will return to this in the closing chapter of this book – is actually a forerunner of the social-democratic program which combines a market economy and state-socialism. He criticizes communism as being "as harmful to [the individual] and to society as the egoism of our contemporaries and the individualism of our laws."[123] And he condemns Bolshevism because it relies on violence to promote social advancement.[124] "It goes without saying that we do not recommend that any dismantlement of the law should take place. The principles of law that govern the market, purchase and sale, which are the indispensable condition for the formation of capital, must and can subsist side by side with new principles and more ancient ones."[125]

These ancient principles to which we need to return are gift-giving and "noble expenditures," by which people in other societies than our own acceded to wealth and power. "It is our Western societies who have recently made man an *'economic animal'* ... *For a very long time man was something different, and he has not been a machine for very long, made complicated by a calculating machine.*"[126]

Ultimately we find ourselves in a situation in which

> a whole section of the law, that relating to industrialists and businessmen, is nowadays at odds with morality. The economic prejudices of the people, the producers, arise from their firm determination to follow the thing they have produced, and from the strong feeling they have that their handiwork is resold without their having had any share of the profit.[127]

To the ancient principle that the wealthy should nobly share their wealth, Mauss proposes to add and develop the new principle of a "State socialism," the need for which is obvious if we accept that it is not enough that the community merely pay the worker for his services. It "owes him ... a certain security in life, against unemployment, sickness, old age, and death."[128] In light of this it is hard to accuse Mauss of having been, at the beginning of the twentieth century, a blind follower of "economic liberalism."

Let us therefore come back to the essential, which is not only to show that Mauss remained to a certain extent aloof from Boas' thinking, but above all that, in striving to interpret the reported facts, he even ventured to challenge the Western concepts of economics and the West's summary views of the economic history of mankind.

One needs only to read Mauss to realize that he was lucid about the limits of the material collected by Boas and those who preceded and followed him. "The attention of Boas and his companions on the Jesup Expedition was focused on the material aspects of civilization, on linguistics and mythological literature ... *The juridical and economic analysis, as well as the demography, either remains to be carried out or at least to be supplemented.*"[129]

In matters of economy and law, he regarded the old Russian, German, French, and English authors he had read, whose works dated from before 1870, as "the best ... The dates of these works impart definitive authority to them."[130] He regretted that too little was known about "social morphology" (today we would say, the social organization of these societies), about the nature of the groups that comprise these societies (clans, secret societies, and so on), and he argued that this should be looked into "before time runs out."[131] He uses the term "feudal classes" to describe these tribal aristocracies, a Eurocentric expression used by most authors (before Marc Bloch) whether liberal or Marxist, Western or Eastern, to describe societies governed by various forms of aristocracy. All were readily dubbed "feudal" or "quasi-feudal."[132] Mauss even adds a "general remark" in his notes, which is very important, to my mind, inasmuch as it shows that he was aware that he did not know enough to understand the relations between the thing given at a potlatch and its owner; this is the nodal point of his work, where we measure his strengths and his limitations.

> A general remark: we know fairly accurately how and why, and during which ceremonies, expenditure and destruction are the means of passing on goods in the American Northwest. However we are still badly informed about the forms assumed by the act of passing on things, particularly copper objects. This question should be the subject of an investigation. The little we know is extremely interesting and certainly denotes *the link between property and its owners.*[133]

All of these passages show just how aware Mauss was of the shortcomings of Boas' work and the other sources he had used, but they do not yet speak to the heart of his concerns, namely the critique of Boas' own interpretation of the facts he was reporting. This is truly where we measure not only Mauss' critical circumspection, but also his effort to construct an *alternate theory, another* theoretical interpretation of the facts reported by Boas.

First of all, concerning the word "potlatch" itself, it seemed to him that "neither the idea nor the nomenclature behind the use of this term have in the languages of the Northwest the kind of preciseness that is afforded them in the Anglo-Indian 'pidgin' that has Chinook [i.e. the trading language used between Indians and Europeans] as its basis."[134] Next, after having examined Boas' glossaries, he notes that "it seems that even the words 'exchange' and 'sale' are foreign to the Kwakiutl language."[135] But that is not his main criticism. This comes paradoxically at the end of a long note in which Mauss has taken the trouble to copy out the famous page in which Boas wrote: "The economic system of the Indians of the British colony is largely based on credit, as much as that of civilized peoples."[136] And Mauss comments: "Boas has written nothing better on the potlatch." But he quickly adds: "By *correcting* the terms 'debt', 'payment', 'reimbursment', 'loan', and *replacing* them with such terms as 'presents given' and 'presents returned', terms that Boas moreover ends up by using himself, we have a fairly exact idea of how the notion of credit functions in the potlatch."[137]

By correcting, and especially by replacing the terms used by Boas, Mauss carries out a theoretical recentering which leads him not only to question economists' concepts and their simplistic views of the economic history of mankind, but to become aware of those limits he himself is unable to overcome, of the point at which his own movement is arrested, where his thinking runs aground, comes to a standstill, as it were:

> Several times we have seen how far this whole economy of the exchange-through-gift lay outside the bounds of the so-called natural economy [not having exchange and/or commerce], that of utilitarianism [i.e. limited to the exchange of materially useful things]. All these very considerable phenomena of the economic life of all peoples ... and all these important vestiges of those traditions in societies close to our own, or of our own customs, *fall outside the schemes* normally put forward by those rare economists who have wished to compare the various types of known economies.[138]

Mauss goes on to say that he joins his efforts with those of Malinowski, who devoted "an entire study to 'exploding' current doctrines concerning 'primitive' economy."[139] But Mauss feels both that Malinowski's criticism does not go far enough in demolishing these doctrines and that the theoretical analysis he himself developed as an alternative is not really satisfying.

> However we can go even *farther* than we have gone up to now. One can dissolve, jumble up together, colour and define differently the principal notions that we have used. The terms that we have used – present and gift – *are not themselves entirely exact. We are unable,* however, *to find others*. These concepts of law and economics that it pleases us to contrast: liberty and obligation; liberality, generosity, and luxury, as against savings, interest, and utility – *it would be good to put them into the melting pot once more*.[140]

As an example, he takes the interpretation of the *vaygu'a*, precious articles that circulate in the *kula* cycle between the Trobriand Islands and the other islands of northeast New Guinea, which I will analyze in a moment.

Lastly, it is no accident that all of the theoretical difficulties cluster around the interpretation of the nature of the precious objects which circulate in gift-exchanges and whose mode of circulation, which may seem strange to us, needs elucidating. Most of these objects are material items whose value does not reside solely in the scarcity of their matter – mother-of-pearl, copper, bone, jade, feathers – or in the labor expended to manufacture and enhance them. The choice of material and the labor invested all count, of course, but less than a certain immaterial reality present in the objects. This reality is imaginary. Its content is comprised of ideas and symbols which endow it with a social power; this power is then used by individuals and groups to act upon each other, in order either to establish new social relationships or to reproduce old ones.

In no case can the imaginary, immaterial content of the things given be reduced to the mere presence of the giver in the thing given. To be sure, it is because the things which are given "are not completely separated" from their owner that they take part of his being with them and that, through these things, persons form bonds, commit themselves to each other. The relations established are "personal," the obligations are between people, and the thing given is the token of the obligations they have contracted. And yet we cannot stop at this level, where the obligation to give flows from the fact that giving creates obligations, which immediately sets in motion a circle of mutual obligations since consenting to receive creates an obligation to give in return, to "pay back," and so on. For while a man can choose to give to one person rather than to another, or to receive from one rather than another, no one in these societies – if he wants to go on existing, that is reproducing himself while reproducing his relations with others – can decide to cease giving and receiving. Behind individuals and their relationships lies another reality, which is social, impersonal, and objective, and which impinges on everyone at every moment, relentlessly.

Mauss saw this, recognized it, and expressed it in one of the few texts in which he attempts to delve beyond the imaginary and symbolic aspects of things that are given in search of an objective reality which cannot be reduced to these imaginary realities, a necessity which cannot be reduced to subjective and intersubjective conscious data, a necessity which could be the source of these other realities and which would explain their existence. Speaking of the "system of gift-exchange" in Melanesian and Polynesian societies, he writes:

> Material and moral life, and exchange, function within it in a form that is both disinterested and obligatory. Moreover, this obligation is expressed in a mythical and imaginary way or, one might say, symbolic and collective. It assumes an aspect that centres on the interest attached to the things exchanged. *These are never completely detached* from those carrying out the exchange. The mutual ties and alliance that they establish are comparatively indissoluble. In reality this symbol of social life – the *permanence of influence* over the things exchanged – serves merely to reflect somewhat directly the manner in which the subgroups in these segmented societies, archaic in type – and constantly enmeshed with one another, feel that they owe everything to one another.[141]

The objective obligation for the component groups of archaic societies to exchange with each other in order to exist was, according to Mauss, expressed "somewhat directly," but in an imaginary or symbolic manner (which I do not regard as being the same thing), by the fact that "the objects exchanged are never completely separated" from their owners. However Mauss tells us nothing about why this obligation should take a mythic form except to say that this is what people believe. Furthermore, the obligation for individuals and groups to "exchange" in order to exist socially is certainly not typical of only segmentary or even more generally "archaic" societies. But above all, if the objects exchanged in gift-giving have a soul, they are not alone in this: sacred objects, too, have a soul, and theirs is even "stronger" because gods, spirits, illustrious ancestors, who are greater than human beings, dwell and act in these objects. And yet these sacred objects, which enjoy an additional portion of soul with respect to valuables that are given, are in general neither given nor exchanged.

Mauss should therefore have asked himself: why, of all these objects endowed with a soul, can those that are in greatest supply be given and circulate between individuals and groups "without ever being completely separable" from their original owners, whereas the others, the most valuable, the most sacred, do not circulate but remain immobilized in the clan and the family treasure? And as these two categories of objects exist in the "segmentary" societies he studied, it may be concluded that segmentation, the division of society into subgroups which are "constantly enmeshed with one another, and feel that they owe everything to one another," *in no way implies that they give everything to one another.*

For him it was obvious that sacred things are not alienable, and he kept his questions and reservations for the problem of why those things that were given and exchanged were not done so completely. In focusing his analysis on a single category of objects (and phenomena), he failed to see that it could not be separated from the other, complementary, category, whose very existence was a necessary predicate for its own.

By excluding sacred objects from his field of analysis, Mauss may have unintentionally created the illusion that exchange was the be-all and end-all of social life, thereby preparing the way for Lévi-Strauss, who further simplified matters in his well-known formula which reduces society to the threefold exchange of women, wealth, and words.

In reality, as I will attempt to show later, no kind of exchange whatsoever fully accounts for a society's functioning or fully explains the totality of the social. Alongside the "things" – goods, services, and persons – which are exchanged stands everything that is not given, not sold, and these are also the object of institutions and specific practices which are an irreducible component of total society and help explain that it functions as a whole.

This brings me to distance myself somewhat from Mauss' description of the potlatch as a total social fact. However, in no way do I contest the importance of this notion, first introduced into the social sciences by Mauss and which brought him well-deserved renown. Mauss distinguishes two degrees, two classes of social phenomena, according to whether they "involve the *totality* of society and its institutions (potlatch, clans confronting one another, tribes visiting one another), [or] in other cases only *a very large number* of institutions, particularly when these exchanges and contracts rather concern the individual."[142]

It is probable that the potlatch concerns all groups of society and in this sense may draw the whole society in its train. And it is certain that the potlatch or the *kula* are even "more than systems of institutions divided, for example, into religion, law, economy, etc.";[143] they are "features" of social systems in their entirety, since, if we apply these analytical categories to such phenomena, we "dissect them producing rules of law, myths, values and prices," and thus risk passing over the unity, the "movement of the whole."[144] But neither the societies of northwest America nor even less those of northeast New Guinea can be completely summed up or expressed by the potlatch or the *kula*, even if the "economy and [the] moral" of both are deeply marked by them.

What Mauss did see clearly, however, was that, once the logic of potlatch is set in motion, once a system of agonistic gift-exchange is put in place and embraces most of the groups comprising a society, nothing seems capable of stopping it. Gradually everything becomes the occasion for potlatch: life, marriage, death. Each gift supposes, presupposes other gifts, in an endless chain which seems to be self-driven.

At this point, for the members of these societies, individuals as well as groups, caught up in this perpetual-motion machine from which there is no escape (except significantly, for a few individuals and groups whose duties and position place them beyond rivalry, such as the families of chiefs who claim to be descended from the gods), it is as if the valuables given and received in potlatch (and the potlatches themselves) had a life of their own which endlessly moves them on, catching up the human beings as they go, turning them from subjects into objects and leaving them dominated by this round of wealth that they themselves set turning.

There is nothing out of the way in these processes. The same is true of our capitalist market societies, where wealth consists mainly of monetary signs and where the money accumulated is, in the last analysis, always the product of production, followed by sale and purchase of commodities of all kinds. These may be material or immaterial; they may have to do with means of production, of consumption or destruction, with people's living or their labor, with the services of a priest or a prostitute; but the specific, concrete reality of each commodity is important only insofar as its use underpins an exchange-value and this is transformed into money which generates money, in other words into capital.

We see the same type of phenomena every day in our own societies. Once, at some point in history, the machinery is set in motion which enables and necessitates the accumulation of capital, the continual transformation of commodities and money into capital and vice versa, it is no longer possible to halt the circulation of commodities and money for long, and it is impossible to arrest it forever. The system reproduces itself "on its own." It is as if money circulated by itself and engendered capital and commodities which in turn produced commodities and capital. We find ourselves, as Sraffa says, "in a world where commodities produce commodities by means of commodities."[145] Marx has said the final word on "it is as if." But the two worlds, the world of gifts and that of commodities, are in fact comparable. To the fetishism of the objects given corresponds that of commodities, and to the fetishism of sacred objects corresponds that of money functioning as capital, as value endowed with its own power to engender value, as money capable of engendering money. This is the mythology of capital.

But we must take the comparison further and examine the difference between the forms of consciousness which exist in an economy dominated by gift-exchange and in a market-driven economy where intellectual and manual labor are also commodities.[146] In societies dominated by the obligation to give (and in the case of potlatch societies by the obligation to *outgive*), objects seem ultimately to take the place of persons, objects behave like subjects. In societies dominated by the obligation to sell and to make money, to make a profit by competing in the sale of goods and services, people are, up to a point, treated like objects. In both instances, however, an identical process has been at work: in each case the real relations people entertain with the objects they produce, exchange (or keep) have vanished, disappeared from their consciousness, and other forces, other, this time imaginary, actors have replaced the human beings who originally produced them.

Whether the sacred things that are not given or the valuables that are given appear to have an in-dwelling spirit which drives them, or the commodities have an exchange-value, a price which fluctuates independently of conscious awareness and the control of those who produce or consume them, we are in either case in the presence of man-made worlds, but ones which have become detached from man and are peopled by phantasmic doubles, duplicates: these are often benevolent and succor man, often they crush him, but in all events they dominate him.

I have shown elsewhere,[147] and I will return to this demonstration in the final chapter, that this production of phantasmic beings who dominate humans is the remote origin of classes and castes, and that it explains why people are willing to work for or to share the product of their labor with those among them who seem closer than they to the gods, with the spirits who bring plenty or misfortune, with priests, with chiefs who are favored by or descended from the gods. In these societies dominated by personal relations, such relationships are no more transparent than the impersonal relations prevailing in the market-based and state-bureaucratic societies described by Max Weber. Their opacity is simply different; for between individuals and groups stand the intercessors who populate their beliefs: gods, spirits, ancestors – benevolent or aggressive, nurturing or cannibalistic – to whom constant prayers must be said, offerings and even sacrifices made. It is hard for an anthropologist to believe that, in societies in which groups and individuals entertain direct relations and where much of the exchange is not conducted for commercial purposes, these relations are any less mystified or more "transparent" simply because they are personal. And yet that is what Marx suggested several times in his *Capital*.[148] I do not follow him on this point.

I come back once again to the imaginary and symbolic content of objects given, of the objects of the gifts and counter-gifts. In order for "things to work," there must be in what is given something more than a gift of oneself to the other. The gift must contain something which appears to the giver as to the initial receiver, and to those who will subsequently receive it, and therefore to all members of the society – who must therefore share this representation from the outset – as a medium, the possession of which, even if it is only temporary, is necessary if one is to continue to exist, to produce or to reproduce social relations which enable individuals as well as groups, clans, families, brotherhoods, secret societies, and so on to continue as part of their society. The thing given must therefore – this much Mauss had foreseen and suggested without analyzing it further – contain more than the "constant influence," the presence of the man who gave it. It must contain *something more*, something which seems to *all* members of society to be indispensable to their existence and which must *circulate among them* in order that each and all may go on living.

Now this something which the objects given must contain, is shared with sacred objects which, on the contrary, do not circulate. This something Mauss called a soul, a spirit, a source of wealth and abundance, of life. And we here come to the heart of the problem. How are we to interpret these valuable gifts which circulate while acknowledging their kinship with sacred objects which do not circulate? I will develop this point at length in the second part of the book and for the moment merely outline my hypothesis.

The precious objects which circulate in gift-exchanges can do so only because they are substitutes twice over: substitutes for sacred objects and substitutes for human beings. Like the former, they are inalienable; but unlike sacred objects, which do not circulate, these do. Not only in potlatches, in (competitive) exchanges of wealth for wealth, but also on the occasion of marriages, deaths, initiations; in these instances they function as substitutes for human beings, "compensation" for a life (marriage) or a death (that of an allied warrior or even an enemy killed in battle).

While they are substitutes for sacred objects and for the supernatural beings that inhabit them, they are also substitutes for human beings, for their substance, their bones, their flesh, their attributes, titles and ranks, for their possessions, material and immaterial. It is for this reason that they are able to *take the place* of humans and things in all circumstances in which it is necessary to *displace* them, or to *replace* them so as to produce new social relations of power, kinship, initiation, and so forth, between individuals and between groups, or more simply to reproduce the old ones, to prolong, or to preserve them. This twin nature of valuable objects makes them hard to define and therefore to think, in our world in which things are separated from persons. But it also enables us to understand why these objects functioned as currencies, without having all the attributes, and that they often became a currency by shedding a great portion of their former functions and becoming an impersonal means of developing impersonal commercial relations, an instrument which circulates only once it has been stamped with the seal of the institution representing the community as a whole and which is the source of power and law: the state.[149]

The reader will understand the necessity of the meandering path he has had to follow in order to understand Mauss' analyses of the potlatch. It was not simply a question of revealing the profusion and riches of a complex text, laden with important facts tucked away in notes and continually opening onto new questions; my primary aim was to make it understood that the ethnographic phenomenon that Mauss thrust into the foreground is the potlatch more than the *kula*, the other ethnographic phenomenon he favored. It is because the potlatch appeared to him as both the extreme and the supreme form of total prestation that he made it the starting point for his study of the *kula* and other similar phenomena; and it is for the same reason that he then turned to ancient history in an attempt to reinterpret the ancient customs and economies of Europe, striving as he did so to work back to "Roman law that predates the era,"[150] before the appearance of the distinction between personal rights and real rights.[151]

For the same reason, he inquired into Celtic custom, and into Germanic law, which seems to have been kept alive by the peasantry throughout the feudal era, since for Mauss, "Germanic civilization … in earlier times had developed to the extreme the entire system of potlatch, but in particular, the complete system of gifts."[152] Likewise, he turned to ancient Hindu law because "[a]ncient India immediately after the Aryan colonization was in fact a land of the potlatch twice over."[153] Twice over, inasmuch as, according to Mauss, the Aryans had practiced potlatch before their arrival in India, and as the two major sets of tribes that made up the basis of the indigenous populations (the Tibeto-Burmese and the Munda tribes) were also familiar with the practice.

As the potlatch paradigm was the centerpiece of his work, it was here that the theoretical difficulties collected. And it is therefore here that the strengths and limitations of Mauss' approach and concepts can be best seized and brought to light. It became evident to me that everything hinged on the interpretation given the nature of the precious objects that circulate in gift-exchange, and that Mauss found his path blocked because he did not seek to bring together and to think, within the same theoretical framework, the sacred objects which do not circulate and the precious objects which do. This criticism does not aim to deny the immense value of his work. It does not seek to destroy but to deconstruct, in order to reconstruct and complete it, either by pursuing the same lines of reasoning whenever possible, or by shifting the problems so as to open new perspectives and to continue to advance.

We cannot however leave the potlatch without mentioning two criticisms that have been addressed to Mauss. One seems to me to be founded, the other somewhat less. The first criticizes him for having glossed over the existence of elements of exploitation in the relations between aristocracy, clan nobles, and the mass of commoners. He uses the term "feudal" to designate this type of society. He speaks of "princes," "vassals," and "their tenants."[154] Elsewhere he even evokes "feudal classes" (very different from Western feudalism), but he goes on to say that these were cut across by clans and brotherhoods.[155] He even speaks of "cross-class" potlatches, but does not elaborate. Mauss was not the only one to draw on the vocabulary of Western feudalism to describe exotic societies ruled by aristocracies. This Eurocentric view was common to all sorts of authors, proponents of Marxism as well as those with a more classic view of history. But his vocabulary is not the issue: Mauss is criticized for having said nothing about the contribution of the labor, staples, and precious goods demanded by clan chiefs from members of non-noble lineages which comprised the clan base. But where did these chiefs and this aristocracy come from? It seems that one was a noble or one was a chief because of the genealogical position of one's lineage in the clan. For instance, the chief belonged to the lineage of the direct descendants of the elder son of the founding ancestor of the clan. The other lineages, whatever their kinship with the chiefly lineage, comprised the mass of commoners. It was the chief who gave the potlatch on behalf of his clan and who requisitioned both the food for the feasts and the valuables that he gave to the chiefs of the invited clans.

But in addition to the mass of commoners, these societies also had slaves, and these, too, Mauss hardly mentions. He simply alludes to the fact that the value of Tlingit coppers was measured in slaves,[156] that sometimes during a potlatch slaves were put to death,[157] or that a potlatch might be given to ransom a captive kinsman, thereby saving him from slavery while restoring the family "name."[158] In short, relations of domination and exploitation did indeed exist in these societies, and this has been emphasized by several authors.[159] It seems to me that Mauss' silence can be explained to a great extent if one looks at the general conclusion to his essay.

In his conclusion, Mauss on the one hand confesses that he did not have the time "to try to perceive at this time the morphological foundations for all the facts we have indicated,"[160] which means that he had not fully grasped the inner workings of the groups engaging in potlatch. But, on the other hand, he stresses the idea that twentieth-century Western society, although obliged to adopt new principles in order to move forward, would also do well to come back to certain earlier principles, and in particular to the practice of *"noble expenditures."*[161] What does the noble-ness of an expenditure signify for Mauss? This is expenditure on the part of nobles, but which is governed by a notion of interest and utility which does not present itself as it functions in our own minds.

> If some equivalent reason animates the Trobriand or American Indian chiefs ... or once motivated generous Hindus, and Germanic or Celtic nobles, as regards their gifts and expenditure, it is not the cold reasoning of the merchant, the banker and the capitalist ... They hoard, but in order to spend, to place under an obligation, to have their own "liege men." On the other hand, they carry on exchange, but it is above all in luxury articles ... or things that are consumed immediately, as at feasts.[162]

And we understand what Mauss intended when we read his description of the rich Westerner: "His expenditures on luxury, on art, on outrageous things, on servants – do not these make him resemble the nobles of former times or the barbarian chiefs whose customs we have described?"[163]

I believe that it is this desire to see "the rich ... come back to considering themselves – freely and also by obligation – as the financial guardians of their fellow citizens"[164] that kept him from examining in greater detail the relations between the "feudal class" of northwest American societies and the mass of commoners.

The second criticism addressed to Mauss was that he had not been clearly aware of the abnormal character of the potlatches Boas had observed at the beginning of the century, a potlatch that had "gone mad," growing more and more aggressive in the wake of the upheavals spawned by the European presence and the pressures it placed on the northwest Indian societies.

The hypothesis that the potlatch observed by Boas was a profoundly altered version has long been argued by ethnologists like Barnett,[165] and by Curtis before him, and it now seems substantiated on all points.

Let us take a brief look at the drastic changes which occurred in these societies, in particular among the Kwakiutl. Their first contacts with Europeans date back to the end of the eighteenth century, around 1780. At that time the Kwakiutl comprised some 20 tribes, who earned their livelihood from fishing, hunting, and gathering. Their economy and technology were characterized by a very high degree of productivity. In winter, each tribe assembled into a town divided into quarters, each one of which was inhabited by a *numaym*, a kin group that Boas, with some reservations, called a "clan," but which bore a closer resemblance to what Lévi-Strauss later termed "houses."[166] Each *numaym* was at the same time a residential, an economic, and a political unit, since the group held fishing, hunting, and gathering rights in common, and possessed immaterial wealth, blazons, ranks, and so forth. A certain number of lineages within the *numaym* were considered to be noble, and it was they who represented their clans at potlatches.

Over the nineteenth century, three series of events profoundly altered the structure of these societies. The population fell by 75 percent owing to the introduction of new diseases and epidemics. The hunting-and-fishing economy (which favored the accumulation of huge surpluses) gave way to a colonial, trade-based economy which induced the importation of large quantities of manufactured goods, thus laying the foundations for the emergence of a class of *nouveaux riches*, capable of competing for status and power with the traditional chiefs. Last of all, the Europeans put a halt to tribal warfare, stopping the capture and sale of slaves; the society found itself with numerous vacant titles and ranks, and growing numbers of newly enriched men whose wealth gave them access to the potlatch arena from which they had traditionally been excluded.

Prior to these changes, the purpose of the potlatch seems to have been to validate the public transmission of the ranks and privileges already acquired. A chief desiring to pass on his rank to his son would invite the chiefs of the other *numaym* of the tribe and publicly distribute valuables and staples, the acceptance of which by the other chiefs was the equivalent of public recognition of the transmission of the title. Potlatches at that time were primarily an intratribal affair. To be sure sometimes two or three candidates might be vying for the same title or function, and in this case potlatches of gifts and counter-gifts would determine the winner. But the potlatch had a much less antagonistic character, and it even seems that the highest positions during the pre-colonial epoch were transmitted outside the potlatch (a fact noted by Mauss).

It was at the end of the nineteenth century that the traditional structures underwent a change, and instead of serving mainly to validate acquired positions, the potlatch became a systematic mode of acceding to new positions, this occurring in the context of a large number of vacant positions and the growing power of the newly rich. According to Marie Mauzé, these alterations in the potlatch took two directions. First of all an increasingly marked individualization: the newly rich, with the help of their families and a few clients, took up the potlatch, whereas this had formerly been the purview of a chief backed by his entire clan, nobles and commoners together; and secondly, a radicalization of the competition: now whole tribes would come to grips in a context in which warfare was forbidden. A new hierarchy of tribes grew up based on wealth, while at the same time a society called the "order of eagles" was created which included "all those who were to be served first," and where the former chiefs found themselves seated alongside the newly enriched.

It was in this context that the potlatch ran away, went mad (it is precisely this madness that Georges Bataille found so fascinating in the potlatch).[167] European missionaries and government agents quickly became alarmed at these gift-giving contests, which they regarded as excessive, unbridled squandering. In 1884, potlatches were forbidden by a law presented as an amendment to the Indian Act of 1876.[168] And it was in this context of European criticism and accusations aimed at the potlatch that Boas, pleading the case that the potlatch was not an irrational custom, wrote his famous text, cited and improved on by Mauss, to explain that the Indians were only doing as the Whites do, investing their capital and making it bear fruit, thereby ensuring the future of their children, and thus misrepresented the workings of the potlatch for a good cause. The Kwakiutl language has, it seems, two terms for gifts. The term *yaqwa* applied to exchanges of practically equivalent gifts; the term *p'asa* meant something like "to give but to flatten at the same time, by crushing the name of a rival, of the receiver." The upheavals of the nineteenth century may well have led to the multiplication of *p'asa* gift-exchanges to the detriment of *yaqwa* giving.

Mauss probably did not take this historical context into account when analyzing the potlatch. Because he focused on the agonistic character of the potlatch, he probably privileged a historically late and pathological form of the institution. Yet Mauss was not unaware of the explosion of European goods in potlatches. We see him even copying out the details of the worth of the famous *lesaxalayo* copper, belonging to "prince" Laqwigila, simply adding that Boas had "studied the way in which copper gains in value through a series of potlatches," but without expressing any surprise at the huge quantity of European manufactured goods (phonographs, sewing machines, wool blankets) on the list, and therefore at their value in dollars.[169]

Indeed, Mauss seems to have been particularly sensitive, not to the chain of brutal transformations which occurred over the nineteenth century, but to the continuity of the potlatch, to the fact that, after two centuries of contact with Europeans, the Indians still did not transfer their wealth through the market but continued to do so *"in the solemn form of the potlatch."*[170] Furthermore, Mauss stresses on several occasions the fact that the oldest documents are still the most valuable for reconstituting the logic of the potlatch, which concurs with the opinion held today. He even ventured to suggest that the potlatch, in its earliest form, was probably less agonistic and closer to the logic of total prestations, in other words to an exchange of equivalent gifts, than it was in Boas' day.[171] This remark has manifestly escaped the attention of most critics, who, on the contrary, criticize Mauss for having too readily accepted Boas' interpretation of the potlatch.

The same problems will be encountered when we analyze the second ethnographic example of potlatch privileged by Mauss: the kula, practiced by the societies of northeast Papua New Guinea.

The kula (a Melanesian example of potlatch according to Mauss)

Let us now take a much more rapid look at the second major ethnographic example upon which Mauss built his theory, the Melanesian kula. "The *kula*," wrote Mauss, "is a sort of grand potlatch,"[172] a "system of inter- and intratribal trade"[173] which involves a large number of the island societies of northeast New Guinea. In 1925 Mauss had known Malinowski's early publications for several years, but he relies above all on his first major work, *Argonauts of the Pacific*, which appeared in 1922 in London. Mauss had read it at the time of publication and, in the "Essai sur le don," is unstinting in his praise for the author. This book, which is "one of the best volumes of descriptive sociology," deals precisely with "the subject that concerns us."[174] Mauss does not hesitate to write that, "in the present state of our observations and historical, juridical, and economic knowledge, it would be difficult to come across a custom of gift-through-exchange more clear-cut, complete, and consciously performed, and moreover better understood by the observer recording it than the one Malinowski found among the Trobriand people."[175] His book "shows the superiority of the observation of a true sociologist."[176]

This admiration for Malinowski's fieldwork and for the fact that, on a more general theoretical level, he "devoted an entire study to 'exploding' current doctrines concerning 'primitive' economy," at the time also referred to as "natural" economies,[177] in other words economies not operating on the basis of commercial exchanges, currencies, and so on, did not prevent Mauss, who had spent years accumulating and comparing information on gift-exchanges in dozens of exotic or ancient societies, from writing: "Malinowski exaggerates the novelty of the facts he describes. First, the *kula* is in reality only an intertribal potlatch of a fairly common kind in Melanesia."[178] How then did Mauss interpret the data gathered and analyzed by Malinowski over the course of several years spent on the Trobriand island of Kiriwina?

The Trobrianders, Mauss says, "today are wealthy pearl fishermen, and, before the arrival of the Europeans, they were rich pottery manufacturers and makers of shell money, stone axes, and precious goods. They have always been good traders and bold navigators."[179] Mauss is aware that the kula is an ancient institution and he does not gloss over the changes forced on it by the introduction of European pearl-fishing. He is also aware that the kula exchanges exist side by side with another set of exchanges associated with marriage, festivals of the dead, and initiations, of which, he notes, "we still await from him [Malinowski] the description ... Consequently the description that we shall give is still only provisional."[180] We will see below that, precisely, in the Trobriand Islands, the kula operated (and still does) in a very special way, independently of the exchanges of gifts and counter-gifts connected with marriages, funerals, and initiations. Malinowski's kula, which set Mauss thinking, is therefore more an exception than the rule among the kula-ring societies.

Here is how Mauss describes the kula: "*Kula* trade is of a noble kind. It seems to be reserved for the chiefs. ... Trade is carried on in a noble fashion, apparently in a disinterested and modest way."[181] Looking back on our analysis of the potlatch, we can understand that Mauss quickly saw an immediate likeness between kula and potlatch: exchanges carried on by chiefs, apparently disinterested but conducted with a view to enhancing the givers' renown, exchanges dominated by rivalry between individuals coveting the same precious object as a gift, giving which, as in potlatch, "assumes very solemn forms."[182]

Next Mauss emphasizes that the potlatch is part of a vast system of prestations and counter-prestations of which it is perhaps only "the most solemn one."[183] Following Malinowski, he cites the exchange of goods (*gimwali*) and the barter between tribes which gives rise to "bargaining ... a practice unworthy of the kula".[184] He also mentions the *sagali*, large-scale distributions of food on the occasion of the launching of a new boat or the construction of a house. But he does not linger over these. Only the kula retains his interest, and in the kula, although he knows this form of exchange entails the circulation of several types of objects, Mauss was particularly taken with the movements of the *vaygu'a*, armshells and necklaces, because for him, these were "the essential objects in these exchange gifts."[185] He sums up the basic rules: the armshells (*mwali*) circulate from west to east, and the necklaces (*soulava*) from east to west.[186] The originality of the game is that an armshell can never be exchanged for an armshell, or a necklace for a necklace. An armshell must be exchanged for a necklace and a necklace for an armshell, on condition that the two are of equal rank and equivalent value.

Mauss does not use the term "rank," though, but prefers to speak of "value." However both terms are needed to describe the nature of these objects. For – and this was left to one side in the analyses of both Malinowski and Mauss – at the outset the *vaygu'a* are made and then exchanged for other items (pigs and the like) and today for currency. An armshell or a necklace therefore begins with an exchange-value. When it comes into the kula, it enters at a certain rank in the hierarchy of kula goods. Within this hierarchy, armshells and necklaces, both objects made from seashells, as a rule outrank pigs or carved lime spatulas, and the shell objects themselves are ordered into distinct ranks. Ten small shells cannot be exchanged for a large one, and least of all for a large shell which has already plied the kula circuit for a generation, which has a name and is charged with the identities of all those who have owned it.

This being said, let us see how Mauss describes the *vaygu'a*. Once again the potlatch looms. "The *vaygu'a* are not unimportant things, mere pieces of money. Each one, at least the dearest and the most sought after ... has its name, a personality, a history and even a tale attached to it."[187] Elsewhere Mauss adds that these objects also have a gender, armshells being female and necklaces, male. The image of kula movement is that of a gendered object seeking a partner of the opposite sex, and their meeting is represented in the Trobriander imaginary as the equivalent of a wedding. "Another symbolic expression [of the kula] is that of the marriage of the *mwali*, the armshells, the feminine symbols, with the *soulava*, the necklaces, the masculine symbols, which stretch out towards each other, as does male towards female."[188]

It is therefore only to be expected that *vaygu'a*, like potlatch coppers, are endowed with a spirit, a soul: "Not only the armshells and the necklaces, but even all the goods ... everything that belongs to the partner is so imbued with it, at least emotionally if not in his inmost soul, that they participate in the contract."[189] But Mauss does not venture further and concedes that "[i]t is not possible to say whether they are really the object of a cult, for the Trobriand people are, after their fashion, positivists. Yet one cannot fail to acknowledge the eminent and sacred nature of the objects."[190] Visibly Mauss would like kula objects to have an in-dwelling spirit (like the Maori *hau*) which propels them back to their place of origin. But he confesses:

Malinowski tells us that he has not found any mythical or other reasons for the direction this circulation [of the *vaygu'a*] takes. It would be very important to discover them. For if there was any reason for the orientation of these objects, so that they tended to return to their point of origin, following a path of mythical origin, the fact would be miraculously identical to the Polynesian one, the Maori *hau*.[191]

Mauss may not have found a *hau* in kula objects, but he managed to identify several points shared by kula and potlatch, the first being the fact that the main goal of these gift-exchanges is not to amass wealth but to increase renown and prestige, to glorify the giver's name. But he also saw that these gifts brought additional wealth to those whose strategy was crowned with success. For, in order to succeed, a man must woo partners and in turn be wooed by partners. He must be able to persuade, seduce, wait, make others wait, show gratitude, all of which is accompanied by more gifts which are added to the giving of the principal *vaygu'a*. In this, the kula resembles a sort of potlatch. But it does so also because of the "extraordinary competition"[192] between partners who covet the same object. And this vying for renown extends beyond the narrow circle of the village or the tribe of those entering the kula. "... the whole intertribal *kula* is merely the extreme case, the most solemn and most dramatic one, of a more general system. This takes the tribe itself, in its entirety, out of the narrow sphere of its physical boundaries ... Yet within the tribe the clans and villages are normally joined by links of the same kind."[193]

Mauss also stressed that the circulation of the *vaygu'a* in the kula ring must never be interrupted: "In principle the circulation of these signs of wealth is continuous and unerring. They must not be kept too long a time, nor must one be slow or difficult in passing them on. One should not present them to any other than certain partners, nor save in a certain direction – the 'armshell' or the 'necklace' direction."[194]

In the end, Mauss found himself once again confronted with the need to define the kind of ownership the receiver of a *vaygu'a* has in the object he has been given. This is a crucial question which he had already attempted to address when analyzing potlatch objects. And again he formulates a number of approximations:

> ... it is indeed ownership that one obtains with the gift that one receives. But it is ownership of a certain kind. One could say that it partakes of all kinds of legal principles that we, modern peoples, have carefully isolated from one another. It is ownership and possession, a pledge and something hired out, a thing sold and bought, and at the same time deposited, mandated, and bequeathed in order to be passed on to another. For it is only given you on condition that you make use of it for another or pass it on to a third person, the "distant partner".[195]

Subsequent research, and the findings of Annette Weiner and Frederick Damon in particular, have enabled us to answer this question. This could not be done on the basis of Malinowski's data alone, and, remarkably enough, Mauss was conscious of this.

> Sociologically, it is once again the mixture of things, values, contracts, and men that is so expressed. Unfortunately, our knowledge of the legal rule that governs these transactions is defective. It is either an unconscious rule, imperfectly formulated by the Kiriwina people, Malinowski's informants; or, if it is clear for the Trobriand people, it should be the subject of a fresh enquiry. We only possess details.[196]

Prophetic words, since that is exactly what occurred fifty years later: in effect, in the 1970s, new investigations were undertaken and have since been continued in the other kula-ring societies. They have led to discovering this rule which was very clear to the Trobrianders but which remained obscure to Malinowski and Mauss.

Yet it seems that Mauss more or less accepted, without placing too much faith in the idea, that things must be clear for the

Trobrianders. Nevertheless, he complains that they use a "somewhat childish legal language ... One cannot credit the extent to which all such vocabulary is complicated by a curious incapacity to divide and define, and by the strange refinements that are given to names."[197] Now this is the same complaint he has about Germanic law and one he had already made about the customs of the Kwakiutl, whom he criticizes for their inability to "isolate and divide up their economic and juridical concepts."[198] Part of this negative assessment of Melanesian intellectual capacities can certainly be attributed to a certain view of human evolution, which places Western peoples, or at least their elites, further down the road of progress. However this same vision of Western superiority does not seem to apply to the traditional peasant communities of Europe, which, for Mauss, were in the nineteenth century still leading a more circumscribed local life with more limited economic and social exchanges than those observed in Melanesian tribes or in southern Asia.[199]

But having questioned the Melanesian capacity for abstraction, Mauss adds this odd formula, which attenuates (or even contradicts) his presumption: "But they had no need to do so."[200] Why reproach them for not having concepts which would be of no use? Mauss justifies his position by advancing a very general reason, born of a speculative and questionable view of their society.

> In these societies, neither the clan nor the family is able to isolate itself or dissociate its actions. Nor are individuals themselves, however influential and aware, capable of understanding that they need to oppose one another and learn how to dissociate their actions from one another. The chief is merged with his clan, and the clan with him. Individuals feel themselves acting in only one way.[201]

The fact that an individual in these societies is a lifelong member of a kin group and that together with the other members of the group he collectively owns land or other resources does not necessarily mean that he is merged with the others and cannot dissociate himself from them or oppose them, but we will not go into that here. Finally, there is one last aspect of the kula that Mauss noted but, as he had done in the case of the Kwakiutl coppers, without giving it special importance. He writes that certain *vaygu'a* are withheld from kula exchanges and offered up to the gods or the spirits.[202] In his view there are then "two kinds of *vaygu'a*, those of the *kula* and those that Malinowski for the first time calls 'permanent' *vaygu'a*, [which] are displayed and offered to the spirits on a platform identical to that of the chief."[203]

Once again Mauss is confronted with the existence of two categories of objects which can be of the same nature (seashells), one of which is comprised of sacred objects, the inalienable property of the clan or the family, and does not circulate, while the other is made up of valuables, the personal property of one man, which circulate in ceremonial exchanges. And, as in the case of the Kwakiutl coppers, Mauss goes on to say of the shells which circulate that, by his own admission Malinowski used the words "exchange" and "payment (in return)" "in a purely didactic way, and in order to make it understood by Europeans."[204] Mauss cannot therefore tax Malinowski with ethnocentrism as he had done Boas. Whatever the case may be, once again the fact that the same objects are put to two different uses does not seem to be a problem for Mauss.

Before presenting the results of the more recent research on the kula contained in the series of studies begun in 1970, let us briefly re-examine Mauss' analysis as based on Malinowski's information. Mauss takes by far the broader view. Indeed he compares numerous societies separated in space (America, Africa, Asia) and in time (Greek and Latin antiquity, Germanic civilizations, Vedic India, and so on). And he rightly, it seems to me, draws a parallel between the kula and the potlatch, finding in the kula a form of gift and countergift exchange motivated by rivalry as in the potlatch,[205] the goal of which is to glorify an individual or a group through the individual. Grandeur and interest are in both cases the two intertwined motivations of these exchanges.

Mauss also situates the kula and its rivalries in a much broader set of exchanges, of services in which rivalry was not necessarily the dominant feature.[206] Here again the parallel with the potlatch (which is also connected with non-antagonistic gifts and countergifts) is justified.

Furthermore, Mauss observes that, like coppers, *vaygu'a* have a name, a personality and a history. To be sure he forces the facts somewhat in order to find a spirit which makes the *vaygu'a*, like the *hau* of Maori *taonga*, want to return to their birthplace. He finds them impelled not exactly by a personal soul, but by "feelings", which are a lesser form of soul, feelings which he describes as being the projection of the owner's emotions and personality.[207] And whereas Malinowski never ceased to find such an institution as the kula strange in its passion for exchanging objects of no use in everyday life, Mauss finds to the contrary. Nor does he follow Malinowski's explicit refusal to regard *vaygu'a* as a form of money because they are not used as a standard for measuring the value of the things exchanged. It was in response to Malinowski, concerning this particular point, that Mauss wrote two remarkable pages, in the "Essai sur le don," on the use of the idea of "money" with respect to the valuables which circulate in primitive societies and in a few paragraphs outlined a history of money and its forerunners.[208]

Nor does he forget that, in Malinowski's day, there were Europeans in the Trobriand Islands and they had developed the pearl-fishing industry. With the Europeans had come large quantities of manufactured goods and European currency.[209] But unlike Boas' potlatch, the kula observed by Malinowski had not undergone radical changes. It has been only in the last two decades that its functioning has begun to undergo far-reaching alterations. And this, paradoxically, because a few Europeans have penetrated the kula mechanism and are using it for financial gain.

However this may be, Mauss and Malinowski must today be set against the findings of the research conducted since the Second World War. We have seen a new series of studies carried out in the Trobriand Islands (including Annette Weiner's work),[210] while at the same time research has been undertaken on practically all of the other kula-ring islands: Woodlark Island (Frederick Damon), Gawa (Nancy Munn), Vakuta (Shirley Campbell), Kitava (Giancarlo Scoditti, Jerry Leach), Normanby (Carl Thune), Tubetube (Martha MacIntyre), Louisiade (Maria Lepowski), and Rossel Island (John Liep).[211]

The findings of these studies have, in my opinion, transformed the view of the kula inherited from Malinowski (and which was largely that of Mauss as well) on four points. I will summarize these here and then propose my own interpretation.

First of all it rapidly became apparent that the kula as practiced on Kiriwina, the site of Malinowski's observations, is highly idiosyncratic. There, only chiefs and high-ranking men (*guyau*) engage in kula, whereas elsewhere Big Men as well as more run-of-the-mill men and sometimes women are eligible to participate.[212] And associated with this is the fact that, on Kiriwina, *vaygu'a* cannot be used outside kula, while in the rest of the Massim region they can. On other islands, the armshells and necklaces can be withdrawn from kula and used in other types of exchanges and for other purposes, primarily to ensure the reproduction of the social relationships which guarantee the continued existence of the local group – kinship, initiations, etc. – but also in rituals designed to replace ceded or deceased persons by a gift of wealth. For instance, on Woodlark, when a man's wife dies, he gives his affines a *kitoum*. A *kitoum*, as we will see, is a valuable object owned personally by an individual (or a group) and which, depending on the circumstances, will be launched on a kula path where it will become, in the case of an armshell, a *mwali*, or in the case of a necklace, a *soulava*; but it can also be used for other ends.

Thus it became apparent that in all kula societies, with the exception of Kiriwina, kula is *directly* bound up with the production of kinship relations and with access to power. On Woodlark, for example, people strive to kula with affines or to marry with kula partners. The introduction of kula relations into matrimonial relations also has a determinant impact on an individual's identity, including "social" gender. On Woodlark, the newlyweds begin by residing with the wife's kin, but the husband is only regarded as fully a man and his children as truly his if his family establishes a kula relationship with his wife's kin. If not, the wife is regarded as "the man" and the husband as "the woman." The establishment of a kula relationship between allied lineages allows the man to take his wife to live on his own lands and to appropriate his children for himself. However, when his wife dies, he must give his affines a *kitoum*, to "replace" her. On Woodlark, again, there is no fixed political hierarchy. One becomes a Big Man by amassing wealth and redistributing it or putting it into circulation in kula.

On Kiriwina, on the other hand, political positions are fixed and inherited. They appear as a ranked hierarchy of clans and subclans; the individuals occupying these positions are there by birth, because of their genealogical position in matrilineal descent groups. Therefore such renown as any of these "nobles" may acquire in kula cannot alter their position in the local political hierarchy. Whereas Big Men are made and not born, one must be born a chief. On Kiriwina kula thus serves "purely" to aggrandize the person engaging in it, to glorify his "ego," to broadcast his name well beyond the boundaries of his village and his island. And because it is engaged in by a minority of men who already hold power in their society and practice kula as a privilege of their rank, Kiriwina kula is directed exclusively outwards, towards other lands, across the seas. As a consequence, kula objects are not used, as they are elsewhere, in the internal exchanges necessary for the reproduction of local society.

And yet, on Kiriwina as elsewhere, such exchanges exist and mark the birth, marriage, and death of an individual. They take on an exceptional dimension on the occasion of the ceremonial exchanges (*sagali*) following the death of a man, and are repeated over several years. The purpose of the gift-exchanges is to "replace" the deceased, to consolidate alliances made fragile by the death, and above all to return to its original *dala* (subclan) not only the body of the deceased but also the lands, the names and the other "properties" of the *dala* that he had ceded during his lifetime by "giving" (*mapula*)[213] them to his children (especially land given to sons). It is the chief of the *dala* of the deceased and his sisters who demand that these belongings (including the bones of the dead man) be returned to their original owner. But this cannot happen unless the members of the *dala* in turn give items of wealth to those who received the use of these belongings, in compensation for their loss. This requires many years and many funerary exchanges in the course of which the deceased's *dala* makes compensation gifts of *beku*, polished stone blades, and yams, which are men's goods, and fiber skirts and banana-leaf bundles, or women's goods.

We have Annette Weiner[214] to thank for this discovery as well as for that of the notion of *kitomu* (or *kitoum* as it is known on Woodlark). On Kiriwina, then, men's and women's goods are used to replace humans and to reproduce their relations. Kula objects remain apart from this process. Everywhere else they enter into the process and are associated with it; here they function as what I have called "human substitutes," as equivalents of the life of a woman or a man. But although, on Kiriwina, kula objects are dissociated from the process of reproduction of kinship relations and regeneration of kin groups, of the *dala* and of their heritage comprised of land, titles, and names, they are not detached. They too are an extension of persons and they bind them together by means of personal ties.

Proof of this can be seen in the fact that, on what we Europeans call the "symbolic" level, *mwali* and *soulava* are male or female. Furthermore, when they are manufactured they are mounted on a support called the "face" of the *mwali* or the *soulava*.[215] These objects have a gender and a face, then. This identification between object and human being also appears in the songs and epic poems that have been collected in the region.

One of these poems, *Yaulabuta*, tells the story of Kailaga, chief of a village on the island of Kitava, who was accustomed to engage in kula with the island of Vakuta.[216] But one day Kailaga became persuaded by a rumor that a Kiriwina chief wanted to exchange a magnificent *soulava* for his *mwali*. Now going to Kiriwina would mean diverting from its path a kula object which should be circulating in another direction. In reality this rumor had been put abroad by enemies from another village on his own island. Nevertheless, Kailaga yielded to his desire and set out for Kiriwina. On the way, his boat was attacked by enemies and he was captured. They lashed him to his canoe and he was roasted alive, like a pig. But before killing him, his murderers stripped off a necklace of boars' tusks that he wore on his chest and brought it back to their chief as a trophy; when they presented it to him they declared they had brought him one of the rarest *mwali* in existence. As Andrew Strathern has pointed out, to speak of Chief Kailaga as though he were a *mwali* is explicitly to affirm the equivalence between a human victim and a kula object.[217] But this particular equivalence rests on a double metaphor, since the necklace was not a *mwali*, a shell armlet, but a necklace made of boars' tusks.

The second major discovery of these last years was made at almost the same time by Annette Weiner on Kiriwina and by Frederick Damon on Muyuw (Woodlark Island).[218] This is the notion of *kitoum*. In order to understand this concept, we must come back to the fact that all of the items circulated in kula (armshells, necklaces) are man-made. To begin with, the shells for their manufacture must be fished from the sea. Only shells of a certain size are selected to be polished, cut apart, and mounted on a support. At this point the object becomes a valuable and the personal property of the man who manufactured it; it is his *kitoum*. It is only after this process that certain of these *kitoum* enter kula exchanges. All kula objects, then, embody a certain quantity of initial labor. Their size, the quality of their mother-of-pearl are "enhanced" by this labor. And it is because of their size and their luster that they will be assigned a particular rank. In effect, all kula objects are classified into three categories which constitute a three-tiered hierarchy accepted throughout the kula islands.

But let us take a closer look at what can be done with a *kitoum*. It can be exchanged for a boat, for example. On Muyuw, an outrigger canoe manufactured in Gawa, a western island, can be had for five top-ranking *kitoum*. People from Kiriwina procure armshells (*mwali*) by going to "buy" (*gimwali*) them on the nearby island of Kaleuna, where they are "manufactured"; in exchange, they give either a fine *beku*, one or more pigs or a large number of yams. A *kitoum* can also be used to "replace" a human being when, for example, compensation must be made for killing an enemy. Today a *kitoum* may also be sold, preferably to a tourist. And finally, it can be engaged in kula. In this case it opens or joins a kula "path", and its progression from gift to gift, its circulation from hand to hand will create or cancel debts, attract other gifts and thereby keep a kula path alive.

The third major discovery since Malinowski's work was precisely this notion of "kula path," *keda*. Let us suppose that the owner of a *kitoum*, for instance a high-ranking armshell which he has made or exchanged for one or more pigs, wants to engage in kula. Since he has an armshell, he must send it in a particular direction in search of a partner who owns a necklace of similar rank and who is willing to exchange it for his armshell. There is no assurance that such a partner exists, and so there is a risk. This risk is accepted as soon as the owner of the *kitoum* chooses a partner to receive his object as a kula object, in this case as a *mwali*.

And so the object is started on a path and passes from hand to hand until it comes into the possession of someone who has a necklace of equal rank, a *soulava*, and who is disposed to exchange it for the *mwali*. The *soulava* then travels in the opposite direction until, some months or some years later, it reaches the man who first gave the *mwali*. That day, a *soulava* which was someone's *kitoum* takes the place, as a *kitoum*, of the *mwali* owned by the original giver. That day the kula path (*keda*) opened by the *kitoum/mwali* is closed and ceases to exist. The former armshell owner, now a necklace owner, may dispose of the latter as he sees fit. The necklace is now his *kitoum*. He can sell it, exchange it for a canoe or re-engage it in kula, but along another path, running in the opposite direction from the first.

What has happened here? Let us suppose that the path of the *mwali* associated four partners: A, who owned the armshell *kitoum*, B who was given it by A and who passed it on to C, who gave it to D, owner of a necklace *kitoum*. There is a big difference between the status of A and D, on the one hand, and B and C, on the other. A and D are both owners of a *kitoum*; B and C are not. When A gives B his *kitoum*, it becomes a kula object, a *mwali* for A and for B; but at the same time it remains for A and for him alone a *kitoum*, an object in which he still has ownership rights. As for B, he received the object as a *mwali* and gives it as such to C, who gives it to D. For B, C, and D, this object is not a *kitoum*. They have no ownership rights in it but they do have the right to give it in order to create or to honor a debt.

However, when D receives the *mwali*, unlike B and C, he decides to give one of his own *soulava* to C in exchange; the *soulava* is his *kitoum*. And he keeps the *mwali* armshell which now becomes his *kitoum*.

```
            mw            mw            mw
 k/mw  A ――――――→ B ――――――→ C ――――――→ D
       A ←―――――――   ←――――― C ←――――― D  k/s
            s             s             s
```

A possesses the object both as a *kitoum* and a *mwali*.
D possesses the object both as a *kitoum* and a *soulava*.
B and C receive and use these objects as *mwali* and *soulava*.

The "indigenous" concept of *kitoum*, then, seems to resolve the problem that continually confronted Mauss, namely "what kind of ownership" do people have in the things they give and in those they receive? For Mauss, this "kind" seemed to "partake of all kinds of legal principles that we, modern peoples, have carefully isolated from one another."[219] Mauss gives an approximate answer, an admixture of facts rather than a definition of the principles at work in these gift-exchanges and a clear picture of their articulation. And yet the Trobrianders' answer to these points is clear, even if it is not "simple."

The logic of these exchanges rests on the combined action of two principles: an inalienable right of ownership in an object – inalienable at least for as long as it has not been replaced by an equivalent object which in turn becomes an inalienable property – and a right of possession and use, which is alienable on condition that the object does not leave the kula framework, is not used for any purpose other than the exchange of gifts and counter-gifts. The combined and lasting action of these two principles explains the manner in which objects travel along an exchange route and the nature of the relations contracted between persons who voluntarily engage in this type of exchange, the tactics and strategies they must marshal, the risks they run, the successes and gains obtained, their losses and failures.

Visibly *not all* partners along this chain of gifts and counter-gifts *have the same rights* in the objects given. At either end of the chain there is one "person" (this can be an individual or a legal entity, a group) who enters the game with two compounded rights, an inalienable right of ownership over the object given because it is his *kitoum* and will not cease belonging to him as long as it circulates as an object of gift-exchange, and a right of use in this object as a gift object, a right which he cedes. Thus for the partners at either end, two things happen simultaneously when they send their object along this path: *the object is at once given and kept.* What is kept is the ownership of the object; what is given is its possession (subject to the restriction that the object in their possession be used only to make other gifts). At either end of the chain, then, two principles conjoin and intervene. In between, the two principles are disjoined but both continue to operate. Possession of the object is transferred from one intermediate partner to another. Each partner cedes it as a gift and to be used as a gift, in the knowledge or the hope that an object will arrive to replace it. And *none* of these intermediaries *may* divert the object for a different use, treat it as though it were his *kitoum*.

It is this indelible presence of the owner of the thing in the thing he gives that is thought by these societies as the lasting presence of the person in the thing. In a society where, in the last analysis, all relations are personal relations, where written contracts do not exist, and where all commitments are made publicly, ownership necessarily appears as an attribute of the person himself and relations of ownership as direct or indirect relations between persons.

Mauss' formula does indeed contain the solution to the problem, then, but this solution is not clearly expressed or exposed because Mauss had not yet completely understood the articulation of the two principles. Try as he would, accumulating words, convoking and parading before us a whole series of legal principles, the kula mechanism and the "kind of ownership" remain partially concealed. We have only to reread the passage in which Mauss strives to circumscribe the relation between the persons and the objects they exchange, to see how inappropriate most of the words used and the legal relations suggested are, and how little they elucidate the solution:

> it is indeed ownership that one obtains with the gift that one receives. But it is ownership of a certain kind. ... It is ownership and possession, a pledge and something hired out, a thing sold and bought, and at the same time deposited, mandated, and bequeathed in order to be passed on to another. For it is only given you on condition that you make use of it for another or pass it on to a third person, the "distant partner."[220]

But the object given in kula is neither sold nor bought, neither used as a deposit nor loaned. It is at once "a property and a possession," but only for the two "remote" partners, those at either end of the chain, who have every chance of not being personally acquainted. They know only each other's names. For the partners in between, the object is received on condition that it be passed on to a third party, and everyone engaged in kula knows that at any moment the original giver may demand the return of the object, thereby breaking the kula path. Of course, observers say this is never done, and no one has an interest in doing it. People are not concerned with getting their *kitoum* back as quickly as possible except in unusual circumstances. Nor are they interested in replacing it as rapidly as possible with a *kitoum* of equal rank. What interests them is to send it as far as possible and to allow it to circulate as long as possible, so that it carries forth the name of the original giver and enhances it, and so that the object becomes charged with more and more life and "value" as it picks up all the gifts and all the debts it has engendered or cancelled by its circulation.

This explains several aspects of these exchanges which seem paradoxical to Europeans. Frederick Damon has shown that when the owner of a *kitoum* gives it to his first partner, the partner's name "goes up" and his own "goes down." But the more often the object is given and given again and the further it travels from its original owner, the greater this person's name "grows."

Lastly, we see that Mauss was right to compare the potlatch, the kula and the circulation of Maori *taonga*. These are three very different sociological realities, but they nevertheless resemble each other in several ways. To be sure, in kula the object never returns to its original place (this is a rule), since the aim of these exchanges is for a like-ranking but different object to take its place. If the object does not return to its place of origin, this is not because its own or its owner's spirit prevents it. The kula object is not a Maori *taonga*. Nevertheless, like the latter, it remains attached to its owner as long as it circulates in kula. This is in fact why kula requires at least three partners and its true nature cannot be seen until such time as a "third party" intervenes as intermediary. As soon as a third person enters the exchange, the duality of the rights of property and possession that are exerted over the kula object become apparent. This is why Ranaipiri's example was well chosen. Mauss had sensed that he had a reason, but was unable to see it clearly.

If there were only two direct partners in the exchange, both owners of a *kitoum* that each wanted to exchange for the other's, then we would have simply a non-agonistic exchange of equivalent gifts. One *kitoum* of equal rank would take the place of another, just as one woman takes the place of another in Baruya sister-exchange. Sahlins had already remarked as much, speaking of the *hau*. In reality, what interests the people of Massim when they engage in kula is not coming together to exchange equivalent items. What they want to do is to create debts, and to make these debts last as long as possible, in order to build up prestige and to aggrandize a name. In this sense kula may be compared with potlatch.

We can now appreciate the very large difference between the practice of non-agonistic exchanges of gifts and counter-gifts and kula or potlatch. In kula, when an object of equal rank and value takes the place of the initial gift, the debt is *cancelled*. Here the counter-gift wipes out the debt. This is not at all the case, as we have seen, with non-agonistic gift-exchanges. Here counter-gifts do not cancel gifts. The object is not "returned," it is given again. These gifts create long-term debts which often outlive the givers, and the primary motive for giving counter-gifts is to restore the balance between the partners, the equivalence of their status, not to cancel the debt. Alternatively, in potlatch or kula, even though the objects may circulate for several years, debts are fairly short-lived; and equivalent counter-gifts cancel debts. This is why those involved must begin all over and give or give back more in order to create new debts, which is the aim of these exchanges.

Now we understand why non-agonistic exchanges of gifts and counter-gifts may occur at the same or nearly the same time. It is because the debt is not cancelled by the counter-gift. In potlatch and kula, on the other hand, because an equivalent counter-gift would immediately wipe out the debt, exchanges are always deferred. A man must take his time in accumulating a counter-gift which will create a new debt. This explains why the people of Massim set out on their expeditions empty-handed. They know that there where they are going they will be given gifts. But they do not take anything with them to give back on the spot. The following year they will go back with gifts to give in turn.

But there is a fourth aspect to the kula, which Annette Weiner also nicely demonstrates. Kula is a game which implies a contradiction between the individual and the global kula system he enters and manipulates. For if a man wants to "win" at this game, he must, as we have seen, possess a highly valuable *kitoum* and must receive another equivalent one. But this is not his "prize." The prize is primarily the renown he wins, but also the "presents," the extra gifts obtained through skillful negotiation. It is also the supplementary kula objects that his successes bring. This "material" supplement is none other than the difference between all the supplementary gifts he had to make in order to seduce his partners and all those given him in order to seduce him. Which means that one individual's success is predicated on another's lack of success. Of course each contestant is motivated by the desire and the illusion that he will be the one to win. But whether any one man succeeds or fails, whether any one kula path is short-lived or long-lasting, for the protagonists it is as if the kula-ring was untouched by these incidents, since it keeps going round and round, of its own accord, apparently reproducing itself, of its own accord, like the market.

We are now in a position to clarify what it means to own a *kitoum* in this society. A *kitoum* is owned outright and fully by an individual; it strongly resembles what in our system is known as "private property," since, as we have seen, the person may do with it as he wishes. He can sell this object, exchange it for others, use it as compensation for a killing, engage it in kula. But he is always acting in a world in which society is the primordial reality, a totality which exists before any of its members and which guides the deeds of the individuals since they reproduce themselves by reproducing society. While a person can dispose of his *kitoum* because it is his personal property, he is not at liberty to dispose of land in the same way. Land belongs to a different category of inalienable goods, those which are held in common by all members of a group – a kin group for example – and are therefore controlled by the others as well. Land is one of those collectively owned inalienable goods which must be kept and cannot be given. The kula object is an inalienable personal possession, the ownership of which is retained as long as another equivalent object has not replaced it; but it is an inalienable possession which can be kept and given at the same time.

In other societies land is like a kula object, an inalienable possession which remains the property of a clan, village community, tribe, Pharaoh, the state, although the use of it may be ceded. Mauss was well acquainted with this rule of right or interest which distinguished between ownership and possession, and he was aware that it was a widespread phenomenon and that it endured in many regions of western or eastern Europe until the end of the nineteenth century. And yet Mauss rejected it as too simple a solution to the enigma of the exchange of precious objects because it did not account for the religious import, for the powers concealed in the objects given, in short for the atmosphere of belief that suffuses them and gives them meaning.

On this point Mauss was both right and wrong. He was wrong in that the distinction between ownership and right of use suffices to explain why the owner of a valuable remains present in the thing he gives, and why this object or its equivalent must one day return to him and again be his property, reproduce his property. He was correct in that a rule of right or interest, whatever it may be, cannot explain the profound nature of the realities it governs. It presupposes their existence, but it does not explain them. The principle alone does not explain why, in one place, it applies to land and in another to shells that circulate, whereas it does not apply to other shells hoarded by clans. Why to precious objects but not to sacred ones, nor to valuables that are sold, alienated for good? This the rule alone cannot explain.

Gift objects and valuables are caught, then, between two principles: between the inalienability of sacred objects and the alienability of commercial objects. Like the former, they are inalienable, and at the same time they are, like the latter, alienable. This, as we will see, is because they function both as substitutes for sacred objects and as substitutes for human beings. They are both powerful objects, like the former, and wealth, like the latter. It is not simply, as Mauss said, reasoning from a common-sense observation, that "one gives oneself when one gives them." In reality what is present in the object, along with the owner, is the entire imaginary of society, of his society. It is all of the imaginary duplicates of the human beings to whom have been attributed (it cannot be said that these are loaned because these duplicates can never give anything in return) the powers to reproduce life, to grant health and prosperity, or the opposite, to cause death, famine, the extinction of the group.

If the rule of right does not explain everything, since it remains to be explained why it applies to what it does, Mauss in a sense did well to ask his two questions. But, as we have seen, in reply he produced two explanations, two theories which, added together, do not quite make a whole. There is a gap between the two which was not filled by the account of the old Maori sage, Tamati Ranaipiri.

We have now finished with Mauss' two ethnographic examples. But I would like to add another example of competitive exchanges from the interior of New Guinea, which were discovered and analyzed by Andrew Strathern more than half a century after Malinowski and Mauss, in order to show how right Mauss was to assume that the work done by ethnologists would uncover many more facts analogous to the potlatch and the kula. This particular fact is the *moka*, a vast system of ceremonial exchanges practiced by a large number of tribes in the Hagen region in the heart of the New Guinea Highlands.

But before leaving the kula, I would like to say that the person who presently dominates this institution in the Massim region is no longer a New Guinea man, but a European, Billy. For several years Billy has both dominated and undermined the kula. This European buys massive quantities of shells in the south of the Massim region, on Rossel Island, and has them shipped by boat back to his workshops, where paid workers polish them and turn them into *kitoum*. Part of these he sells to islanders and tourists alike, but some he engages in kula and makes a profit from all the additional gifts that customarily accompany the circulation of armshells and necklaces. His goal is no longer that of traditional kula, the pursuit of renown; it is simply the accumulation of profit, the pursuit of wealth.[221]

Moka

The *moka* is a system of competitive ceremonial exchanges associating and opposing a set of tribes whose territories lie around the base of Mount Hagen. The population of these groups numbers more than 100,000 people, who speak closely related languages. We owe the analysis of the moka to Andrew Strathern, who has been observing these exchanges since 1960 and has kept abreast of recent developments. The research was conducted in three Melpa-speaking tribes, the Kawelka, the Tipuka, and the Minembi, who are intimately linked by marriages and by moka exchanges.

In this region, a tribe is a set of clans who share the idea (the myth) that they all have the same origin. This social unit acts together in time of war and in organizing large-scale moka exchanges and great ceremonial distributions of pig meat. A tribe is made up of from 800 to 1,000 persons. Clans are territorial groups placed under the authority of Big Men, important individuals who play a prominent role in moka exchange, in marriage alliances, in trade, and formerly in warfare. The economy is based on the production of sweet-potatoes and pigs, to which must be added, since the arrival of Europeans, a series of cash crops, among them coffee.

Before the Europeans arrived, moka consisted of gifts of live pigs and large gold-lip pearl-shells, which were procured by exchanging pigs and other articles with tribes in the south, towards the coast of the Gulf of Papua. Some moka used only pearl-shells, and others combined the two kinds of wealth: pigs and pearl-shells. The difference between pigs and pearl-shells was that pigs were produced by the household, but the pearl-shells had to be obtained through an equivalent exchange, which could be a pig. Before the arrival of Europeans, a pig was worth on average two pearl-shells.

Several types of moka exist, ranging from the exchange of gifts and counter-gifts between two partners to large-scale prestations involving two clans. But there are also intermediate forms.[222] For instance, one Big Man may invite several of his partners and publicly present them with gifts. Or several clansmen may invite all of the partners they have in a number of clans with which they engage in moka exchange. Or finally all the men of one clan hold a moka with all the men of another clan. Often this type of moka took place between relatively hostile groups, in other words ones whose relations alternated between alliance and warfare. But between irreconcilable enemies, there was no moka.

All these kinds of moka, engaged in by one person or by a group, also implied that gifts be given to "help" enter the field. As a rule a man would call on his affines and his maternal kin. But he could also count on his own clansmen and on friends in other clans. Each partner thus collected (with a view to distribution) two kinds of wealth: pigs produced by his own "family" and pigs he had been given by supporters which would one day have to be repaid. Andrew Strathern dubbed these two methods "production" and "finance," with no capitalist overtones in the word "finance."[223] Here, in order to amass the wherewithal to get started in moka, a man relies on others because his own production does not suffice. Big Men, however, are always striving to increase their own production, to accumulate a great part of the gifts to be given on their own. They do this by having several wives and by drawing lower-status men into their orbit, for instance orphans or refugees taken in by a clan following an unsuccessful war which has driven them from their territory. This extra labor is necessary because the number of pigs can be increased only by increasing sweet-potato production. Pigs and people are thus in competition for the same resource, whose production requires a heavy input of labor. There is, therefore, in these societies the possibility of men exploiting women and of Big Men exploiting dependent men.[224]

But in these societies, too, the fact of belonging to a clan provides an individual (a man) with three guarantees. He will receive help in taking a wife, in other words the components of the bridewealth; he will be protected and avenged by his clan if attacked by members of other clans; lastly and above all, he will have the right to use clan land to feed his family and pursue initiatives, in moka or the sale of cash crops. These systems are of course vulnerable to excessive population growth or ill-considered expansion of cash cropping, and so forth.

But what precisely is a moka exchange?[225] Let us take the simplest example, a transaction between two partners, X and Y, in which pearl-shells are the main object given. First X gives Y two pearl-shells and a pig, which itself is worth two pearl-shells.

The first two pearl-shells are called the "front leg" and the "hind leg," which expresses their equivalence with a pig. The pig itself is called "bird-pig" because it is hoped that it will trigger a return gift, at which time the partners will dance on the ceremonial ground adorned with their bird-of-paradise feathers. This gift, which is the equivalent of four pearl-shells then, is called a gift "which initiates" the moka.

The return gift is the "moka," providing that it is greater than the starting gift. Suppose now that Y, having taken the time to get together eight pearl-shells, sends them to X as a return gift. He could also send back only four pearl-shells, but in this case it would be said that he merely paid off his debts but *there was no moka*. What happens when there is moka? The first partner, X, is "richer" by four pearl-shells, but Y is "greater" for having given eight shells.

However they cannot leave the matter there. A second round must therefore be undertaken which Y initiates. He sends four pearl-shells to X, who will later send back eight. If one considers the final outcome of the two rounds, both X and Y have given and received twelve pearl-shells. This means that over time and with the direction switching at each round, the exchanges tend to balance out.

First round

X ⟶ 4 shells ⟶ Y
Y ⟶ 8 shells ⟶ X

Second round

Y ⟶ 4 shells ⟶ X
X ⟶ 8 shells ⟶ Y

But that is of no interest to people, since what they want to do is to demonstrate their generosity, win prestige, get partners, and keep them as long as they can; the system thus harbors an internal tendency to expand. The gift does not grow exponentially, though. For if the difference between X and Y at the end of the first round is four units, this is the starting point for the next round: four units, with a few more thrown in. There are some checks on the expansion, then.

In reality, the *summum* for a Big Man is to give as much as possible without asking for anything in return. From this standpoint, the moka closely resembles the potlatch; the motive of moka partners is not to make a "profit," but to increase the gifts and to create debts. Thus pigs pass from hand to hand, creating debts and encountering other debts which they cancel. But we have seen that the pigs which circulate come from two sources: either from "family" or from supporters. On this point therefore it is easy to compare the moka and the kula. For, although a family pig cannot be identified with a *kitoum*, clearly both are a property to which no debt is attached but which will create debts when put into circulation.[226]

   1 family pig   1 moka pig   1 moka pig

A ⟶ B ⟶ C ⟶ D
A ⟵ B ⟵ C ⟵ D

   1 moka pig   1 moka pig   1 family pig

In Melpa ceremonial exchanges, the gift pigs are frequently lined up in two rows. The first row contains the pigs produced by the Big Man's household, the second, all the pigs given him for the moka, or those he has received in return for the mokas he has given. The extent of his alliance network is thus displayed for all to see. And as in kula (except for the Trobriander version), moka partners become affines and vice versa; the two spheres, kinship and power, are directly conjoined.

Andrew Strathern has followed the evolution of this exchange system and has reconstructed its history from the beginning of the century. From 1933, with the arrival of Europeans, and until 1967, the moka underwent a formidable expansion for several reasons. First of all, Europeans brought in massive quantities of pearl-shells and used them as a currency for paying porters, buying provisions, land, and so on. Very quickly the Melpa eliminated pearl-shells from their moka exchanges and replaced them with Australian dollars, and today with the kina, the new national currency pegged to the Australian dollar (and also the name for the formerly used pearl-shells). Thus the pearl-shell used in the non-commercial ceremonial exchanges gave its name to the national currency created after the independence of Papua New Guinea (in December 1975). And it was Andrew Strathern who, when consulted by Michael Somare, the first prime minister of the newly independent state, suggested that he call it the kina.

Besides the massive importation and devaluation of pearl-shells, the arrival of Europeans also brought about a general halt to tribal warfare and eliminated the principal occasions for moka. At the same time, the growth in cash crops, the relative influx of dollars and then of the national currency enabled many people to enter the moka circuit, even more than previously. Indeed, insofar as the pre-colonial moka was largely based on the acquisition and exchange of pearl-shells whose paths were controlled by the Big Men of the different clans engaged in these exchanges, fewer individuals were involved in moka, and of these, fewer young men ventured to take part and less wealth circulated.

So the moka flourished after the colonial conquest. And the basis of this flourishing, it seems to me, was that for those engaged in moka, land remained a collective inalienable possession which protected them. The survival here and there of inalienable forms of property explains why, after the arrival of Europeans, two parallel economies grew up, one based on gift-exchange, the other on trade. Increasingly individuals and groups could be seen amassing money and commodities for use as gifts, or doing the opposite, selling gift objects as commodities. As late as 1976, Ongka, the Melpa Big Man whose biography Andrew Strathern has written, explained to the latter that the two economies would probably continue evolving side by side for a long time to come. Twenty years later, in 1996, this prediction has only partially come true. Not because the two economies have ceased to coexist (although the market economy has now taken the lead), but because tribal warfare has resumed on a very large scale, requiring more wealth given as "compensation"; and in order to get together the fee, a man must produce and sell increasing amounts; but to do so, peace must last at least a certain time. These societies today find themselves in the grip of new contradictions arising from the coexistence of local tribal powers, which are still quite strong, and a national state power lacking the capacity to intervene on the local level.

But the basis of these exchanges, despite the inflation and the rapid disappearance of pearl-shells, despite the injection of massive quantities of European currency and manufactured goods into these exchanges (Toyota trucks and the like), remains the pig.[227] Not because it is the main source of protein, but because it continues to be used in marriage exchanges and in all other exchanges necessary for the reproduction of local social relations. The pig continues to be a substitute for persons. Pigs are given for a birth, a marriage, on the occasion of a death, and so on.

At the end of this analysis of moka, we find ourselves once more faced with the same problem, that of the nature of the valuables which circulate in ceremonial and competitive exchanges. Whether they are Maori *taonga*, Kwakiutl coppers, Trobriand *vaygu'a* or Melpa pigs and pearl-shells, these objects are all to a varying degree substitutes for human beings.[228] This will again be our starting point for analyzing things that are given, things that are kept, sacred things which, perhaps far from being simple substitutes for persons, are themselves seen as persons, but superhuman ones.

The reader has no doubt also been struck by the presence, in all of the phenomena I have reported, of two principles which combine to engender certain forms of exchange: a rule of right which asserts the inalienability of the ownership of certain objects, and another which authorizes the alienation of the possession, but only for certain purposes. We have thus seen that sacred objects are inalienable and must be kept and not given, whereas precious objects are given while being kept. We have also observed that in all these societies inalienability is based on or legitimized by the belief that there is present in the object a power, a spirit, a spiritual reality that binds it to the giver, and which accompanies the object wherever it goes. It seems to me that this presence is nothing other than the form taken by the inalienability of things in a world where men believe that visible realities are inhabited and controlled by invisible forces, beings who are greater than humans but who resemble them.

Has not humankind entertained an ambivalent attitude on this point from the beginning? Do men not know that objects do not move about of their own accord, without reason? But at the same time do they not do all they can to avoid knowing, to avoid seeing, to reject this knowledge? Why do they not want to know?

I will end the first part of this book by affirming my personal conviction that things do not move about without reason or of their own accord. My position is therefore not the "native" viewpoint. Nor is it that of Lévi-Strauss, who regards the notions of *mana* and *hau* as empty concepts which refer to unconscious operations of the mind. My position is that of Mauss, but only up to a certain point because I am unable to follow him to the end.

Things do not move about without reason or of their own accord

We have seen that a gift object *does not move about without reason*. When it does move, on the occasion of non-antagonistic gift-exchanges, its two-way transfer is the means of creating a two-way relation of reciprocal dependence which is known to entail a certain number of social consequences for the participants: obligations but also advantages. At the same time, when the exchanges are completed, both partners are once again balanced, since if they were of equal status before the initial gift, their equality is restored by the final counter-gift. Giving and giving in return the same object then is the simplest and the most direct way of producing dependence and solidarity while maintaining the individual's status in a world where most social relations are produced and reproduced by creating bonds between persons. The gift followed by a counter-gift of the same object thus constitutes the basic molecule of all gift-exchange, the smallest move that can be made for this practise to have meaning.

But it has also become clear that, if the thing does not move about without reason, *neither does it move of its own accord*, Mauss and Polynesian beliefs notwithstanding. What sets the object in motion, what traces its path in advance, what causes it to leave and then return to its point of departure is the will of individuals and/or groups to produce (or to reproduce) among themselves social relationships which combine solidarity and dependence. Certainly this is not entirely a game, and behind it lie many necessities that are rooted in the social sphere, many social necessities. But man's social being is more than the sum of his needs, of this and that social necessity, for the simple reason that human beings do not merely live in their society and reproduce it, like other social animals; they must produce society in order to live.

Let us come back to these two conclusions, which are in fact the two sides of the same reality. Things that are given do not move about without reason and do not move of their own accord. It goes without saying that these "things" that are given are not necessarily "things" in the sense of material objects having a cultural significance. The "thing" may also be a dance, a spell, a name, a human being, support in a dispute or a war, and so forth. In short, as Mauss emphasized, the category of "giveables" encompasses much more than material objects, and I will say that it takes in *everything* which can possibly be *shared*, a sharing which *makes sense* and which can put someone else under obligation or create a debt. Of course, the question of what object is given is never indifferent or without significance. The nature of the object immediately testifies to the intentions of the givers and the context of the giving: war or peace, marriage alliance or perpetuation of a descent line, and so on.

Things do not move about of their own accord. What sets them in motion and makes them circulate in one direction, then another, and yet, another, is each time the will of individuals and groups to establish between themselves personal bonds of solidarity and/or dependence. Now the will to establish these personal bonds expresses *more* than the *personal* will of individuals and groups, and *even more than what comes under the heading of will*, of personal liberty (individual or collective). What is produced or reproduced through the establishment of these personal bonds is all or part of the social relations which constitute the foundations of the society and which endow it with a certain overall logic that is also the source of the social identity of the member groups and individuals. In short, what appears in the goals pursued, the decisions taken, the actions voluntarily performed by the individuals and groups which make up a given society is not only their personal wills but a-personal or impersonal necessities having to do with the nature of their social relations, which spring up again and again in the process of producing and reproducing them (whether relations of kinship, power, with the gods and spirits of the dead).

Things therefore do not move about of their own accord; they are always set in motion by human will, out this will is itself driven by underlying forces, involuntary and impersonal necessities which are *constantly acting* on individuals, on those who make decisions as well as on those who obey them; through the actions of individuals and groups, it is the social relations which are reproduced and once more linked together, it is the whole of society which is re-created and re-creates itself, and this occurs *whatever form or degree of awareness the actors may have individually and/or collectively of these necessities.*

Let us pause for a moment here and take stock. We can explain why the gift of something is followed by a counter-gift of the same thing or something equivalent without having recourse to the belief that things are possessed by an in-dwelling soul, spirit, or power which compels it to return to its point of departure. I therefore part company with Mauss on this point and agree with Lévi-Strauss' criticism. But neither does our explanation rely on the direct intervention of "unconscious mental structures," which by definition can only be universal and timeless since they are present and operate in every individual and in every people, whatever their context. Unlike Lévi-Strauss, I have drawn on sociological as well as psychological mechanisms; the realities and forces underlying movements of the things given are social ones. They are not connected *directly* by unconscious and universal structures of the mind but *indirectly*, by means of specific social structures, which are therefore not present in all forms of society.

This is not to say that the social is separable from the mental or that it can exist independently and in a sense outside of thought. I have shown elsewhere[229] that a social relation (of kinship or power) can only emerge, develop, be transmitted and reproduced because, from the outset, it contains a *mental* or *ideational* (*idéel* in French) component, made up of conscious principles of operation, of rules to be followed for its reproduction, of representations necessarily associated with it, which found or challenge the legitimacy of its production-reproduction in the eyes of the members of the society. This mental component of social relationships exists at the outset purely through and in individual and collective thought. It is therefore necessarily subservient to both the unconscious and the conscious structures of thought. To think is to establish relations between various aspects of the real, and to discover, invent, and imagine relations between these relations.

But to say that the social does not exist separately from thought is not to say that the ultimate explanation of the social lies in the "mind," particularly in the unconscious structures of the mind. And it is not to say that the social and the "mental," conscious and unconscious, can be explained only by the symbolic, although they can always be reduced to it. For the mental realm, which arises in the thought processes and through them, does not exist in the mind alone. It is actively present in all of the social realities it engenders and which embody it, that is to say which both materialize *and* symbolize it at the same time. A kinship system cannot be reduced to its mental components (descent and marriage rules, residence rules, kin terms, and the like); it is present in every institution, in the ceremonies, in the bodily movements, in the objects through which it gains a concrete social existence and which "symbolize" it. The symbolic here makes the system visible, "communicates" it, but it is not its ultimate source nor its basis.

I therefore diverge somewhat from Mauss' conclusions, without necessarily feeling obliged to adhere to the theses of Lévi-Strauss. But I stress that it is because I have undertaken to *complete* Mauss' anthropological analysis that I have been able to point out its limitations without being driven to the same impasse, without taking indigenous representations of a society for the equivalent of those constructed by an alien mind, striving to be scientific and critical, and unable, on principle, to share these representations (even if it must necessarily take them seriously and ultimately return and explain them as well). Indeed it is readily understandable that if, to this sociological base is added a system of magical-religious beliefs in the presence in things of a soul, a spirit, a force which compels them to act and to move about of their own accord, then it will look as if the things themselves had the persons in tow, as though, driven by their spirit, by their own power, they felt compelled to return more or less directly, more or less rapidly, to the person who first owned them and gave them away.

From the moment most social relations in a society exist as and through the creation of personal bonds, as relations between persons, and from the moment these bonds are established by means of exchanging gifts which themselves entail the transfer and shifting of "realities," which can be of any kind (women, children, precious objects, services) as long as they lend themselves to being shared, all of the objective social relations which form the basis of a society (the kinship system, political system, and so forth), together with the intersubjective personal relations which embody them, can be expressed and "materialized" by the exchange of gifts and countergifts and by the movements, the trajectories followed by the "objects" of these gift-exchanges.

And because gift-giving as a real practice is an essential component of the production-reproduction of objective social relations and of subjective and intersubjective personal relations which are the mode of the former's concrete existence, it is *simultaneously* part of both the form and the content of these relations. In this context, gift-*giving* and the *gifts* given both *re-present, signify* and *totalize* the social relations of which they are at once the instrument and the symbol. And, as gifts are given by persons, and the objects given are originally attached, then detached in order to be again attached to persons, the gifts embody every bit as much the persons as their relations. It is in this sense and for these reasons that gift-exchange is – according to Mauss' superb expression – a "total social fact." It is because it both contains and unites something which comes from persons and something that is present in their relations that these are totalized and symbolized in the giving and in the gifts which materialize this practice.

But add to this the belief that the things which are given have a soul, that they are like persons and can act and move about by themselves, and we can expect to find an entire series of transformations and metamorphoses of gift-giving and of the forms of individual and collective consciousness associated with it. In such a world, one can venture to say that "things" no longer exist, there are only persons, sometimes in the guise of human beings and sometimes in the guise of things. At the same time, the fact that human social relations (of kinship and power) must assume the shape of relations between persons, intersubjective relations, is extended to the whole universe. Nature, the entire universe, is now composed uniquely of (human or non-human) persons and of relations between these persons. The cosmos becomes the anthropomorphic extension of humans and their society. The individual is connected to the whole universe, which goes beyond his individual scope and which contains and extends beyond his society as well. At the same time, however, and conversely, the individual himself contains, in a certain fashion, his whole society and the entire cosmos. The microcosm of the individual contains the macrocosm which both encompasses and is encompassed by him. The part is the Whole, the Whole is present it its entirety in each of its parts. Each of the two, the individual and the cosmos, in a sense mirrors the other, and any action performed on one is believed to affect the other. The whole world, humans included, has become "enchanted."

Thus, when in a society where the bulk of social relations takes the form of personal relations it is prevalently believed that things are also persons, then not only does gift-giving encapsulate something of the essence of these social relations, it amplifies and glorifies their presence and their reality in the individual consciousness. Gift-exchange *amplifies* their essence because the belief that things are endowed with a soul extends this form of relations beyond the boundaries of society, imposing it on the whole cosmos, on all objects and all relations that exist in the universe.

The practice of exchanging gifts is thus extended beyond the world of humans and becomes a basic component of a practice that is religious, in other words of the relations between humans and the spirits and gods who also inhabit the universe. Gift-giving in this case becomes sacrifice to the spirits and the gods, which Mauss designated as the fourth obligation founding gift-exchange. Belief in the soul of things amplifies, but also *glorifies* persons and social relations because it makes them *sacred*. For if things have a soul, it is because supernatural powers, gods or spirits, normally invisible, dwell in them, and with them circulate among men, attaching themselves sometimes to one, sometimes to another, and always attaching men to themselves. But, when it sacralizes objects, persons, and relations, belief in the soul of things not only amplifies and glorifies a universe comprised of personal relations, it *alters* the nature, the appearance and the meaning of these relations. *It effects a metamorphosis.* Instead of appearing to themselves as actors, humans appear to themselves as the target of actions. Instead of merely acting upon others by means of the objects they give, they appear to be acted upon by the objects they give or receive, to be subservient to their will and to their movements. The cause becomes the effect, the means becomes the agent, the agent becomes the means, and the object becomes the subject.

In short, combining this sociological base, this logic of personalized social relations with the belief in thing-persons produces a *general metamorphosis* of reality and an *inversion in the way one thinks* the real relations involved. Objects are transformed into subjects and subjects into objects. No longer is it (only) humans who act on each other, interact with each other, by means of things, it is now the things and their in-dwelling spirits which act on each other through human agency.

It is because he did not carry his reconstruction of the sociological basis of gift-giving far enough that Mauss ended up giving such weight to the magic-religious beliefs that endow things with a soul. Not that such beliefs do not have an important role in society, but *they do not explain the true origin* of the obligation to give in turn what one has received or its equivalent. They explain only *how* the social actors, the indigenous peoples of different cultures think, experience, and legitimize this obligation. What appears here is not only a *symbolic* world. More fundamentally it is the world of imaginary representations elaborated by the actors in order to explain the reasons for their actions, their origin, and their meaning: it is the *world of the imaginary.*

What a contrast between these types of society, these social and mental universes, and today's capitalist society where the majority of social relations are impersonal (involving the individual as citizen and the state, for instance), and where the exchange of things and services is conducted for the most part in an anonymous market-place, leaving little room for an "economy and a moral code based on gift-giving." When most exchanges are transacted through a market, and the value of goods and services is expressed in a universal currency, then debts contracted can be cancelled and things that are bought remain yours. Nevertheless, such a universe must necessarily have other forms of alienated and fetishized representations (and practices) of the social relations that underpin it. But that is another story.

2

Substitute Objects for Humans and for the Gods

~∞~

Once again I found myself confronted with a number of problems which had, in a largely unexpected manner, been raised by my analysis of Mauss' work on the gift.

In effect, it became increasingly apparent that, alongside what can be given or exchanged, it was urgent to look at the things which must be kept, and that the phenomenon of gift-giving itself would be greatly enriched by being examined in the light of what must not be given but must be kept. Now it happens that the things which are kept are quite often "sacred," and it therefore became necessary to inquire into what it is that endows these objects with their sacred character, and hence into the nature of the sacred. Furthermore, there are no watertight partitions between sacred objects and valuable objects produced for the purpose of giving and selling, some of which even ultimately function as "primitive monies." Objects do not need to be different in order to operate in different areas, and it is worthwhile looking at how sometimes the same object can be first sold, then given, and finally stashed away in a family or clan treasure. It is not the object which creates the differences, it is the different logics governing the areas of social life that endow it with different meanings as it moves from one domain to the other, changing functions and uses as it goes.

But there was another problem as well, that of a closer analysis of the sociological and therefore historical conditions of the appearance and the development of antagonistic gift-giving, of the potlatch, and of potlatch societies. On this point I simply listened to Mauss, who had suggested – without provoking much reaction – that the potlatch is an altered form of non-antagonistic gift-giving. The problem was that Mauss had really said too little about the nature of these gifts, about their particular logic, for me to identify the social transformations necessary to the appearance and development of the potlatch. Going from there, and having had the opportunity to live and work in a society which practiced the giving of gifts and counter-gifts, but not potlatch, I postulated that a relatively detailed analysis of what happens among the Baruya, a society without potlatch but with sacred objects, valuable objects and even a kind of "currency object" (salt bars, which are reserved for ceremonial use), should, by virtue of the contrast it provides, enable me to isolate the social conditions in which the potlatch is likely to appear and to establish the social basis of its development. The outcome of this reconstruction, which proceeded by a process of *a contrario* deduction, ultimately would allow me to situate more accurately than Mauss had done the position of "potlatch societies" among the variety of ways in which human society has evolved.

Finally, I turned back to the objects themselves in an attempt to discover what features an object must have in order for imaginary representations of life, wealth, and power to become projected onto and invested in it. The strength of objects lies in their capacity to materialize the invisible, to represent the unrepresentable. And it is the sacred object which most completely fulfills this function.

Of course this type of analysis raises at least two questions for the social sciences. First of all, it challenges a piously received and unanimously respected premise, famous particularly since Lévi-Strauss' introduction to the work of Mauss, namely that everything within man's being is exchange, and that it is by beginning with the necessity for exchange that one can come to understand the way societies function (even if their history, the various forms of their evolution remain external to the field of analysis or are even sometimes repudiated as purely contingent). Secondly, it restores to the social sciences their function of critically assessing the spontaneous beliefs and the illusions that societies and individuals hold about themselves, as well as evaluating the learned theories which do not take these beliefs seriously or do not account for them.

Sacred objects, precious objects and currency objects among the Baruya of New Guinea

The Baruya tribe lives in two high valleys of a mountain chain in the interior of New Guinea, known as the Eastern Highlands. Their reputation as salt-makers made them familiar to many tribes who had never met them but who bought their salt from trading partners of the Baruya. The Baruya's ancestors did not live in the place at present inhabited by their descendants: they lived in the Menyamya region, at Bravegareubaramandeuc, today a deserted spot to which the masters of the initiations return every three or four years, when the male initiation ceremonies are held, to gather magic plants and collect handfulls of clay and ancestral soil which are equally magic, in other words full of supernatural powers and the ancestors' force.

Originally the ancestors of the Baruya formed part of a tribe called the Yoyue, and their name at that time was the Baragaye. At some time, probably around the end of the eighteenth century, they were forced to leave their territory after enemies burned their village and massacred part of its inhabitants. The survivors fled and eventually found asylum at Marawaka, among the Andje, who lived on the slopes of Mount Yelia, at a distance of four or five days' walk. After a few generations, the refugees, abetted by the Ndelie, a clan belonging to the host tribe, drove the rest of the tribe from their territory, and a new tribe appeared which called itself the Baruya, from the name of the clan that exercised the most important ritual functions in the male initiations, those which transform boys from children into adolescents, make them into young warriors. Around the end of the nineteenth century and the beginning of the twentieth, the Baruya continued to expand their territory and invaded Wonenara valley. They waged war on the local groups, with whom they nevertheless exchanged women, and gradually absorbed a number of autochthonous lineages, who left their native tribe and went to live with the Baruya, their enemies but also their affines, thus repeating the Ndelie's conduct a good century before with regard to their own tribe, the Yoyue.

To complete this sketch, I should add that the Baruya do not have a center of power, a paramount chief, like the Trobrianders, or Big Men who amass wealth and women, and try to outdo each other in the giving of gifts and counter-gifts, like the Melpa. They do, however, have men who are more important than the others, Apmwenangalo, "Great Men," whose powers are either inherited (like those of the masters of the male initiations or the shaman initiations), or acquired, through merit (like those of the great hunters, the great cassowary hunters, the great horticulturalists and the best salt-makers). The masters of the initiations always come from the same clans, but the other Great Men may be members of any clan.

So how do the Baruya deal with things that are given, sold, or kept? They have three coexisting categories of objects which, for lack of a better term, I will call sacred objects, "valuable" objects and objects, that function as a kind of currency.

Concerning the things one keeps among the Baruya

Chief among the sacred objects of the Baruya are the *kwaimatnie*, cult objects kept hidden away by the masters of the initiation rituals and taken out and displayed solely on these occasions. Only the clans descended from the Menyamya refugees possess *kwaimatnie*. The autochthonous lineages have none, with the exception of the Ndelie, the clan which betrayed their tribe and helped the Baruya's ancestors, the Baragaye, to seize the territory of the Andje tribe, which had taken them in. Following their victory, the Kwarran-dariar lineage, the lineage of the Baruya clan which conducts the third-stage male initiations, had given a pair of *kwaimatnie* to the Ndelie to thank them for their help, and also to associate them in the performance of the initiations; for it is through these initiations that the Baruya tribe presents itself to itself and to all the friendly and/or hostile neighboring tribes as a whole, as one "body," as they say.

Among the sacred objects were also the dried fingers of the right hand[1] – the hand that draws the bowstring – of Bakitchatche, a legendary Baruya hero who led them into battle against the Andje and in seizing their lands. He is credited with a series of fabulous exploits. For instance, it is said that by the sole force of his spirit he struck down a tall tree which fell across a precipice, allowing the Baruya warriors to surprise and massacre their enemies, who could not imagine they would attack from that side. His fingers, which were carefully preserved, as is often done with the fingers of great warriors, used to be shown, during the initiation ceremonies, to the future Baruya warriors by Bakitchatche's descendants, in the belief that part of the hero's supernatural powers were preserved in them and would give the Baruya strength. The Baruya believe that objects have a spirit, *koulie*, which is at the same time a power as well as power itself. In this sense, the notion of *koulie* corresponds to the Polynesian ideas of *mana* and *hau*.

The Andavakia clan, for its part, used to own a pair of flint stones which were used uniquely when the *tsimia* was built; this is the big ceremonial house erected by the Baruya every three or four years for the initiation of their boys. On each occasion, all village fires were extinguished and, whereas, before the Europeans arrived, the Baruya used to light their daily fire by rubbing, the ceremonial fire was lit by striking, re-enacting the gesture of the Sun, father of the Baruya and of all humans, who struck the first fire and threw the flint stones into the flame. When they exploded, the flints pierced the sexual organ and the anus of the first man and woman, whose organs had until then been walled up; and that is how they became able to copulate and reproduce.[2] Bakitchatche's fingers and the flint stones disappeared when the village in which these clans lived was destroyed by fire, a fire that was ordered by the young Australian officer in charge of the Wonenara patrol post a few months after the Baruya had been pacified.

Informed that the men of this village had taken up arms against the men of Wiaveu, another Baruya village, the officer organized a punitive expedition. On his way, he set fire to the aggressors' village, unaware of what he was burning "inside"; when he arrived at the scene of the battle, he confiscated the attackers' weapons, broke or burned them, and arrested some 50 men and threw them in jail. This battle had actually been sparked by the suicide of a woman from the assailants' village who was married to a Wiaveu man; she had hanged herself after having been surprised with her husband's younger brother. But the officer was not interested in the reason for the conflict. All that mattered to him was that people stop taking the law into their own hands, and that Australian law be established throughout the territory. Henceforth the Baruya were distant subjects of Her Majesty, the Queen of England.

Although they are not "lasting" objects, I would also mention the magic plants gathered at the sacred site of Bravegareubaramandeuc by the masters of the initiations and their helpers, and kept for use in the series of collective ritual meals that take place over the course of the ceremonies. Unbeknownst to the initiates, the celebrants slip dried leaves from these plants into bits of taro or sweet-potato and feed them to the initiates, who may not look at what they are eating. Pieces of these leaves are also placed in the betel nuts the initiates are given to chew. In this case a thin slice of raw liver is also inserted; this is taken from a djatta, a variety of opossum which is very dangerous to catch and which is sacrificed at the time of the construction of the ceremonial house, the *tsimia*. The eating of the raw liver is associated with a practice which is now extinct. Formerly the Baruya used to put captured enemy warriors to death. After breaking their arms and legs, and adorning their bodies with feathers and other ornaments, they would sacrifice them. A band of young warriors brandishing bamboo knives with the handle wrapped in a length of red bark – red being the color of the sun – would charge down a slope and all would simultaneously plunge the knives into the victim's chest. His blood was collected and smeared onto the onlookers, and finally his abdomen was opened and the liver torn out and shared among the men.

All these objects (*kwaimatnie*, Bakitchatche's dried fingers, flint stones, plants gathered on the sacred site of the ancestors) are different from other sacred objects because they contain sacred powers that are to be used on behalf of *all* the Baruya. To these must be added the flutes and bull-roarers, instruments whose sounds accompany the most solemn ritual moments, or at least those that occur away from the village and from inhabited places, deep in the forest or in the cleared grassland surrounding the villages. Only men from the same clans as the masters of the initiations may make and play these instruments. However, whereas the bull-roarers are kept by the men of these clans, carefully wrapped in strips of bark and always carried on their person in a small net bag along with other magic objects, the bamboo flutes are made for each ceremony and then destroyed as soon as it is over. They are smashed, and the bits thrown into the jungle, when the band of men and initiates nears the village. We will see why later.

But first let me say once and for all that alongside these durable or non-durable sacred objects used on behalf of all the Baruya in the framework of the initiations, each clan or lineage has other objects endowed with a more limited "effectiveness," a power which we think of as imaginary and symbolic. Among these are certain stone or wooden clubs that once belonged to famous warriors and which are carefully preserved by their descendants. There are also fertility stones owned by each lineage, which the men of the lineage bury in the gardens they clear in the forest and which they unearth again when they abandon the plot. Of course all these objects are without effect until the proper spells, the secret words, have been pronounced.

A few words about bull-roarers: the Baruya bull-roarer is a slender piece of polished black-palm some 20–25 cm in length, with a hole in one end that is threaded with a length of bark string. The bull-roarers are shown in utmost secrecy to the young initiates when they go through the second-stage initiations. At this time they are told never, on pain of death, to reveal to the women that the bull-roarers are worked by the men, who whirl them over their heads, producing a loud roaring sound which is like *no other sound* in nature, and which is supposed to be the voice of the spirits with whom the men converse and communicate during the initiations.

The bull-roarers are manufactured by the men and passed on as treasures to their sons. But *in the beginning*, the Baruya say, they were *given* to the men (and to them only) by the *yimaka*, the forest spirits. A *wandjinia*, a "man from the Dreamtime," an ancestor from the beginning of time, had climbed a tree when suddenly he heard something whistle over his head and stick into the trunk. He looked, saw something like an arrow and knew that it had been made and shot by the *yimaka*. This arrow was the ancestor of the bull-roarers, their prototype. When the *yimaka* gave men the bull-roarers, the Baruya say, they gave them powers to succeed in hunting and in war, they gave them powers of death. And when the men play the bull-roarers deep in the forest, the initiates' sponsors go and collect the sap (semen and milk) of a tree that reaches up to the sky, towards the Sun, and come back and place it in the young boys' mouth. At this moment, the Sun, the trees, the forest spirits, and the Baruya men unite in the task of re-engendering these boys outside their mother's womb.

All the sacred objects that have hitherto been described are men's objects, or more accurately, *objects appropriated and used exclusively by men*. But a closer examination of the most powerful and most secret of all these objects, the *kwaimatnie*, reveals another reality. A *kwaimatnie* looks like an oblong packet tightly wrapped in a strip of brown bark, which is again wrapped in an *ypmoulie*, the ceremonial headband worn by men, which is dyed red, the color of the Sun. This band is the symbol of the "fire path" which once joined the ancestors of the Baruya, the men from the Dreamtime, with the Sun. The word *kwaimatnie* comes from *kwala*, "man," and *yitmania*, "to make grow." A *kwaimatnie* is therefore an object that contains the power to make men *grow*; and the Baruya relate the word to *nymatnie*, which means "fetus" or "apprentice shaman." There is no such thing as one *kwaimatnie*. They come in pairs, and a *kwaimatnie* is either the male or the female of the pair. The stronger or the "hotter" of the two is the *woman kwaimatnie*. Only the man who "represents" a *kwaimatnie*-owning lineage can be the guardian of this kind. He is the only one who can handle the woman *kwaimatnie*. The male one is left to his real or classificatory brothers, who assist him in his ritual functions. The number and nature of these *kwaimatnie* pairs, and the fact that the more powerful of the two is female, are kept a strict secret from women, children, and first-stage initiates.

Kwaimatnie cannot release their life-giving powers on their own. These are set free only at the moment the representative of the *kwaimatnie*-owning lineage raises them up to the sky, to the Sun, before striking them on the chest of the initiates and sending their force into the boys' bodies. When he brandishes them skywards, the celebrant inwardly pronounces the secret name of the Sun (not known to the women) together with the spell passed on to him with the pair of *kwaimatnie* by the ancestors. The sacred object is thus the visible, material component of a whole comprising two other immaterial elements: a secret spell and a sacred name. Without the spell the object loses much of its power. That is why the ritual masters in this warrior society do not go to war, for fear they will be killed before having transmitted their knowledge to their sons. That is also why the other clans are willing to give them wives without demanding a woman in return, or not too quickly, for they want them to have children, sons, to whom they can pass on the object and the spell.

Outwardly a *kwaimatnie* is a strange-looking object; neither its shape nor its aspect provide a clue to its purpose, its function, and no Baruya must see what is inside, except, of course, the representative of the custodian lineage and the son who is to inherit his ritual functions. *Kwaimatnie* thus raise a series of questions. Where do they come from, according to the Baruya? Why do not all Baruya clans have them? What is concealed inside a *kwaimatnie*? What does its custodian see when he periodically opens the bark packet, rearranges the contents and wraps it up again?

Let us begin by the first question: where do the *kwaimatnie* come from? The Baruya invariably answer: Sun, Moon, or spirits gave them to the ancestors of the Baruya at the time of the *wandjinia*.

Sacred objects as gifts from the Sun, the Moon or the spirits to the Baruya's mythic ancestors

The Baruya have two traditions concerning the Sun and the Moon. One, which is known by everyone (men, women, children, initiates, non-initiates), says that Sun is male and Moon is his wife. Moreover, the Baruya call the Sun *Noumwe*, father, and the Moon, *Noua*, mother. Sun governs light, the day, all that is hot, dry, and semen; Moon reigns over darkness, the night, all that is cold, wet, and menstrual blood. But there is also an esoteric tradition known only to the masters of the initiations and the great shamans: this says that Moon is the younger brother of Sun. Some of the *kwaimatnie* were given by Sun; this is the case of those owned by the Kwarrandariar lineage, the most important of the Baruya clans, which gave its name to the tribe that emerged after the victory of the Yoyue refugees over their hosts, the Andje of Marawaka. Other *kwaimatnie* are said to have been given by Moon: for instance those of the Kuopbakia, which I was privileged to see opened. I will return to this later.

Sun's gift of *kwaimatnie* to the ancestors of the Kwarrandariar is regarded as the act that founded the Yoyue tribe, to which the Baruya's ancestors belonged. The following is the account of this foundation as it was told to me in 1970 by Yarouemaye, a member of the Kwarrandariar lineage, who had just taken over the function of master of the initiations (the Baruya call him a "*kwaimatnie* man") from Ypmeye, his uncle, whose sons were too young to succeed him when he died. This account is very obviously constructed, the events presented in such a way that they clearly legitimize the central role of the clan and the lineage in the celebration of the male initiations:

> In the olden times, all the men lived in the same place, at a spot near the sea. One day, the men parted, and our ancestor, the ancestor of our own lineage, the Kwarrandariar, the Baruya Kwarrandariar, the Kwarrandariar of the Baruya clan, rose up into the air and flew to the spot where we thereafter lived, Bravegareubaramandeuc, not far from Menyamya.
>
> Our ancestor was called Djivaamakwe, and Djivaamakwe had flown through the air along a path red as fire. This path was like a bridge that the *wandjinia* (the spirit-men of the earliest time, the Dreamtime) had built for Djivaamakwe and for the *kwaimatnie* that the Sun had given to our ancestor before he took off. The Sun is the man of the middle. He sees all and everything at once. Djivaamakwe had received three *kwaimatnie*. When he touched the earth, the *wandjinia*, the spirit-men, revealed to him the name Kanaamakwe, the secret name of the Sun. They also revealed to him the name of the spot and the name he was to give to the men he would find there: the Baragaye, the Baruya. Baruya is the name of an insect with blackspotted red wings, which the members of the Baruya clan are not permitted to kill. These wings are like the red path that led Djivaamakwe to Bravegareubaramandeuc.
>
> His men were there. He gave them their [clan] names Andavakia, Nunguye, and so on. Then he instituted the male initiations. He explained that a boy had to become a *mouka* [first stage], then *palittamounie* [second stage], then *tchouwanie* [third stage], and so on, and he gave them all tasks to perform, rituals to accomplish, and made them build a *tsimia* [the ceremonial house]. Then he said to them: "I am the central pole of this house, the *tsimia*. You are beneath me. I am the first, and for all of you now your first name will henceforth be mine, Baruya." The others, the Andavakia, the Nunguye, and so on, did not protest when he raised his name, the name of the Kwarrandariar Baruya, and lowered their names, Andavakia, Nunguye, and so on. They had little *kwaimatnie* ... He

said to them: "Now try your *kwaimatnie*. Try to make them do what I told you to do during the ceremonies."

They said to him: "We are your warriors. We cannot allow you to be killed by the enemies. You shall not go to make war. We shall go and you shall remain among us." For from the moment Djivaamakwe touched ground, there were many wars ... It was because of war, endless war, that Yarouemaye [this is the same name as that of the man who presently holds the *kwaimatnie* and who gave me this account], the son of Djivaamakwe, had to flee Bravegareubaramandeuc and come to take refuge in Marawaka. But he brought with him the *kwaimatnie*, the gift of the Sun.

At Marawaka, our ancestors changed their names. The Ndelie gave them hospitality and settled them at Kwarrandariar. Since that time, we are the Kwarrandariar Baruya. Then the Ndelie helped us to defeat the Andje and to seize their territory and, to thank them, our ancestor at that time, who was also called Djivaamakwe, gave to the Ndelie a third of the *kwaimatnie* given by the Sun, and gave them functions in the initiations. ... And Djivaamakwe ... stood before the defeated enemy, and dressed the young men and placed the insignias on their heads. Then he said: "Those shall be great warriors [*aoulatta*]", "Those shall be shamans [*koulaka*]." He saw and marked those who were to be Great Men.[3]

Several things need to be said about this account. It confirms that Bravegareubaramandeuc is truly the sacred site of the Baruya. Although it lies at several days' walk from their present territory, every three years the *kwaimatnie*-men go with their helpers. They return to the ground touched by Djivaamakwe to gather the sacred plants which they will secretly feed to the initiates at the ritual meals marking the various phases of initiation.

Bravegareubaramandeuc is to the Baruya what Lavinium was to the Romans. Located some 30 km south of Rome, Lavinium was regarded as the capital of the Latins. It was there that the *dii penates populi Romani*, the personal gods of the Roman people, the ancestral gods of the family lines (*patrii*), the house gods (*penates*), were officially housed, probably in the temple of Vesta. Myth relates that Lavinium was founded by Aeneas, who had fled the burning city of Troy carrying the images of the gods, sacred objects and the famous shield of Athena, the Palladium, which Dardanus, the ancestor of the Trojans, had brought from Samothrace.

As Yan Thomas writes, in a remarkable study on the *sacra principiorum populi romani*,[4]

At the beginning of the political year, the Roman magistrates, newly approved by Jupiter and immediately after their investiture by the people, would ascend the Capitol and then proceed to Lavinium to offer sacrifices to Jupiter *indiges* as well as to the public *penates* and to Vesta ... To go back to Lavinium was to go back in time. Or better, to go back to the very beginning, where the kinship line came upon a territory and, settling there, marked the *origo*: the moment when the passage of time came to a standstill on a site, at the crossroads of lineage and territory ... The origin is the meeting of two opposite tendencies, the flow of generations – represented by exile – and the putting down of roots.[5]

I will return later to the sacred objects of the Romans which only priests and Vestals might look upon. Servius speaks of wooden and marble vessels carried off from Troy by Aeneas, which is reminiscent of the objects found entombed with chiefs. But it is the Palladium that merits an explanation. For in claiming to be in possession of the Palladium, the Romans were inventing a mythic origin for themselves, which made them the equals of the legendary Greek heroes and placed the city of Rome on a par with Athens. The political stakes of this filiation are obvious. But establishing this demanded a few contortions, which are reported by Dionysius of Halicarnassus.[6] For instance it had to be imagined that Dardanus had taken two shields from Samothrace, one of which was stolen by the Greeks and carried back to Greece, while the other was carried away by Aeneas when Troy fell. In short, this is not unlike the Kwarrandariar Baruya maintaining that it was their own ancestor Djivaamakwe who gave the other clans their *kwaimatnie*, while denying, as we will see, that the conquered autochthonous clans had ever possessed *kwaimatnie* of their own.

The Baruya foundation myth is also perfectly explicit as to the function and the status of the *kwaimatnie*-men: these men not only institute male domination and transmit to the future warriors the power of the Sun and of the great warriors who died long ago; they also designate those in each generation who will replace them, those who will become the bulwark of the entire tribe, those whose names will grow as theirs have: the *aoulatta*, the *koulaka*, the great warriors, the shamans whose status is not inherited but must be merited, which shows and is shown. This explains why only the custodians of the Sun *kwaimatnie* have the right to place on and to remove from the young men's head the hornbill beak and the curved boars' tusks that symbolize their status as men and warriors. Even the boy's own father does not have this right, proof, were it needed, that initiations partake of a higher social order than kinship. And this is the order of male solidarity, and the political and ideological unity of the whole tribe.

Compared with the men's collective solidarity *vis-à-vis* women and the necessity of maintaining tribal unity, the fact that the autochthonous lineages and clans which joined the Baruya have no role in the initiations seems of lesser importance. But that does not mean that the repudiation of the original groups is not a potential point of fracture within the social body, within the tribe.

The myth thus "explains" the origin of the *kwaimatnie*. For the Kwarrandariar Baruya, it is the *Sun* in person who *gave* them to the *ancestors* of the clans living at Bravegareubaramandeuc. Alternatively, according to myth, the Sun gave nothing to the ancestors of the native populations that the Baruya subsequently incorporated into their own tribe. The Ndelie are an exception because the Kwarrandariar Baruya gave them a pair in repayment for having taken in and protected their ancestors, and in order to associate them in the rituals which celebrate the unity of the tribe and ensure men's domination of women. As luck would have it, the Sun had given the ancestors of the Baruya clan several pairs of *kwaimatnie*, for the day they might need them. Which goes to show that, in the Baruya belief system as in all religions, there is room for a few silences, a little forgetfulness, especially if being deaf, blind, or forgetful is helpful or even necessary for conserving one's power.

There is a clue which is going to enable us to understand what is at stake in this amnesia, and the reason for the unequal distribution of *kwaimatnie* among the clans, for their distribution has a *political* significance. It attests to past events, to a balance of power and to alliances between refugees turned conquerors and autochthones turned allies but on an inferior footing. Here is the clue. I asked one of the ritual masters why the Kavalie, a native lineage absorbed at the time of the invasion of Wonenara valley in the early twentieth century, had no *kwaimatnie*; with vehemence in his voice and a look of disgust on his face, he told me: "But these people come from cassowary droppings, they are forest men, the Sun gave them nothing." Some time later I had the opportunity to ask a Kavalie man, Arindjane, a warrior much feared and admired, why his lineage had no *kwaimatnie*. Lowering his voice, he said he would tell me about it, but later, in a secret place. And so he did. He revealed that, when the Baruya won the war, his ancestors decided that those who had exchanged women with the Baruya should go to live with them, leaving their ancestral clan and their defeated tribe. Then, before going their separate ways, these men buried their *kwaimatnie* on their former territory, in a secret spot in the forest where they await the day when the Kavalie come for them, and once again brandish them over the chest of future warriors.

For the Baruya, however, the Kavalie clan has no *kwaimatnie* and depends on the former to make their children grow and to turn them into warriors. The Baruya *want* to believe that the Kavalie do not have *kwaimatnie* because they *never* had them, because they were not worthy of having them, because they are not human beings like the Baruya. The unequal distribution of *kwaimatnie* is thus a direct reflection of the power relations, of the distinct positions in a hierarchy, in the political-religious totality of Baruya society.

It is therefore not hard to understand why these objects, as well as the knowledge that goes with them (spells, secret names, etc.) are *inalienable* possessions which theoretically are withheld from exchange, from both gift-exchange and from commodity exchange. They are inalienable because they constitute an essential part of each clan's *identity*.[7] They distinguish the clans, mark their differences, and these differences compose a hierarchy.

For all the clans that descended from the Bravegareubaramandeuc refugees, together with the Ndelie, take part in the tasks of initiation, but not at the same point in the ceremonies, not at the same stage, not in the same rites. Overall, the stages and the rites that reproduce them comprise a structure which unfolds between two crucial moments and links them together. The forcible separation of the boys from the women's world and the piercing of their nose (entry into the first stage) is the task of the Tchatche clan; the passage, some years later, of the boys from the world of adolescence to that of "young men", passage from the second to the third stage, is ensured by the Baruya clan. At one point during this second passage, in utmost secrecy, a man places on the young men's head a hornbill beak, which for the Baruya is a *symbol of the penis*; it is mounted on a sort of wickerwork tiara that goes around the boy's head and terminates in two razor-sharp boar's tusks which are pressed into the flesh of the forehead. This is the *symbol of the* woman's *vagina*.

I must repeat that in a hierarchically ranked totality, truly reciprocal relations do not exist, there are only non-symmetrical relations of complementarity and interdependence. In a hierarchy, even though all clans have a place, none occupies exactly the same position as another, or even an equivalent position. Because a particular clan owns a particular *kwaimatnie* and intervenes at a particular point in the initiations, its role is distinct from that of the other clans. Since this role is individual and indispensable, nothing is truly equivalent, nothing can take its place, be substituted for it, or even measured against it. A ranked totality is a set of complementary relations which cannot be switched around or stand in for each other; it is a "whole that forms a system."

But there is no reason to maintain, as Lévi-Strauss does, that because a whole forms a system it is totally dominated by the symbolic, that the signifier (the symbolic) "precedes and determines" the signified. The Baruya political-religious system, the position of their clans in the hierarchy is based on the unequal possession of "imaginary" powers which legitimize this hierarchy. A symbolic logic is a logic of relations, but these cannot be reduced to their symbols. And as symbols are polysemic, the content of these relations cannot be directly deduced from or reduced to the analysis of their symbols. An example of this is the two vagina symbols we encountered in our analysis: the bamboo flutes and the wickerwork ring ending in two boar's tusks. These have nothing to do with each other and can be explained only by the mental construction in which they are enrolled and which gives them meaning. Hence the question we must now ask ourselves, which goes well beyond the case of the Baruya.

Are sacred objects symbols?

If the Baruya's sacred objects are symbols, are they symbols in the same way for the Baruya *and* for us? The *kwaimatnie* are presents given by the Sun to the ancestors of the different Baruya clans at a time when humans were not as humans are now, at the beginning of time when things were just being set in place, at the time of the *wandjinia*, beings from the Dreamtime. Today's men and women therefore owe a lasting debt to the Sun and the Moon, just as they are indebted to their ancestors who received these gifts from the Sun and passed them on. These sacred objects and the knowledge that goes with them cannot be alienated. The Baruya are obliged to keep them. It is these objects which give them an identity and root this identity in the Beginning, in the time of the (imaginary) order of things, the time when the cosmic and social order was first established.

But while the Baruya clans are obliged to keep these sacred objects, they are also obliged to *share* their beneficial effects *with others*. Without alienating the object, source of their powers, they *alienate the beneficial effects* of these objects, they redistribute them to all members of the tribe. They share them, they place them at the service of the whole as a whole, of society. What is alienated is not the object in their possession, it is the effects of the object. The object remains immovable within the clan, holding the clan in place, connected to the Sun and to its ancestors; what is *detached* from the object, what is alienable, giveable, even exchangeable is not its powers, which remain attached, but the effects of these powers, which can be divided, shared, exchanged, added to others, completing them (or made to attack others opposing them).[8]

What the clans exchange are the specific "benefits" that the sacred objects in the possession of each clan can provide to everyone and which they place at the service of all, thereby working together so that the society to which they belong may reproduce itself as a whole, as a society. But these reciprocal exchanges of benefits can never be truly reciprocal, since the benefits that are shared and given are never equivalent. In a hierarchically ordered political-religious universe, there can be no true symmetry.

Alternatively, in the Baruya kinship system, as we have seen, reciprocity, symmetry in the area of exchange is deliberately sought and laid down as a principle. So where do sacred objects stand? *Between two types of gift*, but without being giveable. They hold this position because they were originally a gift from the gods to the ancestors of men. The gods therefore remain their true owners, and they have the right to repossess their gifts. But because these gifts were given by the gods to men, they can no longer be given by men to other men, except in special circumstances or for extraordinary reasons. On the other hand, what men may (and even must) give are the benefits, the positive effects emanating from the powers contained in these objects from the beginning. Once a sacred object has been received from the gods, it is difficult for men to turn around and give it to other men and, to quote Mauss, it is clear that "*it would be difficult for it to be otherwise.*"[9]

So, are these sacred objects symbols, and if they are symbolic of something, what is it, and to what extent? From this point, the analysis must navigate between two shores, between what is symbolic for the Baruya and what is symbolic for us, who do not believe in their beliefs. For the Baruya, the powers to make bodies grow, powers given by the Sun in the form of these *kwaimatnie*, are truly present in the black stone, in the eagle bone and in the human bone wrapped in bark cloth and tied up in a headband. The black stone is not the *sign* or the *symbol* of Venus and female powers. It *is* Venus, it is these powers. It contains them.

On the other hand, the fact that a particular *kwaimatnie* is held by a particular ritual master is indeed the *sign* that his clan has been set apart, has received special powers from the Sun and the ancestors. Just as the hornbill beak is a sign, the symbol of the penis, and its position above the boar's tusks, symbol of the female vagina, is seen as a sign of male dominance (or at least as the sign of the men's will and desire to dominate the women), so too the *kwaimatnie* held by the representative of a clan is the sign of this clan's position in the hierarchy of political and religious relations that order Baruya society, the sign whose public meaning all members of the society are capable of decoding, of deciphering, but whose secret sacred meaning is closed to most of the tribe. The other clans understand its public meaning, but not its secret one. Ultimately, the sacred must always remain secret, indecipherable, must only hint at a meaning which lies beyond all possibility of expression and representation.

For the Baruya, *before* becoming signs and symbols, sacred objects are *things which possess a spirit and therefore powers*. The word for spirit and power is the same: *koulie*. The symbolic is indeed "preceded" by the imaginary, then, and this is as true for the Baruya as it is for us. But for us, who do not believe in their beliefs, these become purely "symbolic." The fact that we do not believe in their beliefs concerns only us and may point to a critical consciousness of their religion, or even an irreligious consciousness of religions, of all religions, of all religious beliefs and practices. But the fact of not sharing a belief does not abolish the belief. Moreover, this belief in the presence of real ("spiritual") powers in objects is the most direct proof that the Baruya's concept of power necessarily includes "kernels of imaginary materials," that the hierarchical political relations among the clans, on the one hand, and between men and women, on the other, can exist only if they are *legitimized* by relations with a supernatural world, *with the origin of things*; in short by social representations of the imaginary foundations of the order of the universe.

This is the crucial point. For the Baruya, the organization of society, the rules of conduct, the values they espouse, in a word, the prevailing order, appears to be self-evident, legitimate, the only one possible; and this is because they *do not think of themselves as being the authors of this order*, because they believe that beings more powerful than themselves invented it and handed it down to their ancestors, who were different from present-day humans. And therefore it is the sacred duty of the Baruya to preserve this order and to reproduce it.

But these supernatural forces – Sun, Moon, and the men and women of the original time who spoke with them face to face – have not disappeared. They are still present, they still coexist with humans, and act upon them, working for or against them. Their continued presence among humans is attested by the existence of the sacred objects, the *kwaimatnie*, and by the spells and rites that go with them. The objects, spells and rites are there to represent what cannot be represented, to say what cannot be said, and to attest to its existence. The imaginary past of the origin of things is still present because it has become the foundation of the cosmic and social order, an invisible reality, but one which is co-present in the present. The origin has become the foundation, a point in time, and a reality beyond which it is henceforth impossible to go. The past of the origin transcends time, goes beyond it, encompasses it. It partakes of the sacred (of timelessness and perhaps even of eternity). Hence the importance of origin myths in Baruya culture, of the origin of men, women, fire, the flutes, weapons, cultivated plants, and so forth, which tell and retell of the supernatural character of these origins.

This point is capital. We have the right to assume, without being accused of dismissing the Baruya's explanations, that their ancestors *produced* in some far-off time, the type of society that their descendants presently reproduce. But the ancestors of the origin myths are not like those genuine ancestors, nor like their present-day descendants. They are duplicates of today's humans, but of another nature since they speak face to face with Sun and Moon, and receive gifts directly from them. When a supernatural origin is imagined for the social sphere, the social becomes sacred, and society is legitimized as it stands. Its order must be preserved and reproduced. But when the sacred nature of the origin appears, real humans disappear and *imaginary duplicates of these humans* appear *in their place*, beings in the image of humans but endowed with greater powers and entertaining imaginary relations with the "spirits which give life" to all things, to all the powers which make up the universe.

Of course the features we have just analyzed for the Baruya are found in all human societies, including those which attribute the origin of the laws that govern them to the sovereign people rather than to the gods. We are therefore in the presence of a universal phenomenon, of a general mechanism involving more than the unconscious structures of the mind. In order to be reproduced by all members of a society, social realities must appear, if not to everyone at least to the majority, as legitimate, as the only ones possible, and this certainty is not wholly self-evident unless the origin of these relations seems to lie outside the human world, in some sacred, changeless order, and changeless because it is sacred. Of course these representations will not be the same, the sacred will have a different nature in accordance with whether the changeless order to which the society ascribes its origins is "divine" or "natural." In the latter case, the "Law" or laws will be fetishized, and this will take the place of the worship of the father gods and mother goddesses of the human order.

Lastly, if we are to measure the extent to which the Baruya regard their sacred objects as merely symbolic realities, the degree to which their contents manifest a belief in the imaginary access of clans and individuals to the time when the world and society were founded, we need to know what is "really" concealed inside a *kwaimatnie*.

The privilege of seeing what is "inside" a *kwaimatnie*, was granted me several years after I had begun working with the Baruya, when one of the masters of the initiations, a man some 50 years old from the Kuopbakia lineage (Bakia clan), known for its brave warriors and effective war magic, came with his eldest son, a boy of 16 or 18, to keep the promise he had made me one day to show me what was "inside" a *kwaimatnie*. What happened and what was inside?

What is concealed inside a sacred object

Even before he arrived, I had felt that something unusual was afoot. A heavy silence hung in the air. The village was suddenly deserted. Everyone had left, having caught wind of something serious in the offing. Then the man arrived. His son – who lived in the men's house at the upper end of the village with the initiates – was with him. I was not expecting this. The two men came into the house and sat down, one at either end of the table. I put my head out to make sure no one could listen in, and saw two or three men from the Bakia clan, armed with bows and arrows, discreetly posted around the house so that no one could approach. The man opened his netbag and took out a long object wrapped in a strip of red bark. Without a word, he laid it on the table, untied the strip and began undoing the packet. This took some time. Carefully and delicately his fingers spread the bark. Finally he opened it completely, and I saw, lying side by side, a black stone, some long pointed bones, and several flat brown disks.

I was unable to say or ask anything. The man had begun to cry, silently, keeping his gaze averted from what lay before him. He remained in that posture several minutes, sobbing, his forehead on his hands which were resting on the edge of the table. Then he raised his head, wiped his reddened eyes, looked at his son and, with the same delicacy and the same precautions, reassembled the packet and wrapped it in the red *ypmoulie*. It was over. I was then allowed to ask a few questions, from which I learned that this *kwaimatnie* was powerful because it was female, and that *kwaimatnie* came in pairs. That was all. The man got to his feet, his son followed, and they left.

What had I really seen inside the *kwaimatnie*? The black stone was shaped like an adze blade, long and polished. The pointed bones were from an eagle. Now the eagle is the Sun's bird, which brings him the Baruya's prayers and spirits. For the Baruya, the eagle is more than just a majestic bird. It is another form of Djoue, the wild dog that accompanied Kourambignac, the first woman, the primordial woman, as she wandered the earth before humans appeared.[10]

But there was also a human bone, one from the forearm of one of the Kuopbakia's prestigious ancestors. It was obviously not a bone from the mythic ancestor who had received the Bakia's *kwaimatnie* directly from the Sun. The bone was sharpened and may once have been used to pierce the initiates' septum. The black stone, according to the Baruya, is inhabited by the spirit of a heavenly body, Venus, the morning and evening star. But who is Venus? She is a woman who was given as a present by the Baruya to the python, the master of thunder and rain (and menstrual periods), one day when he appeared on earth in the guise of a huge, terrifying wild boar who ravaged men's gardens and threatened them with famine. We call this story a myth, the Baruya say "short speech," in other words an account which relates in a few words the origin of things. It goes like this:

> One day the Baruya heard a loud noise in their gardens. They all came and they saw a gigantic python that they killed with arrows. They carried it away and cut it into pieces which they put into the earth oven to cook with taros and vegetables. That evening they opened the oven and shared out the meat and taros. They began by eating the taros and vegetables, leaving the meat for the next day.
>
> Next morning one of the women awoke very early and decided to eat some meat. There was nothing left in her bag. "Who stole my meat?" The other women heard her, looked in their bags to check and found that their meat too had disappeared. Everyone went back to the site of the oven and there they saw the snake which had gathered itself back together and was coiled up as though sleeping. Terrified, they drew near to it and asked: "What do you want of us to go away? What can we give you? Taros?" The snake did not move. "Salt?" The snake remained motionless. "Some cowries, necklaces, shells?" The snake remained there, its head bowed. Finally they asked it: "Would you like us to give you a woman?" At these words, the snake reared up, and that meant, "Yes." It looked toward the sky. "In which direction will you be leaving us?" It looked once more up into the sky. The Baruya led out a woman, heavily adorned. The

snake motioned her to pass ahead of him, but she said: "No, you show me the way." Before following him, she took a stone that had been heated in the fire and placed it in her bag. They climbed up to the sky and found themselves near a big house. The snake motioned to the woman to go in. "No, you go first, it's your house." While the snake was moving about inside, the woman took the big stone from her bag and blocked the door with it. Then she started down the column of smoke by which she had arrived as quickly as she could. But halfway down, she was turned into Venus, the morning and evening star. Meanwhile, the snake was wandering around inside the house. When he came to the door, he bumped his nose against the stone. He burned himself terribly and he cried out. That was the first thunder. The same snake made the first rain by urinating and the first rainbow.[11]

This is how Venus came to be. Venus is the star whose course is linked with the path of the Sun, whom she immediately follows (at dusk) or precedes (at dawn). She is therefore a Baruya woman who was given by the men but who did not remain a passive victim of this sacrifice, since she had the idea of taking along the stone which she used to wall up the big snake, indirectly causing the appearance of thunder and rain.

The conclusion is clear and it is *the most secret of all the Baruya's secrets*: inside the sacred object which manifests men's power is contained the *women's powers*, which the men managed to appropriate when they stole their flutes. Ever since these primordial times, men have had the capacity to re-engender boys outside the woman's womb, but they must constantly keep the women apart, separated from their own powers, alienated, as we say, from themselves. This explains the presence of the flat brown discs inside the *kwaimatnie*; they are the inedible fruit of a tree that grows in the forests of the hot southern valleys of the Baruya territory. On the side of these brown discs is a mark which looks like the iris of an eye; the Baruya call it "baby's eye." They use these pits in magic spells for giving or for restoring life. And they sometimes suck them to purify the mouth after they have been discussing women or sexual matters.

Which brings us to the flutes, other cultural objects whose "voice" plays an important role in the initiations and which, like the bull-roarers, are utterly forbidden to be seen by women, who are supposed to be unaware of their very existence. So what are the flutes for the Baruya?

Men tell the women that they are the voices of the spirits which join them in the forest when the time comes to initiate the boys. As in the case of the bull-roarers again, the young initiates are also

forbidden, on pain of death, to divulge to the women and uniniti-
ated children that these are not really spirits but instruments made
by the men, which they smash when they are through playing them.
But where did these flutes come from? Here is what the initiates are
told:

> In the days of the *wandjinia* [the men of the Dreamtime], the women
> one day invented flutes. They played them and drew wonderful
> sounds from them. The men listened and did not know what made
> the sounds. One day, a man hid to spy on the women and discovered
> what was making these melodious sounds. He saw several women,
> one of whom raised a piece of bamboo to her mouth and drew the
> sounds that the men had heard. Then the woman hid the bamboo
> beneath one of the skirts that she had hung in her house, which was a
> menstrual hut. The women then left. The man drew near, slipped into
> the hut, searched around, found the flute and raised it to his lips. He
> too brought forth the same sounds. He quickly put it back and went
> to tell the other men what he had seen and done. Later the woman
> returned and took out her flute to play it, but this time the sounds she
> drew were ugly. So she threw it away, suspecting that the men had
> touched it. Later the man came back, found the flute and played it.
> Lovely sounds came forth, just like the ones that the woman had
> made. Since then the flutes have been used to help boys grow.[12]

When the initiates have been told this myth, the secret name of the
flutes is revealed to them, *namboula-mala. Mala* means "struggle,"
"fight." The word *namboula* means "tadpole," but it is also used
among men to designate a woman's vagina. Why this allusion to
tadpoles and the vagina? Another myth explains the reason:

> In fact the women existed before the men, who one day appeared to
> them, on the shore of a lake, in the form of tadpoles. The women
> decided to make *pulpuls* [grass skirts] and miniature bows and arrows
> for them. They left these by the lake. The next day these had disap-
> peared and later these tadpoles metamorphosed into men.[13]

Today, from time to time, bands of Baruya women go down to
the river to catch tadpoles, which they give to the young boys. Every
night the female shamans are said to turn into frogs and gather
along the rivers around the edges of the Baruya's territory; here they
keep the spirits of sleeping women and children from straying across
the border and onto the territory of enemy tribes, where they could
be captured and devoured by their shamans.

But most important of all is that, according to the Baruya, it was
the women who invented bows and arrows, the weapons used in

hunting and warfare. It is said that they gave them to the men, who now have the monopoly on their use. But that is not all they did. According to a myth collected from neighbors of the Baruya, the Watchakes, who belong to the same culture, it was from the corpse of a woman murdered by her husband and secretly buried in the forest that the cultivated plants and the different varieties of bamboo used as cooking "vessels" grew. Fundamentally these myths are making and reiterating two essential claims.

First, that, from the very beginning, women, as a gender, have always possessed greater powers of creation than men, and this in two fundamental areas: on the one hand, they have the power to give life, the capacity to carry children in their womb, to bring them into the world, and to nourish them; on the other hand, they invented the material elements of "civilization:" weapons, clothing, cultivated plants. In short, it is due to women that humankind no longer lives in a savage state.[14]

> In those times, men and women ate nothing but wild fruits and plants. Their skin was black and dirty. One day, a man went off into the forest with his wife. On the way he killed her and secretly buried her corpse. He returned to the village and said that his wife had disappeared. Later, he revisited the scene of the crime and saw that all sorts of plants had sprung from the ground where he had buried the corpse. He tasted their leaves and found that they were good. When he returned to the village, the others said to him: "What have you done to get so fine a skin?" He looked different but he said nothing. The next day he went back to the forest and again tasted the plants. His skin became finer and finer. When he came back to the village, the others begged him to explain what he had done to have so fine a skin. That went on for several days, until one day he told the other villagers to follow him. He led them to the tomb where the plants grew and showed them which ones were good to eat and which might be suitable for cooking [allusion to the bamboo whose stems are used in steaming vegetables]. Since that time, men have taken to cultivating and eating these plants, and their skin has changed.[15]

The Baruya do not then oppose woman and man as two beings, one governed by nature (woman) and the other by culture (man). Rather, for them man is the one who has remained closer to the natural wild state. Furthermore, whereas women spend the bulk of their time in the villages and the gardens, the cleared spaces, men spend a large portion of their time in the forest. That is where they hunt, initiate the boys, place the bones of their dead in tree hollows. That is where they pray to the Sun and mingle with the *yimaka*, the spirits who gave them their bull-roarers. Fundamentally then, the men combine both the forces of "civilized" life, agriculture, sedentary existence in the villages, and the forces of wild, mobile life, in the forest.

But the acknowledgement of the original superiority of women in the myths is also a pretext, a "ploy." In reality this acknowledgment legitimizes the violence inflicted on women, a violence which is an essential principle of the organization of Baruya society, one of the basic principles of the order that this society intends to promote and to which it wishes to remain faithful, by invoking the authority and the will of the ancestors who handed on these rules. But how can this recognition of women's original superiority be a pretext for violence? How can it legitimize their subordinate role in the exercise of political power, in the appropriation of land and in the alliances contracted between various kin groups?

Once again the answer lies in Baruya mythology. Their myths tell us that women did indeed invent the bow and arrow, but they go on to say that the women held the bow backwards. Because of this they killed too much game, and the men were forced to intervene. They took away the bows and turned them around. Henceforth, they killed game only when they needed to and only as much as they needed, and women were no longer allowed to use bows. The thesis is clear. To be sure, women are endowed with primary creative powers which are greater than those of men; but they are also the source of disorder, or excessiveness, a constant threat to communal life, not only the life humans share with each other but the life they share with the beings that coexist with them in the same universe: animals, plants, and so forth. Men acknowledge their inferiority to women on one level, but regard themselves as superior when it comes to bringing order, measure to society and the universe. This is why the relationship between men and women is not conceived merely in terms of opposition between complementary terms. For one of the terms opposes the other by subordinating it, and therefore, in a certain fashion, by encompassing it. It is because their power contains or encompasses that of women that the Baruya consider it legitimate for men to represent both genders, themselves and women, and therefore legitimate for them to be the ones who govern society.[16]

But in order to bring order to society and govern it, men had to intervene and compel women by physical, psychological, and social violence. All these forms of violence however are regarded by men as nothing more than the consequences of the primordial violence that their Dreamtime ancestors inflicted on the first women when they made off with the flutes. What happened there? The flutes ceased once and for all to play for the women and would henceforth sing only in the hands of the men. Which means that women's life-giving powers became detached, as it were, from them, from their bodies, that women were separated, disconnected from themselves by the first aggression committed by a man on one of their number. And the memory of this aggression lives on in the word *mala* of the expression *namboula-mala*, which designates the vagina-flute.

It is this primal scene of the expropriation of women's original powers by trickery and violence that is continually recalled by the flutes which accompany the initiates' movements through the forest. Following this theft, men were greater and more powerful than they had been in the beginning. To the death-dealing powers that had been given them by the *yimaka* and which are present in the bull-roarers, Baruya men added women's life-giving powers present in the flutes and in the black stones of the morning and evening star, Venus. The Baruya's formula for political power is clear, then. To their own powers, men must add those of women, they must combine the two types of power in order for their sex to be not only the superior one, but so that it can also encompass the other. It is at this cost that one part of society, men, can come to represent the whole, and that women may be excluded from any direct action on the whole as such, on the society as a whole, in other words be prevented from exercising political power.

But if men were to seize women's power to make life grow as well as their civilizing powers, a man (and therefore all men) had one day to violate a basic taboo, he had to enter a menstrual hut, a space forbidden to men, to search under blood-stained skirts, to touch an object polluted with blood and to raise it to his lips. It was at the cost of violating a rule laid down from time immemorial as necessary for governing relations between the sexes that men were able to lay hold of the means of re-engendering boys independently of women, outside their mother's womb. And this explains the Baruya's ambivalence towards menstrual blood. For this blood is associated with women's life-giving power (and with their civilizing power since it was women who "invented" the flutes), but at the same time it threatens men with physical and social death, with the loss of their identity and superiority. For the Baruya think that if a man's body, and particularly his genitals, were to come in contact with a woman's menstrual blood, he would be drained of his power, of his strength, not only of the powers the men stole from the women, but also those that the Sun, the Moon and the *yimaka* gave them personally. Men think and feel menstrual blood as an absolute threat, and that is why women must live outside the village during their periods, that they are shut away during that time in a space situated between the village and the forest.[17]

In order to re-engender them, to make them grow faster and better in a world that will be exclusively male until they marry, small boys are given another highly secret food: the semen of older boys, of young unmarried men who have reached puberty, and who are in the last years of their initiation and their life in the men's house. This semen from the body of young men never having had sexual contact with a woman is therefore a purely male substance, a source of life and strength free of any female pollution. This substance circulates between the generations and links each new generation of men to their elders, and through them to the ancestors and to the Sun. It is a chain made up of gifts and debts: of gifts given by the elder boys to the younger ones, and of perpetual debts, since those who receive, the young boys, are not yet sexually able to give in return, and when they become able a few years later, at puberty, it is not allowed. They will give their semen to the next generation of boys who enter the men's house. Once again the givers are superior to the takers, but in this case the takers cannot give in return to their givers.

The differences in the relations between donors and recipients reflect the difference that exists between the area of kinship relations and that of power relations between the genders, between generations, between clans, and more generally relations of political power. Whereas in the production of kinship relations, young men from the same generation exchange sisters, thereby becoming, with respect to each other, both givers and takers, superiors and inferiors, in the construction of the general domination of men over women, which is also the construction of their "male" personality, men of different generations are in a non-equivalent position, each one being both a recipient with respect to the older men and a donor with respect to the younger ones. And whatever their age, all are, on another level, indebted to the ritual masters, the *kwaimatnie*-men who initiated them. The latter in turn owe a debt to the Sun and to the Moon, his wife (or according to the shamanic esoteric version, his younger brother), who gave Kanaamakwe, the founding hero of the Baruya tribe, all the *kwaimatnie*.

In the Baruya's thinking, in their accounts of the origin of the flutes and the basis of men's power resides an essential idea which connects their conception of the origins of their social order with all that we have said about the inalienable character of sacred and precious objects. Sacred objects, as I have shown, are inalienable and may not be given. Precious objects are inalienable, but may be given.

In this case, however, what is given is not the ownership of the object – this remains attached to the original owner – but the right to make use of the object. The donor gives the use-right and keeps the ownership. He keeps while giving. Now in the case of the flutes, repositories of the original female powers, we have the same logic, but in reverse. Stealing is the opposite of giving. But behind the gift and the theft lies the same logic.

The men's theft of the flutes

The flutes were not voluntarily given by the women to the men, they were stolen from them. This theft was committed at the cost of violating the rules of communal life, of the proper conduct between the sexes: the taboo on menstrual blood. Yet, though men managed to lay hold of women's powers, they were incapable of appropriating them fully. These powers remain fundamentally attached to women; it is in them that they have their primal, inalienable source. In reality, what men seized was merely the use of these powers, not their ultimate ownership. And because this right of usage was not given but was acquired by violent means, it must be kept through reiterated acts of violence. It is because the powers that were stolen from women remain originally and essentially female, even in the hands of men, that they can never be completely appropriated by the latter. And were men to relax this violence, this constraint they exercise over women, for a single day, a single month, a single year, disorder would once again well up and subvert society and the cosmos.

This is why generation after generation of men must expend so much energy, time, and material resources in organizing the large-scale initiation of their boys. It is also why they must perpetually conceal from the women that they do what they do by means of women's powers. This is why it is the female *kwaimatnie* that is the stronger and hotter of the pair; and finally, this is why the men sentence themselves to live both in the denial of women's real powers and in the fear that the imaginary powers they attribute to women will come back to life. In dealing with women, man is torn between envy and contempt.

We see the extent to which the logic of Baruya thought is based on the notion of the inalienability of things and powers with respect to their original owners. It is because the Baruya men seized only the use of the women's powers and not the original ownership that they must constantly reiterate the violence that enabled them to take what they had not been given. And what was taken by violence can be kept only by violence.

Having completed this analysis of the sacred objects which, for the Baruya, are possessed by men but which are actually handled by only a few, we can now compare what their mythology says with what really goes on in society. In the myths we see the *imaginary magnification* of the male person.[18] We see men take pride in having detached, by an act of violence, the powers which rightfully belong to the other sex and having attached them, by an act of violence, to their own being. First they inflicted a mutilation, then they attached to themselves that which they had detached by violence, by trickery, from the being of the other. This mutilation, this forcible disjunction of women from their original powers, is an imaginary act of violence, perpetrated by the mind in the mind.

But it is this imaginary, mental violence which in the first instance legitimizes all the real violence done to women: the fact that they do not inherit their ancestors' land, that they are excluded from owning and using *kwaimatnie* and therefore have only indirect access to the Sun and to the forces governing the universe, that they do not have access to the means of armed violence, to weapons, nor do they have the right to manufacture their own means of production, their tools. Even the digging stick, a simple but indispensable instrument for planting or harvesting tubers, is not of their own making. It is made by their father, if they are not married, or by their husband, if they are. Last of all, they do not have access to the production of salt, which is a medium of exchange in Baruya society.

The imaginary, then, is clearly an essential condition for, and a pivotal point in, the construction of social reality. The imaginary is made up of everything human beings (of both sexes) *add* in their minds to their real capacities, and of all that they mentally *subtract* from them. But in the purely imaginary interplay of mentally attributing to women original powers of which they are then mentally dispossessed, there has occurred something more than a "play" of the mind. The entire configuration of the real relations between the genders has been legitimized. This is not to say that myth is the "real" source of social reality, but that this reality cannot crystallize and reproduce itself without a myth which represents this particular organization and legitimizes it. For there is a considerable social force present in myths, which constantly fashions those who believe them. By recounting the extraordinary events that gave rise to the present-day order of the cosmos and society, by attributing these events to actions of larger-than-life characters, myths endow this order with a sacred, supernatural character which is the most convincing and impressive proof of its legitimacy and inviolability. Myths are therefore one of the most effective sources of the assent that all members of a society accord the norms that organize it and which are imposed on them from birth, on women as well as on men, on the younger people as well as on their elders and, among the Baruya, on clans without *kwaimatnie* as well as on those with *kwaimatnie*, or more generally on the governed as well as on those who govern.

Foundation myths are an essential element of the mental portion of the real, one of the imaginary components of social reality. It is this mental element, this imaginary component at the core of power, which is constantly present in sacred objects and which these in turn constantly re-present to the personal or collective consciousness of individuals. Sacred objects are therefore objects gorged with meaning, with the very meaning of the origin of things, objects which are not necessarily beautiful and which do not need to be, or at least, if they are perceived as being beautiful, it is a sublime beauty, a beauty which transcends all criteria of beauty. This is the case of the Baruya's *kwaimatnie*. One can now understand the emotion that overcame my friend, Kuopbakia, when he carefully unwrapped the packet containing his ancestors' *kwaimatnie*. What was it if not the emotion that comes over the believer at last contemplating the sublime object of his faith, the face of Christ imprinted on the Holy Shroud, or a fragment of the "True Cross," in short when he suddenly finds himself face to face with the unrepresentable, when he sees the invisible?

On the sublime[19]

This analysis restores emotions, feelings, and beliefs to their rightful place in the interplay of social relations and makes them meaningful once more; it also runs counter to the interpretation of Lévi-Strauss, who criticized Mauss for having

> [sought] the origin of the notion of *mana* in an order of realities different from the relationships that it helps to construct: in the order of feelings, of volitions and of beliefs, which, from the viewpoint of sociological explanation, are epiphenomena, or else mysteries; in any case, they are objects extrinsic to the field of investigation.[20]

The emotion inspired by a sacred object is neither a mystery nor an epiphenomenon. It partakes of the same whole; it is an essential component which cannot arise from or be triggered by the sight of a "symbol in its pure state," by a signifier that is devoid of meaning, but "liable to take on *any symbolic content whatever* [italics added]."[21]

These are not processes governed *directly* and essentially by the "laws of the human mind," the rest being, in Lévi-Strauss' words, "residual." We are dealing with a certain type of relations *between man and himself*, relationships which are therefore *at the same time social, intellectual, and affective*, and which are materialized as objects.

These relationships between man and himself are such that humans occupy *two* positions at the same time, one in space and the other in time: furthermore, these positions are simultaneously occupied by man's imaginary duplicates. And as man divides himself, he populates the universe with beings conceived in his own image, but endowed with powers to which present-day humans have no access (except through magic), powers which their mythic ancestors, however, possessed as a matter of course. In this respect, man's relations with the surrounding world are but the projection onto things of an aspect of himself. And because of this, things are never "truly things," external to man, since they necessarily take on the appearance of persons, and, transformed into persons, are addressed by humans as persons (in prayers, through sacrifices, and so on). The circle is completed. The ideas fit the things. The things and the events fit the ideas. The truth proves true. The obvious cannot be denied. Man finds himself a prisoner of the world of his representations and his desires, of his volition. And in the course of this process, his social relationships become constructed in such a way that the opacity necessary for them to exist and to reproduce is produced at the same time.

We are therefore not dealing with purely intellectual phenomena, but, on a deeper level, with the role of thought in the very process of producing social relations, with the mental portion of social reality. In other words, these processes are set in motion not only as a function of "a certain way that the mind situates itself in the presence of things,"[22] but also because of a certain way that man situates himself with respect to himself, because of certain stakes implicit in the nature of his social relations, which move him to construct representations of himself and the world in the content of which, however, certain aspects of these relations are passed over in silence, others idealized, others transformed into inviolable conditions for the survival of society, metamorphosed into the Common Good.

This type of situation exists in every society, including of course our own, where, alongside myth and religion, scientific knowledge both experimental and mathematical is developing at a rate hitherto unknown in human history; and these have *direct* effects on the material conditions of existence, since, unlike the case of Antiquity and the Middle Ages, today nearly all techniques of production, destruction, and communication derive from the sciences.

In our contemporary societies, man's double existence, the inversion of relations between subject and object, between the individuals who produce and their products, can be seen in two principal areas: the economic sphere, where relations between humans are both present and eliminated in what has become the eminently sacred object, money, especially when it functions as capital, as money which generates money "on its own"; and the political sphere, since despite the fact that it is the citizens who elect their representatives, and these representatives pass the laws, the Law as such, and its institutional support, the state, are still imbued with an almost sacred character.

It seems to me of the utmost importance to stress the fact that all of these processes whereby man and the world are split and duplicated are ultimately *materialized in objects.* To be sure, all of these man-made material objects are a mixture of tangible, intelligible realities, and of mental and cultural concepts, all embodied in matter. However we are not for the moment dealing with cultural objects in general but with sacred objects in particular. The latter can be presented as having been made either directly by gods or spirits, or by men following instructions provided by the former, but in any case, the powers present in these objects were not made by man. These objects are gifts from the gods or the ancestors, gifts of powers henceforth residing in the object.

It is as if it was not humans who assigned meaning to things, but rather the things, whose meaning derives from beyond the world of men, which transmit this meaning to humans on certain conditions. In other words, the synthesis of that which can and that which cannot be expressed, of that which can and that which cannot be represented takes place *in an object,* external to man but which exerts the greatest influence over him, his conduct, his very existence; in other words again, the sacred object brings us to the extreme point at which the *opacity necessary* for the production of society is fully realized, where the misapprehension necessary to the preservation of society *runs no further risk of recognition.*

Men ultimately find themselves alienated to a material object which is none other than themselves, but an object into which they have disappeared, in which they are necessarily and paradoxically present through and by their absence. This is not the social and material alienation directly imposed from without by a master on his slaves or by a conqueror on the people he has subjected by might. It is an alienation which arises *within* each person because it springs from the relations that fashion man's social being, the relations that obtain *between* all members of a single society, who make this society.

To a greater degree even than sacred texts, *sacred objects* realize the *synthesis of the real and the imaginary*[23] *which make up man's social being.* For this reason they are loaded with the ultimate symbolic value for the members of the society which has produced this code; and yet they can never be reduced to the state of pure symbols or of mere objects.[24] This explains why sacred objects do not have to be "beautiful" or to be enhanced by humans in order to arouse the emotion inspired by the presence of the gods and the ancestors. The same does not hold, as we have seen, for the precious objects which circulate in gift-exchanges, and especially in antagonistic gift-giving or potlatches.

This also explains the theoretically unique character of sacred objects. Even when these come in pairs (or in other multiples), as with the Baruya *kwaimatnie*, the pair owned by a clan is in principle unique and indivisible. And in societies where it is the custom to make copies of sacred objects and to multiply these copies, the archetype of these objects, which is at the same time the prototype, is carefully preserved somewhere, if only in people's minds.[25] One has only to think of the gold reserves held in banks when gold was the standard for the other forms of money (bank notes and so on) which circulate in commercial exchanges.

Concerning things the Baruya produce to give or exchange

Salt, the Baruya "money," is extracted from the ashes of a cultivated plant,[26] a kind of salt cane that they transplant into naturally or artificially irrigated zones. Once the canes have been cut, filtered and dried, they are burned; the ashes are mixed with water and the salty solution is slowly evaporated in large salt ovens. This process (which takes two days and a night) yields around fifteen bars of crystallized salt weighing between 2 and 3 kg a piece. The crystallization is entrusted to a specialist, who tends the fire, eliminates the impurities that settle in the salt, and so on. For the duration of the operation this man does not return to his house and is not allowed to have sexual relations with a woman. Were he to violate these prohibitions, the salt would turn to water, and its owner would be unable to exchange it. All Baruya clans have salt-cane fields established along the rivers. The specialist, in possession of a magic, is given one or two bars of salt in compensation for his work.

The salt in question is not sodium but potassium. It gives food a salty taste, but in high doses it is a violent poison. It is not used in daily consumption but exclusively in *ritual* contexts (for instance male and female initiations). That is why its consumption is associated with key stages in the life of individuals, which are themselves linked with key moments in the reproduction of society.

Salt is regarded as a source of strength, which accumulates in the liver, a blood-filled organ which, for the Baruya, is where the individual's whole force is concentrated. More secretly, salt is associated with semen, with men's strength. This is why the salt-maker is a man and why he must abstain from sexual relations when he is making salt. Among the Baruya, salt has two uses and two modes of circulation. Within the tribe it is shared, redistributed through the giving of gifts. Ultimately it is consumed, but only in ritual contexts. For example, the fathers of the initiates give chunks of salt to the men initiating their sons for them to chew and spit onto the ceremonial foods. A shaman who has driven a bad spirit from someone's body may also be given a bar of salt, or at least if he so desires. In short, salt is redistributed mainly between kinsmen, neighbors, co-initiates. It never circulates between Baruya as a commodity, but as a gift object for which *no one expects* a direct or even a deferred counter-gift.

However the bulk of Baruya salt is not produced to be given or consumed within the tribe, but to be exchanged as a commodity with neighboring tribes. The Baruya regularly set out on two- or three-day expeditions, their bodies painted with magic signs to protect them from enemy sorcerers and evil spirits; they go to the homes of their partners who guarantee them hospitality and protection, in tribes which were yesterday's enemies and could be tomorrow's. The exchanges are conducted in front of the door, in a space which temporarily serves as a peace zone and a marketplace. The salt is exchanged for several categories of goods: means of production (such as stone or steel tools), means of destruction (bows and arrows), means of social reproduction (bird-of-paradise feathers, cassowary feathers, cowries, pearl-shells, large shells, all used as ornaments and finery to adorn initiates, warriors, girl initiates, married women), expendable items (barkcloth capes, string bags) and young pigs.

In sum, in these exchanges salt functions as a commodity which is distinct from all others insofar as it *alone* can be exchanged for all other commodities. It is therefore more than just a commodity used in barter. In a certain manner, it serves to measure the exchange-value of other commodities since it is exchanged for them at stable rates which constitute their "price." An average-sized salt bar can be exchanged for four large barkcloth capes, or formerly for two polished stone blades for making adzes, and so forth. Of course salt also serves as a unit of measure because it can be broken into large or small pieces; it can be divided without destroying its use-value, which cannot be done with a barkcloth cape or a stone adze.

But it seems to me that salt serves as a currency for another reason as well: because, for the Baruya's neighbors as for the Baruya themselves, it contains a magical-religious life-force, something having to do with the world of the *kwaimatnie*, of sacred objects. Moreover, both the Baruya and their neighbors use it exclusively in ritual contexts, even if their rites are different and they do not always belong to the same culture. Nevertheless, it must be stressed that, when the Baruya *sell* their salt, they do not feel *personally bound* to the people with whom they have exchanged it for tools or capes. They have and indeed are supposed to have personal ties with the "correspondent" who houses and protects them and announces that the Baruya have come with salt. But they feel no obligation to those who buy their salt; salt, as an object, is completely detached from its owner. Commercial exchanges, for the Baruya, then, have an impersonal character. In certain exceptional circumstances, it is true, salt is not exchanged as a commodity between the Baruya and a neighboring tribe but given as a token of peace. The salt bars given on these occasions can be neither exchanged nor consumed: they are there to recall a peace agreement, they actually contain an oath, and giving them calls for a counter-gift from the former enemies, which seals the friendship and equality restored by the peace treaty. In short, the salt bars are no longer good for consumption or good for exchange. They are given to be kept and to bear witness.

It must be noted, too, that the tribes which buy the Baruya's salt do not in turn use it as a privileged medium of payment in their own exchanges with the more remote tribes which do not trade with the Baruya. Furthermore, the Baruya produce no more salt than they need to procure the things they do not produce themselves, or do not produce in sufficient quantities. They never make and stock salt in order to procure commodities with the sole purpose of selling them for a profit. In other words, while salt is in a certain manner a currency-commodity, it is a currency which never *functions as* capital, as money that is invested in order to make money. Although salt is the only commodity the Baruya exchange for all their needs, it never ceases being an object of barter; it is a privileged commodity, to be sure, but one whose exchange-value is not sufficiently separate from its use-value for it to be a full-fledged currency.[27]

Baruya shell necklaces and "valuable" objects

There are, however, objects for which salt is exchanged and which, like salt, can be exchanged for other objects, but in a much more limited fashion. These are the large, flat mother-of-pearl shells that adorn the chest of initiated men, and the large, round milk-white shells which decorate the women's breast from the time they begin having periods and have been initiated. These objects, too, contain a magical-religious power associated with the reproduction of life.[28] But no one among the Baruya amasses them for the purpose of potlatch-type gift-giving.

Yet this is precisely the type of objects that the Melpa, the Enga, and other Highland groups of New Guinea used to accumulate – before the arrival of the Europeans – for the purpose of displaying them alongside hundreds of pigs in the large-scale ceremonial exchanges, the great competitive distributions of wealth (like the Melpa *moka*, the Enga *tee*) which both linked and opposed these societies. The contrast is therefore striking: for the Baruya do not stockpile their salt, whereas they could,[29] and they raise pigs but do not use them in their ceremonial exchanges, where only game hunted by the men is featured, they practice no competitive exchange of gifts and counter-gifts, and every adult man and woman owns a certain number of shells intended for their sons (pearl-shells) and daughters (large round shells). Why such a contrast? Why is it that what is practiced elsewhere using the same objects – pearl-shells and pigs – is not and cannot be among the Baruya?

The reason, it seems to me, lies in the very nature of the kinship and the political relations which organize Baruya society, and in the relationship, the direct link, between the ones and the others. The first are based on the principle of the exchange of women between men, between lineages; the second consist of male *and* female initiations which establish and legitimize the men's collective and individual domination, their solidarity and unity *vis-à-vis* the women of their own tribe and *vis-à-vis* the men of neighboring tribes, all of which are potential or real enemies. This social structure precludes all competition, through gifts of wealth, for access to the positions of power.

Baruya marriage rests on the direct exchange of two real or classificatory sisters between two men. Through this exchange an alliance is contracted between two lineages and two clans. Marriage within the same "clan" is also allowed, but between distant lineages. A man may not take a wife in his mother's lineage, thereby reproducing his father's marriage. And two brothers may not take wives in the same lineage. Each must ally himself with a different lineage.

By applying these principles, each Baruya lineage finds itself linked, in each generation, with several other lineages; these alliances change from one generation to the next, old alliances gradually fading, but eventually being reproduced after three or four generations. Let us examine what, in these principles, rules out the competitive use of goods. First of all it is the fact that the Baruya do not exchange women for wealth but for other women. There is no bridewealth, no wealth comprised of valuables or pigs as a direct substitute for the woman, for a human being. A lineage which has given a woman without receiving one in return has a right to the daughter of the woman given, who will thus return and marry a man from her mother's lineage, a matrilateral cross cousin.

Through this gift and counter-gift of women, the two lineages are indebted to each other and obliged to help each other, to come to each other's aid, to exchange services, to share salt and pigs, and to invite each other to work land in common. The reciprocal exchange creates a bond between the lineages and, in some instances, a man may settle in his affines' tribe, even if they belong to an enemy group. Marriage alliance undermines political solidarity, then, and both the Baruya and their neighbors are skilled at playing on kinship ties to sow division in the enemy camp.

But kinship relations and marriages between lineages and clans do not suffice to make a society, by which I mean a whole unified with respect to itself and to the outside. That requires political-religious relations, which integrate all clans, all generations, all individuals into the same structure, a framework constructed by the male and female initiation ceremonies by means of which the Baruya present themselves to themselves and to their neighbors – both friends and enemies – as a whole.

And they apply the same logic of equivalence to war. The death of a Baruya can be compensated only by the death of an enemy. Just as there is no valuable or amount of wealth that can be exchanged for a woman, there is none that can pay for the death of a warrior.

It is not that the Baruya do not know about exchanging wealth for a life or a death. *On the contrary, they are quite familiar with the principle.* When they want to conclude a trading pact with a remote tribe with whom there is no risk of being alternately at war and at peace, they marry a woman from this tribe and, in exchange, give a large number of salt bars and dozens of cowry fathoms, in short "money" and "wealth." They are therefore familiar with the principle of marriage with bridewealth, although they do not practice it among themselves and with their immediate neighbors, in other words within the sphere of their political relations.

There is another context, this time within the tribe but exceptional, in which the Baruya exchange wealth for a life. This is when a person wants definitively to sever ties with his own lineage and, having married a woman from another lineage, wants thenceforth to be considered as a member of his affines' lineage. If this lineage and his own agree, the transfer and the symbolic binding of the person to his new lineage take place during a ceremony in which a "bridge" made of salt bars, cowry strings, pearl-shells and so forth is constructed and then given by his affines to his lineage of birth. From that time on, the man and his descendants no longer have the right to use their ancestors' land, to work it, or to hunt on it. Far from being ignorant of the principle of exchanging wealth for a life or a death, then, the Baruya know all about it but *have no intention* of extending it to the sphere of their political-religious relations.

It is therefore not the presence of pearl-shells or the capacity to procure them, nor is it the capacity to raise a large number of pigs that explain the *existence* of large-scale *competitive* exchanges. To be sure their development supposes favorable technological and ecological conditions, but it is a certain type of relations that people entertain with each other (and not directly with nature) which explains their appearance and then their development. And these relations must be sought, precisely, in the area of kinship and in the political-religious sphere.

Thus, among the Baruya, even though the direct exchange of women among the lineages affects the economy and morality – since it entails other gifts, exchanges of services, the sharing of goods – society *as a whole* is not founded on "an economy and a moral code based on gift-giving." For the kinship relations which constitute the domain in which the principle of gift and counter-gift operates do not constitute a field open to competition. It would make no sense for a Baruya to give *two* of his sisters in exchange for *one* wife. A woman must take the place of a woman, and, ideally, one (healthy, well brought-up) woman is equivalent to another.

Furthermore, the political-religious relations between clans and lineages, their participation at distinct inherited positions in the performance of the initiation ceremonies, in the production of this imaginary collective architecture which both realizes and symbolizes the political unity of the tribe over and beyond its divisions into separate kinship and residence groups, all of this precludes competition for a limited number of positions of power and prestige. When such a field does exist, and when the means for acceding to these positions is the competitive giving of amassed wealth, we are dealing with a society in which the economy and moral code have every chance of being marked and driven by the giving of gifts and counter-gifts. We now see why, for the Baruya, amassing shells and pigs was not *socially* necessary, even though it was possible.

Gifts between friends

In Baruya, *nya'mwei* means a male friend and *nya'mwe* a female friend. The word *kwaiyeuwaalyaigeu* may also be used for a man. The first two terms can also be used for "brother" and "sister." A male friend is (like) a brother, a female friend (like) a sister. The third term refers to the world of male initiations, to the bonds of solidarity that unite co-initiates (*nyakwe*): it is expected that they will help each other and share their food as they shared the cold, hunger, frights, fears, and ordeals.

Relations between friends, then, lie somewhere between the relations that unite very close kin of the same generation and those linking co-initiates. But let us not forget that one chooses one's friends, but not one's brothers, sisters, or co-initiates. Between friends, whether of the same or the opposite sex, one gives and shares, and each knows they can count on the other. In short, friendship is a relation between non-kin, usually (but not necessarily) of the same generation, who show their feelings by offering mutual assistance and by exchanging gifts and presents (*yanga*). The term *yanga* features in both the idea of sharing (*yanga mudeumo*) and of exchanging (*yanga yeunako*). But when something has been given definitively, has been truly separated from its giver, it is designated by the term *seuhumale*.

Gifts between friends concern only the individuals involved. They therefore do not contribute to the reproduction of basic social structures, kinship relations for example, as does the practice of *ginamare*, sister-exchange between two men, the exchange of women between two lineages. Gifts and assistance between friends come under the heading of subjective ties between individuals who choose each other; but this choice has no other motivation or obligation than the strength of their feelings, the attraction that they arouse in and feel for each other. One social constraint is imposed on friendship, however: sexual relations are excluded. In this respect friendship resembles the relations of intimacy between brothers and sisters, between consanguines. It resembles them in another respect as well, in that friends give without expecting immediate reciprocation and even without being concerned with reciprocation, somewhat like parents and children.

Here we catch a glimpse of why, in Western societies, gift-giving between friends continues to exist and to be valued, whereas the other types of giving, which are obligatory because they are necessary to reproduce basic elements of society, such as kinship relations, no longer exist. The giving of gifts between friends, which is a minor feature of Baruya culture, remains a strong paradigm in the individualistic West because it is seen as a spontaneous, individual, subjective, and altruistic act, free of collective obligations and objective social constraints, which therefore does not serve to reproduce society on a deep level. In the West, gift-giving between friends stands alongside another gift which is strongly privileged by the Christian West, and that is the gift of his life by Christ, the son of God, to redeem people's sins and to save them from everlasting damnation, the supreme example of the absolute gift freely given.

Recapitulation of the things that are given, those that are kept and those that are exchanged among the Baruya

At the top of the list come sacred objects together with the names and spells that go with them. The lineages claim to have received some of these from the Sun, the Moon, and nature spirits as gifts that they must keep and not give. All of these realities which are theoretically withheld from gift-giving and exchange constitute the mental and ideological basis of the power relations, the political-religious relations, which obtain, on the one hand, between the sexes and, on the other, between clans, and which are relations of domination.

Some of these objects were given directly to men by the powers of the universe: these are the *kwaimatnie*, the bull-roarers, and so forth. Others were originally given to women (flutes) but were stolen by the men. All are now in the hands of men, who keep them. But while keeping them, they bestow on all Baruya the life-forces which these objects contain and which can be of benefit to the population. Although the objects are exempted from gift-giving, then, their benefits are given and exchanged.

Among the political-religious relations intended to ensure male domination is the giving of semen, which takes place in two entirely different contexts: on one hand, the semen given the boy initiates by young men never having had sexual contact with women; and on the other hand, the semen a man must give his wife from the moment he marries, with the idea that his semen is stored in her breasts, where it becomes the milk she will give her babies. A man renews these gifts each time his wife gives birth and sometimes each time she menstruates, in order to restore her strength. The Baruya child is thus considered to be the product of the semen of its father, who makes the body of the child in its mother's womb and then nourishes it by repeated sexual intercourse throughout the pregnancy. But the father's gifts of semen to the fetus are not sufficient to make the whole child, and it is the Sun, father of all Baruya, who completes the embryo *in utero* by making its hands, its feet, and its nose (the seat of the spirit/soul).

The Baruya reciprocate prayers to the gods and the spirits. Periodically, when an epidemic ravages the tribe and people die by the dozen, the shamans sacrifice a pig and bury one of its feet near the house where they invoke the spirits. The Baruya like to recall that they gave a woman to the great python, master of thunder, rain, and menstrual blood, and that this woman became the star, Venus. But it is clear that the debts owed the spirits and the invisible powers can never be cancelled, or even "balanced."

Alternatively, in the sphere of kinship, the reciprocal gifts of women balance but do not cancel each other, thus restoring equivalence of social status to the individuals and groups involved in the exchange. Finally, in salt we have an object produced for the purpose of redistribution among the Baruya through a series of gifts, or for use as a sort of currency for buying the necessities the Baruya either do not produce or do not produce in sufficient quantities. Among their purchases are the cowry necklaces or large flat shells which come from the sea by a long chain of intertribal exchanges. These shells are used as finery, and the Baruya give them to their sons or daughters upon their initiation or marriage.

Baruya society thus offers us a variety of forms of gift-giving. Gifts in which the recipients (gods, spirits) dominate the donors (humans) because they will always be superior for having given the *kwaimatnie*, the secret knowledge, and so forth. Symmetrical gifts between wife-takers and -givers, asymmetrical gifts of semen between initiates in which the men of one generation will always be indebted to their elders while their juniors will always be indebted to them. Manifestly when we come to the potlatch societies, we are dealing with an entirely different configuration, but we can now make an attempt to define the conditions in which these societies emerged.

Hypothesis on the emergence and the development of potlatch societies

For potlatch societies to appear and develop, two conditions are necessary. First of all, in the area of kinship, marriage must no longer be implemented through the direct exchange of women, and bridewealth must, for the most part, have replaced "sister" exchange. Secondly, a portion of the political-religious power has to exist in the form of titles, ranks, names, and emblems placed in competition and open to those who successfully establish their superiority over others through prodigal giving, by amassing more wealth than others in order to outdo their rivals in gift-exchange. Give more than your rivals, return more than your rivals: this is the recipe, and it relentlessly drives the system to its limits.[30]

In order for this to come about, the safety catch of direct exchange of women has to have been removed. The number of exchangeable "sisters" (even "classificatory" ones) is always very limited, and unless one imagines a brother exchanging all of his sisters in order to multiply the number of wives he can take, thereby sentencing his brothers to bachelorhood, the sphere of *direct* exchange of women is quantitatively restricted beforehand. Furthermore, this exchange is also qualitatively limited because it is two *concrete* persons that are exchanged.

The problem vanishes when, in exchange for a concrete person, wealth is given – valuables or pigs that are raised not for consumption but for exchange. The elements of the problem are completely different: on the one hand, we have a woman, on the other, valuables or pigs which can be multiplied by producing more or by procuring them by other means. One the one hand, we have persons, on the other, all sorts of "things" which function as substitutes for these persons.

When a woman is exchanged for a woman, it is an exchange of two beings of the same nature, whose social value is presumed, *a priori*, to be *equivalent*. Their upbringing ensures that all girls will be hard workers, faithful wives and good mothers; that they will all be equivalent. But even the best upbringing cannot guarantee that a woman will not be sterile or that she will give birth to viable children, and it is most often the women who are accused of sterility, for a Baruya man *cannot* be sterile.

But when a woman is exchanged for wealth, the equivalence takes on another, more abstract character. Persons are equated with things, things are equated with persons. But the two terms of the equation do not share the same mode of existence. Persons are produced in the framework of kinship relations, wealth is produced in the framework of the social relations which organize production and exchange. Once women can be exchanged for wealth, "a veritable political economy of kinship" becomes possible. Wealth procures women, and women procure wealth. Women themselves become a form of wealth.

Without going into the actual problem of the meaning of bridewealth, and even less that of the dowry which, in certain civilizations, is provided by the girl's parents when she goes to live with her husband,[31] I will give one example, which will suffice to illustrate my hypothesis and bring us directly back to the world of potlatch, and more particularly to the *moka*, the ceremonial gift-exchanges practiced by the Melpa.[32]

Among the Melpa, when two families or two lineages have agreed to marry two of their children, the amount of the payment is negotiated in several stages. Goods are exchanged between the families, but in addition a certain number of large shells and pigs are given to the bride's parents and these are not to be repaid. Several of these pigs are described as *kem kng*, which Andrew Strathern translates loosely as "pigs for the girl's vagina"; a certain number of shells are called *peng pokla*, which means "to cut off the head" (of the girl), in other words to separate her from her parents; one pig is given especially to the mother of the bride, which is called *mam peng kng*, "the pig of the mother's head."

The logic behind these equivalences is clear. Wealth, pigs, and shells are transferred without a return payment, both to sever (in part) the bonds that connect the young woman to her family and to gain access to her sexual (and other) "services." At the same time, however, live pigs are exchanged between the two lineages and others are given to the girl by her parents so that the couple may start raising their own pigs. The intent behind these gifts is no longer to repay the gift of the woman with wealth, but to prepare to make the affines into moka partners.

Indeed, for the Melpa, a marriage is not fully established until the groups and individuals linked by this alliance become partners in the moka exchanges and vie as well as cooperate with each other. This example clearly shows why marriage in potlatch societies could never be based on the direct exchange of women: for this would "block" the competitive aspect of the exchange of material wealth. Here marriage alliances and the interplay of kinship relations are subordinated both to the perpetuation of the moka and to the expansion of its base, which consists of many dozens of clans and thousands of individuals, in short a base of another order than that of kinship. We are now talking about politics.

To put it another way, the practice of bridewealth, the absence, or the presence of no major social importance, of the direct exchange of women, *does not suffice* to pull the society into the exciting but perilous round of gifts and counter-gifts of wealth; it is not enough to subordinate the economy and the moral world of individuals and groups to the constant transfer of riches from hand to hand, from group to group or from individual to individual. There must also be a certain number of positions of power that are *accessible by competition* between groups and between individuals, and the condition for success in this competition must be the capacity to *amass wealth and to redistribute it*, to give it away.

It is by giving away wealth that a man acquires power and fame, just as it is by giving wealth that a man acquires wives. Under these conditions, the objects which constitute wealth function not only as *substitutes for persons*, for human beings, but also as *substitutes for sacred objects*, which are the ultimate source of all human power, their possession attesting the privileged relation a man enjoys with the gods and the ancestors.

When two types of structure intersect and mesh – kinship relations in which the alliance between two lineages engenders the transfer of wealth on the part of the wife-takers and in which direct exchange of women plays only a minor part and is sometimes explicitly forbidden,[33] and political relations in which a number of individual and local groups can, by vying to outgive each other, use wealth to accede to positions of power and prestige, either within their tribe or in a much broader, intertribal, or regional framework – then the conditions seem to be present for the emergence of a society in which the groups and the individuals who represent them can pursue their interests by making a show of their disinterestedness and vying to outgive each other.

In this type of society, the field of competition between groups and individuals has become immense. It cuts across all kinship relations and extends to a portion of the political-religious relations. But the underlying logic is still the same: that of social relations which exist and are reproduced only between persons and groups, groups which for the most part act like persons and are regarded as such. There is no trace here of impersonal relations, like those of contemporary Western society, those entertained between citizens equal before the law and the constitutional state.

By political-religious powers I mean a certain kind of powers which are exercised over the entire society and on behalf of the entire society in order that all of the kinship groups and all of the local groups that constitute it *may be reproduced together*, as a whole, united *by and over and above* their internal divisions, their conflicts of interest and their disputes. The field of political-religious relations overspills and encompasses that of kinship because matters of local-group interests or kinship-group interests are dealt with *on another plane*, which is largely independent of the domain of kinship.

But why, in this type of society, does the exchange of gifts and counter-gifts become the *privileged* instrument of the *struggle* for power and fame? The first reason, it seems to me, lies in the fact that giving puts others under obligation without the need for violence. Gift-giving, we have seen, creates an interdependence between the two partners and at the same time puts one (the recipient) under an obligation to the other (the donor), installs him in a socially inferior and dependent position until he can in turn give more than he has received.

But, whereas for the Baruya the goal of heeding the principle of "a woman for a woman" is to enable *all* men to have at least one wife and thereby enable all lineages to reproduce themselves,[34] in societies which practice competitive exchanges of wealth, the avowed goal is to enable *only a few* individuals and groups to accede to the positions, titles, and ranks up for competition, which implies that the number of these ranks, titles and positions is well below the number of groups and individuals vying for them.[35] The consequence of this relative "scarcity" of political goods compared with the number of participants is that those who enter the game and want to stay the course and win are socially obliged always to give more than the others or to give increasingly rare objects, more valuable than those given by the others. Another consequence is the emphatic, ceremonial style of the gestures which accompany the giving of gifts and counter-gifts.

We now understand why, in this type of society, it is difficult or impossible for the majority of individuals and groups *not to get drawn into* the game of gift and counter-gift or to get themselves out. The only ones (partially) exempted are those whose elevated rank raises them well above the arena or those whose inferior or servile position excludes them from below. For the rest, to avoid giving is to forfeit one's own honor and that of the group one represents.[36] It becomes impossible to refuse to give or give in return. Thus the act of giving contains a violence which is not only that of the individual, since it springs from beyond the individual, from the social relations which ordain that the struggle for power and fame is to be waged by means of wealth. Gift-giving contains this violence in both senses of the term: it carries the violence within itself and at the same time maintains it within certain boundaries, allowing it to be manifested in the public, political arena.[37]

Having come around to Mauss and the "Essai sur le don" once more, we are now ready to look back over the ground we have covered and, in a certain manner, take the measure of Mauss' merits and limitations. Mauss was the first to highlight the importance of the gift, of gift-exchanges in the way human societies operate – ancient societies or modern, Western or other. He was the first to make a clear distinction between two kinds of gifts: non-antagonistic gifts and counter-gifts, and antagonistic gifts, which he called "potlatch," a term with which he was not entirely satisfied. He also made another important suggestion – but one which aroused little interest in those who did not think human society evolves or who did not regard this evolution as an object worthy of scientific reflection – namely that antagonistic gift-giving was a transformation of non-antagonistic gift-exchange, a form in which rivalry, the struggle of wealth, prevailed over sharing. For Mauss, the potlatch could not have characterized the first forms of human social organization, but was an institution which developed later, sometimes to the extent of marking the entire "economy and moral code" of a society.

Yet his analysis has its limits. To be sure, Mauss made it remarkably clear that in the giving of gifts and counter-gifts, some things occur which may seem odd to a Westerner accustomed to a world in which things have long been separable and separated from persons. He was justifiably surprised that the donor of an object retained ties with the thing he had given as it continued to pass from hand to hand and to be given anew. But he never found the key to the enigma. Or rather he believed he had found it in the concept of *hau*, the spirit of things, and in the account of a Maori sage as he interpreted it.

This trail might have led Mauss to the solution, but the fact is that it did not. His lack of success was due not only, as his critics claim, to his fascination with a "mystical-religious" explanation of the phenomenon, but to the fact that he did not seek a more accurate reconstruction of the sociological basis for the way a certain type of objects circulated, that he recognized the importance of the imaginary meanings these objects carried for the social actors but did not work back to the sources of these meanings, to their role in the production and legitimation of a social order. For every social order, if it is to convince itself and others of its legitimacy, needs both to pass over in silence certain aspects of its workings and to thrust others to the fore by loading them with imaginary meanings and symbolic weight; in short, every social order needs to invent a social and material device which will produce and maintain the (partially illusory) representations that every society generates of itself and of other societies.

This machinery for producing useful and effective illusions cannot be uncovered and dismantled without a detailed understanding of the way the social relations function. However, the "Essai sur le don" lacks a fine-grained, sociologically faithful analysis of the area of social practice in which the ceremonial gift-giving competitions take place, of the identity of their real actors, and of their effects on the reproduction of society. In spite of the space he devoted to two scientific examples, the northwest American Indian potlatch and the kula of the Trobriand Islanders, Mauss never actually penetrated the mechanisms of their kinship systems, or of their rites of birth, initiation, or death. He never detailed the architecture of their ranks, titles, and other positions of power. He saw that some, the highest-ranking men, stood above the struggles of the potlatch, he perfectly understood and saw that these positions exempted from competition were associated with the ownership of sacred objects that were not given or exchanged; but there he stopped, describing the bare facts, but not investigating them.

It was by following the very trail that Mauss had indicated and by undertaking a detailed analysis of a society which engaged in gift-exchange but not in potlatch that I began to perceive more clearly, by contrast, the conditions which enabled the appearance, development, and flourishing of societies characterized by an economy and a moral code of agonistic gift-giving, of potlatch-giving. These conditions appeared to be quite well defined. As I have said, in the area of kinship, direct exchange of women had to be absent[38] or of minor importance, and in its place alliances between lineages and individuals had to proceed from the giving of wealth for women. In the area of political-religious relations, there had to be a significant number of powerful positions and functions which were not fixed and hereditary but open to competition, and the instrument of this competition had to be the giving of wealth.

Taken separately, each of these conditions is necessary but *not sufficient* to launch societies on this course. But taken together, linked in a chain combining and multiplying their effects, they become the structural conditions, the social basis of societies characterized by an economy and moral code based on potlatch-giving. Historically, then, one or several social and mental revolutions had to have occurred for equivalence (wealth = a person) to have replaced identity (a person = a person), and for non-equivalence rather than equivalence in giving to have become the goal. I will return to this later.

In conclusion, let us come back one last time to the problem of equivalence between "realities" of different natures. When one exchanges wealth for a woman, one is not merely substituting things for persons, one is also doing the converse, substituting persons for things, and above all one is breaking up the narrow character, the boundaries imposed by nature on the "things" exchanged: a woman for a woman, a dead warrior for a dead warrior. A more abstract relation of equivalence is established, since, on one side stands a concrete person, a woman, who cannot be divided even if she can be "used" in various ways, and, on the other side, pigs, pearl-shells, and so on, which can be added, subtracted, multiplied, divided. But this abstract relationship between a concrete human being and equivalent specific things also has its boundaries. These are erased when *all* things or nearly all, all services or nearly all have become commodities which can be equated because they are measured by the same standard. But this happens only when there is a currency which functions as a universal currency, when everything or nearly everything that is of use to humans can be bought or sold, and when humans themselves, or at least parts (or uses) of their body, have a price measured in the same currency. When this happens, the whole society becomes one great marketplace. We have come to this point in the Western world and in some parts of Asia. And the rest of the societies in our world are heading in this direction; today not one can escape the direct or indirect pressures of the conditions of capitalist development. I nevertheless do not share Mauss' conclusion that "we can and must return to archaic society,"[39] even though, like him, I believe we must go beyond "the cold reasoning of the merchant, the banker and the capitalist."[40]

What is the place of potlatch societies in history?

At last, it should be possible, it seems to me, to assess the place of potlatch societies in history. Of course the history I am talking about is not the specific history of each of these societies. It is the history that begins to take shape, to be reconstructed when, through the specific histories of individual societies, parallel evolutions begin to emerge which make sense because they suppose irreversibilities which are no longer singular and accidental but structural and necessary. Now these parallel irreversibilities, which are linked to convergent structural transformations, occur in societies which have had no contact with each other and which quite often do not even belong to the same epoch.

This means that history entails evolution. Not that laws for the evolution of human society are inscribed in nature or in the mind of God, laws which precede history and predispose societies to move in one direction or another. Nor is it history that drives history. It is human beings themselves who do the driving; they cause things to change, they modify their relations among themselves and with nature. But one thing does not turn into something else willy-nilly, and at any one time in any one society the number of possible transformations is always very limited. It is impossible – sociologically, mentally, materially, and therefore historically – for a neolithic society organized more or less on the lines of the Baruya as they were living before 1951, the date of the arrival of a young Australian patrol officer named James Sinclair, to have transformed itself *directly* into a society organized according to market-economy principles, governed by a state and having mastered several sources of energy, among them nuclear power.[41] Simply raising this possibility is enough to show that it *makes no sense.* Therefore some societies must have gone through *several stages,* in space and over time, for such transformations to have come about and for other societies to have access to the same results *without having to go through* these stages. This necessity of going through certain stages is what is called "the conditions of evolution" or "historical necessity." No society is exempt: if some are able to skip certain stages, it is because others have gone through them.

All of today's existing societies result from transformations of societies which have gone before and which sometimes continue to exist side by side with new forms. All present-day social structures are transformations of other structures which characterized the same or other societies at other times. Transformation means both the conservation and the destruction of certain parts of old structures, but also the emergence of new realities which combine with the old ones and give them a new meaning and new functions.

In this perspective and after having taken these many theoretical precautions, I will quote, without necessarily espousing his position, Mauss' conception of the place of potlatch societies in history. Mauss believed that they corresponded to

> a regime that must have been shared by a very large part of humanity during a very long transitional phase, one that, moreover, still subsists among the peoples [of the Pacific and northwest America] ... this

principle of the exchange-gift must have been that of societies that had gone beyond the phase of "total prestations", from clan to clan, and from family to family, but have not yet reached that of purely individual contract, of the market where money circulates, of sale proper, and above all of the notion of price reckoned in coinage weighed and stamped with its value.[42]

Between the economic structures of societies based on "total prestations" and

the individualistic and purely self-interested economy that our own societies have experienced at least in part, as soon as it was discovered by the Semitic and Greek peoples ... there is an entire and immensely graduated series of institutions and economic events, and this series is not governed by the economic rationalism whose theory we are so willing to propound.[43]

For Mauss, then, all we can expect to find in the operation of Western societies today or in the way they functioned in the past are fragments of this gift-based economy[44] or forms of gift-giving present in other areas of the economy and which are not necessarily vestiges.[45]

I can only agree with Mauss' idea that the struggle of wealth did not have a place or a basis in the early phases of the evolution of human societies because the "individual" accumulation of wealth was not possible or was not an accepted principle of economic and social life. But I will not go any farther, for several of the claims advanced in these passages call for some strong reservations. I will develop two of these.

In the first place, although ethnographers have discovered a number of other examples of potlatch-like exchanges (for instance the moka) in the last century, these do not seem to have characterized "a very large part of humanity." Their number remains small in comparison with the truly great number of examples of gift- and counter-gift-exchanges practiced to cement solidarities rather than to develop individual and group rivalries. Furthermore, it has not been shown that the potlatch culminates in the massive public destruction of wealth, as in the case observed by Boas which so fascinated Georges Bataille,[46] who saw both these lavish gestures and the Aztecs' sacrifice of thousands of prisoners to Quetzalcoatl, the god of corn and rain, as attempts to experience eternity here and now. This example of potlatch – if indeed it ever existed in such a paroxysmal form – is definitely an exception. It is the product of a social mechanism that has broken down, run amuck, the unexpected consequence of exceptional circumstances, of the intrusion of European wealth and political-colonial domination into the workings of the Indian societies of the northwest coast.

As far as that goes, in certain areas of New Guinea, in Eastern Highlands Province, for example, after the European arrival and the development of cash crops, the traditional system of competitive ceremonial exchanges (which knit the many tribes of the region into one vast political and religious network) rapidly became transformed into a sort of system of commercial dance festivals dubbed *sing sing bisnis*. It is worth asking why the change was so radical, insofar as, contrary to all appearances, the transformation was not of an economic order. Traditionally these exchanges would draw a considerable crowd of participants from all nearby groups to the ceremonial grounds of the host tribe (which changed each time). Hostilities between certain groups and even wars would be suspended for these occasions. Everyone worked together to coordinate preparations for the exchanges, to augment their production, and to attend the rituals. For, during these festivities, apparently unlike the moka-type systems found further to the west, the sacred character of these encounters was affirmed. The sacred flutes, powerful symbol of fertility and male domination, would play throughout the preparations and during the ceremonies, and male initiations would be conducted in conjunction with these events. Offerings were made to the ancestors and to the dead to thank them for their generous gifts to the living of a plentiful supply of food, of wealth which was obvious from the number of pigs slaughtered and redistributed, the shells given to the visitors or brought by them. It was also a time for conducting the end-of-mourning rites and negotiating marriages. In short, these periodical events were at the same time an end and a beginning, the chance for each group to display its warriors, its might, its wealth, and its vitality, all of which were, ultimately, materialized in the capacity to give more and to reciprocate more than all others.

These ceremonies were also an occasion for the leaders to show off their influence and their power to all the other groups, since it was they who supervised the redistributions of goods and gifts, and accompanied them with long speeches. Then suddenly everything changed.[47] In the 1960s, the pig-festivals began disappearing one after the other. The process began with the Kamano, after the missionaries and the Australian patrol officers had forced their men to publicly show the sacred flutes to the women and the young non-initiates.[48] Gradually the population converted to Christianity, and the rites ceased.

It was in this context of forcible desacralization that a new system appeared in place of the former ceremonial exchanges, which combined the economy of the gift with one of commercial profit: this was the *sing sing bisnis*. A local group, led by a "sponsor" invites other groups to come and dance on its ceremonial grounds. Each dancer pays to participate. The host group distributes gifts, but it also sells beer, pieces of pork, and European goods bought for the purpose of reselling them with profit that day. As he comes onto the dancing ground, the leader of the group which has agreed to organize the next *sing sing bisnis* presents the sponsor with a generous gift, which will be returned when the latter comes with his group to take part in the next festival.

This example shows that the massive intrusion of (European or other) commodities and currency alone does not destroy a gift-based economy, or drive the potlatch to its limits, or cause it to disappear. Other, non-economic, factors are necessary, cultural and ideological transformations which have a deep-seated effect on the society.

The example of Japan shows us that, when a culture is not deeply affected by direct interferences (one might even say aggressions) on the part of foreign societies and cultures, gift-giving can continue to exist alongside an impetuous development of the capitalist market economy and the logic of profit.

The Japanese tradition of exchanging gifts goes back thousands of years and is practiced at every level of society, playing a considerable role in the everyday life of all persons. A gift must be made on the occasion of all major life-events (birth, marriage, building a house, death), at the beginning of every new year, in the middle of the year, and at the year's end. Besides these formal and obligatory gifts, small, informal gifts are given on all manner of occasions, when paying a visit, and so forth. The basic and original feature of this generalized exchange of gifts is that every present demands a present in return, which must be of equivalent value. As Jane Cobbi writes, "the Japanese do not seek to outdo each other in the value or the quantity of gifts they give ... they do not value the spirit of competition in gift-giving ... it is more likely to give rise to derision or displeasure than to admiration."[49] Paradoxically, "a large gift" can be given between persons who are very close because the imbalance is not "seen as a threat" to their intimacy. We have here, then, a form of generalized gift-giving which is the opposite of an economic and moral system based on potlatch.

The huge development of Japan's capitalist market economy, especially since the Second World War, has had two somewhat contradictory effects on this tradition. On the one hand, the market seized upon it and created a veritable gift industry which is growing apace and which offers an ever-increasing choice of gifts to satisfy the tradition. At the same time, however, the expansion of gift-giving has come into conflict with new economic behaviors which appeal to saving and productive investment. As a result, campaigns to "simplify" the practice of gift-giving and to reduce traditional social obligations were launched in the 1960s. This example shows that the economy of equivalent gifts was initially strengthened by the expansion of capitalist market relations, as had been, for example, the economy of potlatch-giving.

The second objection is that neither human history nor its evolution can be reduced to "a lengthy transition" between the time when societies were organized around non-antagonistic gift-exchanges and the modern era, characterized by commercial exchange and personal contract, principles of organization which are supposed to have appeared in antiquity, among the Semites, the Greeks, and the Romans, in short around the shores of the Mediterranean, and which, many centuries, detours, and avatars later, have finally blossomed out in Western society in the last two centuries.

We know today that all societies have some "individual" form of contract and that, in all societies, some of the objects or even some of the knowledge necessary for social reproduction comes from other societies by way of barter or other more developed forms of market relations. Nowhere are these relations unknown; all that differs is their importance in the *internal* workings of the societies concerned.

Furthermore it is clear that, while human society has evolved, this evolution has not followed a single line, but has taken several paths. In my view, it was along two of these paths – that of Big-Men societies and that of societies in which more or less hereditary tribal aristocracies appeared – that the calculated acts of generosity, the "wars of wealth" reminiscent of the potlatch, multiplied. Speaking of such societies, Mauss mentions in the same breath German nobles, Celtic chiefs and Trobriand Island aristocrats. To be sure, to say "aristocracy" is to say lavishness and display of generosity, but generosity and lavishness do not necessarily mean potlatch, if the latter is defined as enabling a man to acquire a title or a rank and not merely to show them off. Other historical evolutions took place elsewhere which did not lead to the development of a market economy either, and which restricted the space available for the practice of potlatch.

Mauss had perceived this clearly, noting that "the basic elements of the potlatch can therefore be found in Polynesia, even if the institution in its entirety is not to be found there,"[50] and after having advanced the suggestion that the potlatch may have existed earlier in Polynesia, he added this note, which for once alludes to the nature of the political structures of potlatch societies:

> Indeed there is a reason for its [the institution of potlatch in its entirety] having disappeared from part of this area. It is because the clans have *definitively become hierarchized* in almost all the islands and have *even been concentrated around a monarchy*. Thus there is missing *one of the main conditions* for the potlatch, namely the *instability of a hierarchy* that rivalry between chiefs has precisely the aim of temporarily stabilizing.[51]

The assertion that clans in Polynesia had "definitively become hierarchized" in almost all islands now appears somewhat hasty, and the cases in which they were "concentrated around a monarchy" were rarer than Mauss believed. This is true of Tonga, but not of Samoa, for example. But what seems accurate in Mauss' thesis is the statement that, throughout Polynesia, when individuals or clans wanted to be recognized as the best subjects of a chief or the best followers of a god (or, if they were themselves chiefs, as the best "vassals" of another chief), they felt obliged to give more than the other clans, more of their possessions, more of their harvest, as an offering to the chiefs and to the gods. And even in relations that presumed equality of rank between the partners, as in a marriage between two clans, the same obligation to assert one's superiority led (and still leads) each partner to give a little more than the other, a few more women's items, or a few more men's items, depending on which side of the alliance they were on, but nevertheless taking care to not upset the overall equivalence of the exchanges imposed by the equal status of the two parties. It was thus possible to attempt to give one's way up the ladder of rank, but that did not suffice to win a new title.

Warfare, on the other hand, did extend this possibility. When a chief brought the population of another district under subjection, he would seize the losers' titles and redistribute them among his lieutenants, while he refashioned his own genealogy to give his ancestors the appearance of having always enjoyed rights in the new territory. Violence was thus more effective than gift-giving in modifying positions in a hierarchy, but, in Polynesia, the latter expressed in all cases a fundamental asymmetry at two levels, between gods and men, on the one hand, and between chiefs and commoners, on the other. And this double asymmetry was inescapable, set fast "in the nature of things."[52]

However, in Polynesia, commoners are almost always related to chiefs. Chiefs descend from the eldest sons and daughters of a founding pair of ancestors, a brother and a sister, a man and his wife, and even a god and a mortal woman. Commoners are the descendants of the younger sons and daughters. Such relations of kinship between aristocrats and commoners were not found in the structures of the great states and empires which, from ancient China to the Inca and Aztec empires destroyed by the Spanish conquest, subjugated millions of individuals belonging to different tribes and to ethnies having different languages and cultures. The offerings of first fruits presented to the chiefs and the gods became an obligatory tribute, raised and entered into the accounts by a bureaucratic and/or military machine. Voluntary service in the common interest of the members of a local community became obligatory labor designed to reproduce the state and to maintain the reigning ethnic groups, which had become sorts of castes or tribal classes owing their dominant position to a monopoly on the principal religious, military, and bureaucratic functions in these empires.[53]

In this type of universe, gift-giving was still present, and the magnificence of the gifts was still of political consequence; but gifts as a means of acquiring a title, a function in a political-religious hierarchy, gift-giving as potlatch, occupied an even smaller place than in the "Polynesian chiefdoms."[54]

So how can it be explained that, among the Baruya of Melanesia (who have no aristocracy or kings) and in Polynesian societies (which have both), it was not possible for the potlatch to develop, whereas all of these societies abounded in gift-exchanges? To my mind, it is the fact that, in these societies, however different they may be, the political-religious hierarchy among the kinship groups and the local groups tends to appear as a framework, a rigid structure, immutable, inherited but also hereditary. In this case, the basis of potlatch societies would be the absence of a definitely established political hierarchy and the presence of kinship relations which entail transfers of goods and wealth in order to seal an alliance. It is at this level that their workings could be explained, and not by the belief that things have a soul.

But these two conditions are not of the same nature and they do not operate on the same level, insofar as kinship relations alone do not suffice to make a society. A society exists only if it forms a totality, and somewhere it must be represented as such, at a level on which the interests of the kinship groups or the other individual groups that compose this society are subordinated to the *overall reproduction of this whole*. This is the level of political relations, whatever their form and content. But at the level of the whole as well as at that of its parts (families, clans, and even castes or classes), there are two opposing principles which must always be combined: exchanging and keeping, exchanging for keeping, keeping for transmitting. In every society, alongside those things which circulate, which move about, there must be fixed points, points which anchor the social relations and the collective and individual identities: it is these which allow the practice of exchange and which set its limits.

What is a valuable?

Societies which practice gift-exchange and potlatch have invested a great deal of ingenuity and refinement in selecting and inventing objects which seemed to them capable of being both the vehicles and the symbols of power. But in every case, these objects must fulfill several functions: (a) they must be substitutes for real persons; (b) they must attest the presence within themselves of powers emanating from imaginary beings (deities, nature spirits, ancestors) believed to be endowed with powers of life and death over persons and things; (c) they must lend themselves to comparison with each other so that, by their quantities and/or their qualities, they provide their owners with the means of measuring themselves against others and of raising themselves above the rest.

Above and beyond the diversity of their forms and concrete raw materials, all objects selected to materialize wealth and power must present a number of characteristics which enable them to fulfill these functions and to serve as a support for the fusion/inversion of the relations between humans and things entailed in these functions.

These objects must first of all be *of no practical use* or *unusable in the daily activities of living and earning a livelihood*. Some do indeed appear to be weapons or tools, but they are never used as such: the ceremonial stone axes of New Guinea are one example.[55] This means that the competition for power and fame takes place somewhere *beyond* the subsistence sphere. Let us not forget that we are dealing with societies capable of producing, on a regular basis, considerable *surpluses* of products from the land or the sea. We should also note that the land, streams, seashores, and other production sites are not usually appropriated by individuals, but by one *community* (whatever its nature: lineage, clan, caste) and do not enter into gift- or market exchanges. And finally, let us not forget that we are looking at societies in which, owing to the very nature of the work processes and the relative simplicity of the forms of social division of labor involved in them, most individuals and groups satisfy the bulk of their needs *on their own*, mobilizing their own labor and resources. Whoever fails to do so is a *rubbish man*, a worthless person, a piece of garbage, and there is no question of his taking part in the mechanisms of giving and returning wealth and attempting to win power.[56]

The second characteristic of these objects is their *abstraction*. This is the case of the pearl-shells used in Melanesia and the Pacific, or the abalone shells which may have been the ancestors of the coppers used by the Chinook, Salish, and other tribes on the northwest coast of America.[57] But the same is true of the boar's teeth "money," the tusks that have been forced to grow in a spiral and which are used on Malekula and in the Solomon Islands in ceremonial competitions for titles and for ranks in the initiation societies.[58]

The "abstract" character and the deconnecting of these objects from everyday life seem to me to be the prerequisites for their being able to "embody" social relations and thought systems and then to re-present them, to present them back to the social actors in a form which is material, abstract and symbolic. Abstraction and disjunction from the world of subsistence and daily life facilitate projection and make it easier for the objects to encapsulate imaginary kernels and symbols which belong to the mental aspect of the functioning of the social relations which provide access to wealth and power.[59]

In what is, in my opinion, an exemplary study of the pearl-shells which served in Highlands New Guinea as both wealth and power symbols, Jeffrey Clarck[60] revealed for the first time the complexity of the imaginary and symbolic meanings these objects carried, and which explain their use in the production of kinship and political relations.

These meanings are in a manner of speaking materially stamped on the object and on the bark stand on which it is displayed. The naturally yellow shell is rubbed with ochre powder, its bottom lip is trimmed with white sap which soon turns black, marks are incised beneath the upper lip. These are all delicate operations which transform the object and not only give it a meaning but enhance it. Just what is this meaning? Yellow is a female color, associated with a yellowish substance thought to be found in the woman's uterus and which is an essential ingredient of the fetus at the time of its conception. Red is the color of wealth, but also of virility; and sacred stones associated with health and fertility are coated with ochre, and so forth. The white of the sap is associated with semen; the black, like the color red, is associated with virility. The marks incised close to the female lip of the object are like the joints of the bamboo, like the glans of the penis. But we will not pursue this analysis any further. It is enough to note that, once again, what is hidden in this androgynous object and cloaked in male attributes is "femininity, femaleness," essentially women's reproductive capacities detached, as it were, from their bodies and reattached to those of men.[61]

The third characteristic of these objects is their *beauty* as it is defined in the cultural and symbolic universe of the societies that make use of them. Now beauty can be the vehicle for two functions. It can valorize, enhance, and glorify the object's owner: worn or given ostentatiously, it displays the quality and the status of the person wearing or giving it. But the beauty of an object is also a source of emotions which create a kind of intimacy between the object and its owner, and contribute to a feeling of identification between the individual and the thing he exposes[62] to the gaze of all.

The beauty of a shell, its singularity are not purely accidents of nature: in order for it to become an exchangeable object, a shell must be worked – polished, pierced, mounted, decorated; a copper must be poured, molded, fashioned. Exchange-objects are therefore unequally beautiful and unequally singular, and their value varies accordingly. To be sure, this value is linked with their singularity, but it can also be the result of an accident of nature, or the fruit of labor, or the effect of having been owned by a famous person.

But whatever its source, the value of a precious object is always "represented" in objects of "equivalent" value for which it can be exchanged. In most cases valuables are classified by rank, and it is rare that an object from a higher category can be exchanged for several of a lower class. Each category of goods constitutes, to borrow Paul Bohannan's[63] expression, separate "exchange spheres," no two of which occupy the same place in the reproduction of society. One, for instance, may have to do with kinship, another with political relations. Furthermore, it should be remembered that the logic of gift-giving aims to call attention to social ranking, and ranks mark qualitative differences which no quantitative manipulation may obliterate.[64]

Ultimately the most valuable objects are unique and, given that their value increases with the number and the importance of the persons having owned them for a time, they no longer need to be beautiful; they merely have to be old. They then become "one and indivisible," just as sacred objects tend to do.

To finish with this point, I will examine two examples of exotic "moneys." Once again, let us note that, if a currency is to circulate as a medium of payment or as wealth, it must be authorized, as it were, by its ties with some reality which does not circulate, which is kept out of the exchange sphere and which appears as the true source of their exchange-value.

The first example is that of the Lau, on Malaita Island, where Pierre Maranda did his fieldwork, and it is to him that we owe our information. Among the Lau, each clan possesses an inalienable treasure which is kept by the clan chief. This treasure is composed of a fathom of shell money and a string of large dolphin teeth, also used in exchanges. These are wrapped in very old pieces of bark cloth.[65] The whole treasure is called *malefo aabu*, "taboo money." In effect it is forbidden to use this money for any purpose whatever. Were this taboo to be violated, the clan would dwindle and die.

This money is therefore associated with the "foundation" of the clan and contains some of the powers, *mana*, which underpin its existence. Another object, called a "spirit bundle," is also associated with the clan's foundation and is another source of its *mana*. This is a bundle of cordyline leaves containing a relic of the clan ancestor or an object believed to be associated with him. The "spirit bundle" is also carefully kept either in the chief's reception house or in a sacred shelter built for this purpose, but always in the men's space.[66]

The second example is that of the shell-money of New Caledonia, described earlier in the twentieth century by Maurice Leenhardt, which combines all the attributes of the wealth-objects we have been analyzing.[67] These shell strings substitute for persons, enter into marriage payments, are used to compensate the death of warriors killed in battle, and to conclude peace treaties. They also serve as a currency in more secular exchanges. While they are themselves divisible, they draw their power from a sacred object which is indivisible, a sort of basket to which they are attached.

This shell-money consists of strings of black or white shells the length of a man's height, which are divided into parts designated by the terms used to describe the human body. People speak of a money's head, trunk, or foot. These strings of shells can be divided in half, or into shorter lengths, which are detached and distributed, with the possibility of replacing the missing segments on the next occasion and recomposing the entire string. The money strings are supposed to represent the body of an ancestor.

They are kept in a sacred wicker basket in which they are laid after having been attached to a hook called "the ancestor's head". Divisible and alienable, they are believed to draw a life-giving strength from this ancestor head, a force which flows into them through the tie which fastens them to the hook. The basket, hook, and shell-money as a whole appear as a sort of material synthesis of all our analyses. The baskets and hooks are carefully conserved as treasures by the clan chiefs. These are sacred and inalienable. The money strings, on the other hand, circulate in gift- or commodity exchanges. They are alienable and alienated. But the basket and its hook never circulate; they constitute the permanent source of the ancestor's life-giving presence, the stable point which allows the rest to circulate.[68]

The basket and the hook therefore assume the function of sacred object, source of the exchanges but itself withheld from the exchange circuit. Whether it is gifts or commodities that are being exchanged, the same strings of shells function, in the first case, as wealth for giving and, in the second, as money, a medium of payment for services or commodities. The same type of object can take on two distinct functions because it enters into two distinct fields of social relations. For, and this is a crucial point, in all of these societies, commodity exchanges and gift-exchanges exist and coexist as two modes of exchange and two areas of social practice which are *consciously* and *purposely* kept distinct and separate, even though the same type of objects circulate in the one and the other, and between the one and the other.[69]

It has been a long time since Malinowski showed that, in the Trobriand Islands – alongside the competitive kula exchanges of *mwali* and *soulava*, the armshells and necklaces that circulate in opposite directions – there exist commercial exchanges, *gimwali*,[70] which are not conducted with the same partners, and which involve haggling and use shells as currency, and also commercial exchanges in which money does not feature,[71] *wasi*, in which farming tribes from the interior and seafaring tribes from the coast barter their respective products. We have also seen that the Baruya produce quantities of salt which they use as currency in their exchanges with neighboring tribes, but which never circulates as money or as merchandise within their own tribe.

Do our analyses enable us to say something about the origin of currencies, about the origin of money? I believe they do. Monies are precious objects, valuables which have gradually made their way into commercial relations as these have gained ground, grown until they could no longer be contained within the too narrow framework of even the more complex forms of barter. Monies are precious objects (and as a consequence in contact with sacred objects), but which have ceased being *both* alienable and inalienable and have become definitively alienable, like the commodities they already serve to acquire, to make circulate, or to stock. Monies are precious objects which have already enjoyed a long career in types of relations other than commercial exchanges, and which have gradually become detached from these non-commercial relations, thereby permitting objects which have themselves become detachable from persons to circulate in impersonal relations between individuals or between groups. These objects we call "commodities." Now when the formula for the exchange of goods is no longer barter but the purchase of goods for resale, and when these goods turn up in the hands of veritable merchants, they necessarily undergo a metamorphosis, when they are bought and when they are sold, into a given quantity of a valuable against which the relative exchange-value of each commodity is measured. This object which is the symbol and the obligatory intermediary of developed commodity exchanges is what we call "money."

It should come as no surprise that, in many societies and cultures, gold and silver have been used as money. These are metals which, over the centuries, have been used to adorn the bodies of the gods and the men (and women) in positions of power, and which were of no use in daily life. They could not be made into tools. The Egyptians viewed gold as "the flesh of the gods,"[72] and Pharaoh was called "Golden Horus," for his divinity could be expressed only by the undying brilliance of the precious metal which shone like the Sun, the father of all the gods. In other parts of the world it was the mother-of-pearl lining the fine, large shells that captured the imagination of societies which saw in the iridescent whiteness the presence of life, the trace of the sperm of the gods and that of men in societies which, as a rule, had not yet discovered the art of smelting ores.

In order for a precious object to circulate as money, its "imaginary" value must be accepted and shared by the members of the societies trading with each other. A currency cannot exist, cannot circulate as "legal" tender without having "force of law." And laws are not made by individuals. A money must harbor the presence of the gods, be stamped with their symbols or with the seal of the state or the effigy of a king. Even today, on the dollar, the only money known and accepted worldwide, is printed the reference to God, the god of the Bible.

Now Mauss had understood this perfectly well, as is shown by his superb "Note on the principle concerning the use of the notion of money", which takes up two pages of small print in the notes to the "Essai sur le don" and outlines a history of money.[73] But in my view, something has always been lacking in his analysis, as in those of many others who came after and who encountered the same problems. And this is his failure to recognize that, in order for there to be movement, exchange, there had to be things that were kept out of exchange, stable points around which the rest – humans, goods, services – might revolve and circulate.[74]

On the metamorphosis of an object of trade into a gift object or a sacred object

It is to Michel Panoff that we owe a very fine analysis of this process, which he observed among the Maenge of New Britain. In this region, rings (*page*) cut from giant clam (Tridacna) shells and strings of beads (*tali*) made from seashells used to be circulated or hoarded. The Maenge, a tribe living on the southern coast of the island, purchased these with dogs or a certain number of coconuts from the mountain tribes of the interior, who had themselves bought them with salt and taros from the Nakanai, a northern coastal group. The Maenge were unaware of the origin of these shells and of the existence of the Nakanai, and they could not know that the latter procured them by organizing seagoing expeditions to buy the *page* on New Hanover Island and the *tali* on New Ireland, in other words hundreds of kilometers from New Britain.[75] It was only around 1914, when a number of men were recruited among the Maenge and the other tribes in the south of the island to work on the big German plantations in the northeast, that the Maenge learned the true source of these objects.

Until then they believed they were the work of supernatural beings who kept them in a mysterious place before giving them out to humans. The Maenge knew that these supernatural beings had not distributed the objects to their own ancestors but to those of the tribes from whom their ancestors had bought them. Pierre Maranda called my attention to an even more tangled web. On the island of Malaita, the shell money is manufactured for the most part by the Langa Langa, who are in charge of the "minting," as it were. What makes this money valuable are the purple disks, whose number per string is carefully calculated and which are made from the lips of a shell (*romu*) which the Langa Langa collect twice a year from the lagoon territories of a clan of the Lau tribe, on the occasion of major expeditions involving several canoes. The divers spend several days at the site. The chief of the Lau clan allows them to fish for the shells in exchange for half of the money strings featuring the *romu* shell disks. Clearly the commercial spirit is alive and well at the scene of manufacture of the money strings, and the Lau know how to "profit" from their situation, since they cede the use of their lagoon to the Langa Langa in exchange for 50 percent of the production. But let us not forget that the same Lau hoard moneys in their sacred treasures which they cannot under any circumstances alienate.

Several theoretical conclusions can be drawn from this series of converging facts. Malinowski, Armstrong, Mauss, and many others were astounded by the complexity of the classifications these societies established between the different types of exchange and the different types of objects that circulated in them.[76] It seems to me that the source of such complexity and complication should be sought among the reasons which compel these societies to make a conscious distinction and to maintain a deliberate separation between the sphere of commodity exchanges and that of gift-exchange, while keeping both of these spheres associated with, but separate from, the sacred. These reasons are found, as I have shown, in the area of kinship and political relations. Matters are all the more complicated because a single type of object can often function first as a (valuable) commodity, then as a gift-object, and then as a treasure. Hence, to my mind, the great importance of the Maenge material reported and analyzed by Michel Panoff because it throws a direct light on fundamental social and mental processes.

These facts show in what contexts and through what social and mental mechanisms objects having no practical everyday use, useless when it comes down to subsistence, which have gained entry into society, without ceremony but as valuable commodities, little by little take on human attributes, or those of persons more powerful than humans – deities, nature spirits, mythic ancestors – once they have gained the areas of social life in which their use is necessary, in which they are looked to. Like human or supernatural persons, they acquire a name, an identity, a history, and powers. The vast majority of these trade objects initially characterized by mysterious origins and possessing an exchange-value will circulate as substitutes for persons, living (brideprice) or dead (bloodprice), or serve as instruments in the reproduction of the social, kinship, and power relations entertained among the clans that make up Maenge society, clans which would be unable to reproduce themselves without these exchanges.

But these exchanges are not the only condition for the perpetuation of the clans. There is another, which is just as indispensable but less visible because it does not enjoy the public and even ostentatious nature of the exchanges of goods, but remains in the background. This condition is the relations each clan must entertain *with itself*: the gestures, the ceremonies, the efforts by which each reproduces its identity, ensures its continuity, maintains a constant connection *with its origins.* It is when the exchange object reaches this point, when it enters the domain, no longer of exchanges between the living, but between the living and their dead, and the living and their gods, that the object of trade *becomes sacred.* Already distinct because it has no use in daily life, already distinguished because it is ascribed supernatural origins, the object of trade now ceases to circulate and comes to stand at an essential place in the society, at the place to which each clan feels obliged to return periodically because it comes to encounter itself, to confirm its being, its identity, its substance, preserved from time and conserved in time, in short it comes to confront its origins.

To sum up: it is when the object of trade enters this place, and is used to reactivate this imaginary and symbolic relationship with the origin, that it becomes sacred and acquires an even greater value for having moved into the religious area of power. For the sacred – contrary to the views of Durkheim, who made too stark a separation between religious and political – always has to do with power insofar as the *sacred is a certain kind of relationship with the origin*, and insofar as the origin of individuals and of groups has a bearing on the *places* they occupy in a social and cosmic order. It is with reference to the origin of each person and each group that the actual relations between the individuals and the groups which compose a society are compared with the order that should be reigning in the universe and in society. The actual state is then judged to be legitimate or illegitimate, by right, and therefore acceptable or unacceptable. It is therefore not objects which sacralize some or all of people's relations with each other and with the surrounding universe, it is the converse.

In the Maenge example, we clearly see how people *project* onto things and *embody* in the matter and form of these imported objects the imaginary kernels and the symbols of the real relations they entertain with others and with the world around them. This entire social process is at once a mental process which mobilizes both parts of thought, above and beyond thought, the two parts of the human psyche, the conscious and the unconscious. Individuals are not conscious of projecting and reifying the realities that are part of their own social being. They are confronted with things which have a name, a soul, force, powers, things which have come from the individuals themselves, but which the latter regard and treat as beings who are different from themselves, as having come from somewhere else, as strange beings, aliens. Or, more accurately, they find themselves face to face with person-things, both alien and familiar. They are familiar because, in a certain sense, people see themselves in the exchange objects and the sacred objects, but alien because they see but are unable to recognize themselves.

People generate duplicate selves but do not recognize themselves in their replicas, which, once they have split off, stand before them as persons who are at once familiar and alien. In reality these are not duplicates which stand before them as aliens; these are the people themselves who, by splitting, have become in part strangers to themselves, subjected, alienated to these other beings who are nonetheless part of themselves.

3

The Sacred

~∞~

What is the sacred?

The sacred is a certain relationship with the origin of things in which imaginary replicas step in and take the place of real humans. In other words, the sacred is a *certain type of relationship that humans entertain with the origin of things*, such that, in this relationship, the real humans disappear and in their stead appear duplicates of themselves, imaginary humans. The sacred can appear only if something of human beings disappears. What disappears is man as co-author, along with nature, of himself, man as author of his social way of existing, of his social being. For humans are so constituted that they not only live in society, like other social animals, but that they produce society in order to live. When they split themselves into imaginary humans, more powerful than real humans but beings who do not exist, and real humans, who appear incapable of doing what their ancestors and they themselves nonetheless actually once did (domesticate plants and animals, make tools, and so on), something happens which makes real humans appear no longer as actors and authors, in part, of themselves, but as acted upon. Man's replication of himself is accompanied by an alteration, by an *occultation* of reality and an *inversion* of the relationship between cause and effect.

But when real humans disappear from the origin of things, when man becomes divided by his own thinking process into superhuman beings more powerful than humans, and imaginary beings less capable than real humans, when human reality splits in two and real humans become in part alienated from themselves, a mechanism has been triggered which does not depend on thought alone. Of course the fabrication of these imaginary beings, the elaboration of the rites which celebrate them and bring them back to live for a time – symbolically for us, in reality for the Baruya – among humans, all of this involves thought at work, a conscious effort which *at the same time* calls upon unconscious structures of the mind. But in my view that is not the essential. In the production of mathematical mental structures, too, or works of art, conscious thought intervenes and at the same time calls upon unconscious structures of the mind. The essential lies in the fact that myths are an explanation of the origin of things *which legitimizes* the order of the universe and society by replacing the real humans who domesticated the plants and animals, invented tools and weapons, with imaginary humans who did not actually do these things but received these favors from the hands of the gods or the founding heroes.

It is as if human *society* could not exist unless it obliterated from the conscious mind the *active presence* of man *at his own origin*. It is as if society could not subsist unless it repressed into the collective or individual unconscious, beyond consciousness, the action of man at the origin of himself. It is as if the survival of societies, or at least their survival as *legitimate* societies, as realities which all their members *have an obligation* to preserve and reproduce, were *threatened* by recognizing, by taking as the point of departure for a reflection about society, the essential fact that humans (and not the gods or nature spirits or mythic ancestors) are in part their own authors.

If this makes sense, the question of the unconscious can be formulated in other terms. It would not be the human *mind* which, by the workings of its unconscious, universal and anhistorical structures, is *at the origin* of this disappearance of real humans and their replacement by imaginary beings who communicate on an equal footing and by right with the spirits of things. It is *society* as a whole which transcends individuals and provides them with the material and cultural conditions for their existence, that is the prime source, the origin, because this obliterating of real humans and replacing them with imaginary beings, this repressing beyond consciousness of the active role of man in the origins of society, this forgetting of the presence of man at the origin, is necessary in order to produce and to reproduce society.

In order for such a mechanism to work, and if indeed it exists, it needs to operate largely unbeknownst to the individuals who experience it. Like *the object it represses*, it, too, *must be repressed*. This is where the unconscious – which, in my view, takes in much more than the unconscious structures *of thought* – comes in. Or at least, not to reify or substantivize the unconscious, this is where the psychic mechanisms begin to operate which repress *and* conserve beyond conscious awareness the realities which the conscious part of the human mind will not (or must not) recognize. The unconscious intervenes, but as a *means, not* as an origin, as an *instrument*, not as a basis. One cannot simply state, as Durkheim did, that society is the source of the sacred. It also has to be shown that the *sacred conceals something from* the collective and individual consciousness, *something contained* in social relations, something essential to society, and in so doing the sacred distorts the social, makes it *opaque* to itself. It is even necessary to go further and to show that there is something in society which is part of the social being of its members and which needs *opacity* in order to produce and to reproduce itself. It would therefore be essential, for social reasons, that the social conceal itself from itself, become opaque and take on a *sacred* character. Fantasies about the origin are decidedly not the origin of fantasies.

The sources of this opacity among the Baruya are clear. The rituals in which the *kwaimatnie* are publicly displayed are male initiation rituals, which are closed to women, one half of society, and which consecrate and legitimize the general domination of women by men. At the same time, these rites also legitimize the fact that a number of clans and kin groups which are part of the Baruya tribe are excluded from positions of responsibility in the rituals which celebrate both the Baruya's unity with respect to their external enemies and the solidarity of Baruya men *vis-à-vis* women.

The sources of opacity in Baruya society therefore have to do with the existence of two relationships of exclusion which form part of the very foundations of their society, that are the basic *principles* of an organization which, in order to be reproduced with a minimum of conflict, needs the consent of all, and first and foremost of those who suffer the negative consequences of these exclusions. For it is just as important not to reify society as it is not to substantivize or reify the unconscious. It is not *society* which conceals something of itself from men; it is real human beings who conceal something of their social relations *from each other*. If social relations are "good" as they stand for part of society, the governing part, they *must* also be good for the rest of society, in other words for everyone.

Something which is involved in the very nature of social relations, something which lies at the very heart of these relations, which is part of the groundwork of society, and which necessarily and continuously entails negative consequences for part of society, cannot appear *as such* in the representations individuals and groups produce of their society. In this case there are two ways reality can be transformed: either something disappears from the representations, no longer appears in public discourse; or this something appears, but transformed into a totally positive reality, into an indispensable component of the common good, "necessary" for the existence of society and its reproduction, and all the more indispensable, all the more inviolable because it seems always to have existed, since it is part of those things that the men of the Dreamtime, the Baruya's imaginary ancestors, bequeathed to their descendants for their good. And it is all the more inviolable because, associated with the origins of the society, it partakes of the sacred nature of these origins and appears as the Law, given, entrusted by the Sun and the other powers of the universe, to the Baruya so that they might model their life on it and pass it on to their descendants.

This then is the function of the imaginary men (and women) who take the place of the real men and women of the original time. They *give them back* their own laws and customs, but in a sacred form, idealized, transmuted into the common good, into a sacred principle which brooks no argument, no opposition, which can only be the object of unanimous consent. It is all of this which is present (and presented) in the sacred objects, the *kwaimatnie* held up to the Sun before being struck on the chest of the initiates.

By now it should be obvious that *kwaimatnie* are not symbols in their pure state, signifiers devoid of signification; they are signifiers full of signification, gorged with meaning, *at once* presenting *and* disguising the content of social relations, stating the order that should prevail in society, an order which unifies and materializes, in an *object*, a piece of matter – wood, bone, stone, or whatever – everything that society is supposed to say *and* to hide about itself. It is because it is the *visible synthesis* of everything a society wants to present *and* to conceal concerning itself that the sacred object combines and unifies the contents – imaginary, symbolic and "real" – of all social relations. And it is because it is the cultural object which condenses and unifies the imaginary and real components of social reality more intimately and effectively than any other object that it is at the same time the strongest symbol, the most replete signifier, the richest, most meaning-full term of a language, which extends beyond articulate speech, beyond the language spoken in the society, and speaks just as eloquently through the gestures, bodies, and the natural and manufactured objects which surround them. Because it expresses the inexpressible, because it represents the unrepresentable, the sacred object is the object charged with the strongest symbolic value. Our analysis of Baruya sacred objects has led us to a position diametrically opposed to the theses of Lévi-Strauss and

Lacan, who give the symbolic primacy over the imaginary and the real, who believe in symbols in their pure state and who, like Lévi-Strauss, see the notion of *mana*, or *koulie* for the Baruya, of a "power-spirit" contained in things, as concepts whose function is to "fill a gap between the signifier and the signified" without themselves having any particular signification.[1]

Objects gorged with signification, objects endowed with a "sublime" beauty which transcends all categories of beautiful, such are sacred objects, objects in which man is both present and absent.

Concerning sacred objects as the presence–absence of man and society

Throughout this analysis we have skirted one essential aspect of sacred objects. To be sure, they are the support for and the sign of the relationships of dependence, indebtedness, and gratitude that humans entertain with the imaginary beings, "true owners of the objects and goods of the world," who shared their use with men and who, when they gave these sacred objects, also gave men some of their own powers. But we must be careful not to lose sight of our point of departure which explains why sacred objects are to be kept and not given: the fact that possession of these objects gives *men*, or at least some men, *powers* and sets them apart from the other members of their society. To own these objects is to be in possession of part of the powers of these mightier-than-human beings, it is to satisfy a desire for power, to show one's will to *control* the forces that govern men, to act on the course of events, on fate. After all, does not *kwaimatnie* mean "to make men grow," and do not the Baruya initiation masters place at the service of the whole Baruya society and at the service of men's domination of women within this society the powers contained in the *kwaimatnie* given their ancestors by the Sun?

In the sacred object there is, then, the admission of a desire for power, for the capacity to influence the course of events and to place them at the service of mankind. With the sacred object, the same inversion that is found at the representational level continues at the level of the action of the rite. For it is there where man has *no effect* on reality – for instance, he cannot "really" multiply the species of wild animals he hunts or fishes, or make the waters of the Nile return every year carrying fertile silt – that he (wants to have and) believes he has the power to act on the beings who do have this power. Hence the fertility rites, the Australian Aboriginal rites for multiplying the species of plants and animals, hence the rites performed every year by Pharaoh when, after taking his sacred boat up to the headwaters of the Nile, he would speak the ritual words that were supposed to make the waters return the following year. It goes without saying that, for this power to appear "real," the belief has to be shared by everyone and that, from time to time, "real" proof must be offered of the efficacy of the rite and the object. For, as Mauss so nicely puts it, "in the end society always pays itself back with the counterfeit coin of its dreams."[2]

It is for this reason – the deep-seated presence of desire in all belief – that, for Mauss, the notion of *mana* cannot be reduced to anything "too intellectual" or "too far removed from the mechanisms of social life." Behind the "categories of thought" which underlie magical judgments, which impose a "classification of things," establish "lines of influence or boundaries of isolation," there are, "at the very root of magic, affective states which generate illusions, and these states are not an individual matter."[3]

Yet affective states cannot engender categories of thought by themselves, and they cannot produce illusions unaided: illusions cannot take shape or signify without the work of thought. And part of this signification lies in whatever drives humans to split, to duplicate themselves, to imagine themselves at once weaker and stronger than they really are, to be present, but by their absence, in their cult objects, subservient to the powers that populate the universe, but at the same time endowed with part of this power.

Everything that is mentally subtracted from the real relations humans entertain with each other and with nature, together with with everything that is mentally added to these relationships, makes up man's imaginary being, the imaginary core of his social being, a fantasy content and a constant source of imaginary realities which have become social *reality*. The complement of man's opacity to his own reality is the magic world which springs up in place of the real world. Of course this enchanted world and its enchanted humans do not arise from the personal, private, and unique history of each individual. They are spawned, not by the accidents of a singular history and the complex material of intimate, personal relations between individuals, but by the nature of their *social* relationships, by something that is objectively present and acting in these relations but which must disappear from the conscious representations individuals produce of these relations, or must appear only in the guise of something else.

This process of occultation and metamorphosis is not only a condition for the formation of the individual as such: a singular, unique being; it is first and foremost a condition for the emergence and reproduction of the society in which this individual is born, of the common, general social relations which underpin his social existence and which every person must, up to a certain point, internalize and reproduce if he wants to go on living in society. Must I reiterate that the real, historical origin of a "form of society," of a configuration of social relations which regulates, in a common and general manner, the life of all members of a society, whatever their gender or age, is a collective and largely unintentional process which cannot be the "plan" of any one individual as *such*, as a singular, unique individual separate from the rest? This process has to do with what each individual has *objectively in common* with all others without having chosen it, with what he shares with others, whether or not they are known to him, by *the fact of belonging to the same society*, in other words, his social being. And it must be remembered that the real, historical origin of a new form of society always emerges in a field of possible transformations which are *not* infinite in number and which no individual or group of individuals can know in their entirety.

Concerning repressed things which enable humans to live in society

It is as if man's social existence were due entirely to *two processes of repression*, which constitute the two *sources of the formation of the individual and the collective unconscious*. The first process concerns sexuality and its repression, the second (political and economic) power and its exclusions. The two are intimately linked in all societies. Among the Baruya, for instance, sacred objects are used to establish and to exalt a social order which is at the same time a sexual and a political-religious order, an unequal relationship between conquering and autochthonous clans. In numerous other societies, the main divisions do not oppose dominant and dominated clans, but castes or classes. To be sure, the latter divisions are broader than the existing differences between individuals and exclusions of some because of their gender, but they nevertheless contain these in a form redefined and reshaped to fit the occasion.

While there are (at least) two sources of repression, there is only one human psyche which carries out these repressions, these displacements of meanings and symbols, these metamorphoses. That is why individual and collective psychology (or what Freud called metapsychology) are interlinked. It is clear that Freud and Marx are still the main sources of inspiration for any analysis of these processes, to which must be added numerous elements from the works of Mauss, and of course Lévi-Strauss and Lacan. But there are many other themes in the works of these thinkers which I do not espouse.

There remains the unavoidable question: to what extent do humans not recognize themselves in their replicas? To what extent do they believe in their beliefs, and are convinced that it is someone other than themselves who forces them to keep silent about, or turn a blind eye to, what is negative for some in the way society functions? To what extent are they convinced that it is necessary to exclude, repress, metamorphose, sublimate the facts for the supreme good of all, and that the restriction of access to power (and/or wealth) to only one part of society is in the divine, supernatural order of things?

To cite a few facts that we have verified many times, the equivalents of which can easily be found in our own societies: Baruya women having reached a certain age know more about the men's secret rites than they are supposed to know. What is asked of them is to not show that they know, to feign ignorance in public. When one day the Baruya men reveal to the initiates that it is not the spirits who produce the terrifying sounds they hear in the forest but men whirling a tapered piece of wood over their heads, they threaten them with death if they tell the women. But they also tell the initiates that the *first* bull-roarers were not made by men, that, in the beginning, these were arrows that a forest spirit shot at a mythic ancestor of the Baruya who in turn passed them on to all Baruya men (but not to the women).

There is therefore room, alongside (and within) good faith, for bad faith, room alongside blind belief for calculating, interested, manipulated belief. It is possible to know but to have an interest in seeming not to know; it is possible to not know and to have an interest in seeming to know, and so forth. But more important than these manipulations is the knowledge that it is in the social relations themselves, in the structures of society and not in those of the mind thinking for itself and by itself, that one finds the reasons and the forces which drive the mind to all these ruses: to eclipse, repress and reduce to unquestioning tasks a whole part of reality, and particularly that which concerns the human origins of human relations and the objects that circulate in and symbolize them.

It is in this perspective that it seems to me particularly significant that the processes of producing these precious objects and the processes of "consuming" them, in other words the circumstances, times, and places in which they are used as precious objects, tend to separate, to become detached in space and/or in time, in such a way that the *human origin of these objects tends to fade* and then disappear, and that, in place of the humans who manufactured them, "supernatural" beings appear, "culture heroes" to whose intelligence and generosity today's humans are indebted for possessing these objects of value and power and for being able to use them for their own needs. The distance between the place of production and the place of consumption may be spatial, as in the case of the Maenge of New Britain and the tribes of New Ireland, or temporal, as with the Baruya's *kwaimatnie* and bull-roarers, the originals of which were not of human manufacture. In both instances, though, the same process in various forms is repeated: man is not the author of his works, is no longer his own origin. To be sure, he can *see himself* in these sacred objects because he knows the *code*, but he cannot *recognize* himself in them, cannot recognize himself as their author and maker, in short as their origin.

This obliteration of man from his own origins and his replacement by supernatural beings which are duplicate selves, and behind which real man disappears, is the work of *myths* which explain the origin of cultural possessions: the origin of fire, hunting weapons, cultivated plants, domesticated animals, and so forth. Time and again, as Lévi-Strauss showed in his four-volume *Mythologiques*, it was *following* some exciting adventure involving supernatural beings, traitors, or seducers, at the time when jaguars were also men and married jaguar-women, and so forth, that men *began* to differentiate between the raw and the cooked, to make dug-out canoes, to grow crops, to exchange their sisters, to practice good table manners. Humans invented nothing. They were given everything. Now it is up to them to preserve what they received.[4]

Concerning the unequal gifts that, from the outset, gods, spirits, and humans have given each other

If, as we have tried to show, the sacred is a relationship humans entertain with origins, with the origin of themselves as well as of everything around them, and a relationship such that real humans are both present and absent, it is worth our while to re-examine a few origin myths in order to discover the nature of the *debt* humans imagine they owe to the powers and forces which made the universe and man as they are. The words used to designate these powers vary and are also worth discussing. The myths speak of nature spirits. They speak of gods and goddesses. They speak of divinized ancestors, and so on. The reader will have noticed that I was in no hurry to call the Baruya's Sun or the python who commands the rain and thunder "gods."[5] But I will leave this question to be explored elsewhere. Here I would simply like to investigate the nature of the gifts these powers made to men, and to compare them with what men present to the gods – and not necessarily "in exchange." Once again we find ourselves before Mauss' famous fourth obligation, that of humans to make presents "to the gods, to the spirits of nature and to the spirits of the dead"; since "it is they who are the true owners of the things and possessions of this world."[6]

The gifts men make them are prayers, offerings, and often sacrifices, the offering of an animal or a human life. But here we must be careful. Sacrifice is not a universal practice. There exist religions which do not practice sacrifice: such seems to be the case in many societies which procure their living by hunting and gathering. This was pointed out for the first time to my knowledge by James Woodburn, a specialist on one of the last hunter groups in Africa, the Hadza, at a conference convened by a number of theologians and anthropologists to examine the notion of sacrifice.[7] These hunters live on the flesh and blood, on the body of wild animals, and strive to maintain a relationship of respectful amity and gratitude with the "animals' masters" and to kill game "in moderation" for their needs.

These peoples do not necessarily regard human beings as "superior" to the animals they hunt, on which their life depends. Sacrificial religions are ones in which the gods lord it over men with all their might and make themselves feared. But, as Alain Testart also stresses, for there to be sacrifice, there must be victims, and these are often either dependent humans (prisoners of war, children, women) or animals, in particular domesticated ones.[8] Let us not forget the discussion about the "plow ox" in ancient Greece and the meaning of the Pythagoreans' refusal to eat the meat of sacrificial animals.[9]

We will begin our evocation of the gifts circulating between the gods and men by a myth from Melanesia which describes the self-sacrifice of a supernatural being known as "Old Afek."

Afek, the "Old Woman," the "Great Woman," the "Ancestress," or the "Widow," is widely worshipped throughout the interior of New Guinea,[10] in the highland valleys of Telefomin, Oksapmin, and the neighboring area. Afek is said to have come from the east and to have crossed these regions on her way west. As she went, she cut valleys and leveled the ground. She drove the original occupants of the place, a spirit people, into the bush where they live in hiding even today. Along the way she left signs of her passage, and one day let drop from her netbag (uterus) pigs and taros (the traditional tubers that arrived in New Guinea several thousand years before the sweet-potato, which the Spanish navigators brought from South America in the sixteenth century). Some of the pigs changed into marsupials (sacrificed along with the pigs during the initiation rites). Her menstrual blood left a deposit of red earth today used to paint the initiates' bodies. Then she dived into the ground and continued along until she surfaced further to the west and, on that site, built the cult house that is there today.

She made other journeys underground, and wherever she emerged, a place of worship stands today. The path connecting all these sites leads to the biggest religious center, located at Telefolip.

At Telefolip, she diverted the river, drained a swamp, and forbade the planting, in that spot, of sago palms, which grow in the hot lowlands along the coasts of New Guinea. An old man had joined her. She killed him and then brought him back to life. She divided each cult house in half; she entrusted the man with "the arrow half" and she kept "the taro" half for herself. Further along, she encountered two humans who had eaten some fruit from the banana palms she had planted as well as some of the tadpoles that belonged to her. She killed them both, ate one and then smeared their blood on the posts of the Telefolip cult house, which she then finished building.

Later she met up with the old man and, before parting, the two carried out the first "commercial" exchange, for the old man had returned from the kingdom of the dead with shells and stone blades for making adzes. Afek went to live with her brother, Olmoin, who slept at night in a woman's house and raised pigs as women do now. One day, Afek decided to decorate her brother's body and put him through the initiation rites. From that time on, men's and women's roles were set forever. But her brother had a gigantic penis. She cut it down to size and made love with him. The blood from his penis fell onto two plants, which she gathered and concealed in her body. The blood spilled on one was the blood of fertility, the blood on the other was the blood of aggressivity. Afek gave the blood for aggressivity to men.

Afek and her brother lived in Telefolip for a long time. He stayed in the village preparing the meals and cooking the taro. She, on the other hand, went hunting every day. One day Olmoin followed her and spied on her. He saw that the animals came up to her of their own accord. It is since then that animals no longer come and give themselves to humans. They now run away when they hear hunters. Another day the brother again followed his sister and came upon her with her legs parted, giving birth to all varieties of animals. To each kind she explained how it should live and behave thereafter.

But Afek eventually caught her brother spying. She killed him and exposed his body on a platform. As the body did not decompose, she created maggots and thereby brought death, rotting, and decomposition into the world. Some of the maggots crawling on the corpse changed into shells and valuable objects. Then she gathered up her brother's bones and distributed them among the various cult houses she had built. Ever since, these bones have been used in rituals for making taro grow. Afek had had a large family with her brother. Her children were the ancestors of all the groups in the area. To each group she gave a distinct but related language and customs. When she died, she ordered that her head remain in Telefolip, and that her pelvic bones be placed in the cult house that today belongs to the Ulapmin tribe.

This sums up the corpus of myths, of which we have numerous versions. These myths were associated with initiation and fertility rites which have until now been held in utmost secrecy. Here is one of these rites, as recently described to Lorenzo Brutti[11] by elderly informants who, in telling him about this rite, denied that they still practiced these customs, since they had now heard the "tok bilong Papa God," the word of Jesus Christ, the true God.

This rite used to be performed in times of prolonged drought and famine, the last of which dates back to the Second World War. It consists of sacrificing a young man who already has two or three children. The rite was collected among the Oksapmin. They explain that Afek ("Yuan-an" in their language) came from the southeast and crossed the region diagonally to the northwest, performing as she went all of the deeds described in the myth above. When she was done, and before going on, she ordered the men to kill her and to keep her bones, which they were later to divide up among themselves and place in the cult houses.

Before she was killed, however, she explained to the men what they must do when nothing grew in their gardens and the taros withered and famine threatened. They were to choose a young man from one of the two villages situated at either end – west or east – of the path she had traveled, a strong young man who already had several children, preferably sons. It was up to the elders to decide if they needed to perform the rite and to choose the victim. The victim was aware of nothing. His best friend was charged with drawing him into a trap in which young male initiates laid hold of the victim, bound him, and tied him to a tree in the forest, a wild pandanus. There they would break his arms and legs, and then kill him by sticking seven bat-bone needles into his kidneys, his lungs, his neck and his head. Last of all, his heart was torn out and wrapped in wild pandanus leaves and taken from one cult house to the next, where each time it was passed over the flames of a fire. The men smeared themselves with the victim's blood in order to become strong and have fine gardens. The rest of the blood was for feeding the insects that live in the ground and destroy the crops.

Then the victim's body was cooked along with a pig that had been sacrificed at the same time. The pig's flesh was eaten, but not that of the man, because the Oksapmin did not practice endo-cannibalism: they ate their enemies but not their kinsmen. Then the man's bones were collected and shared out by the different clans, who buried them near their villages. The bones were stuck into rocky outcrops on barren land that needed regenerating. The juxtaposed killing and cooking of a man and a pig is eloquent proof that, in New Guinea, the being closest to man, his substitute, is the pig. And, as we have seen, while shells are substitutes for humans, they can also take the place of pigs.

This ritual, which has since "disappeared," is directly inspired by the myth we summarized, and particularly by its ending. The sacrifice of the man reproduces Afek's self-sacrifice. In each case, these real or imaginary deaths appear as the condition for the reproduction of life – the life of taros, the life of men – when it is in danger of dying out. But the difference between Afek and humans is that Afek dies without ever dying. After dying at Oksapmin, she went off to live other lives and to perform other feats. Humans die and go on living after death, but in the same place, as known ancestors or as part of the nameless mass of ascendants.

Let us now try, in a few words, to "qualify" this imaginary being, Afek, and her deeds. She is a woman, the "Old Woman," the "Great Woman," but a non-human woman. She appears out of nowhere and, as she crosses a region, she transforms it. She does not create. She refashions a world already there, inhabited by spirit folk and probably by human-like beings who, moreover, steal her "belongings," and whom she kills. She produces, from her vagina, taros and the plants that men will later cultivate, as well as all the wild animals they will later hunt (marsupials) or domesticate (the pig). She hunts, but it is not really hunting. For the animals which came from her, from her body, return to her of their own accord. She is a woman, the first woman, and she "civilizes" the world. She leaves behind commandments, rules not to be violated. Furthermore she is in possession of all powers, male and female. And it is she who endows men with their masculinity, which she detaches from herself, in a certain manner, and attributes to them. She gives them the use rather than the outright ownership of this maleness, though, since she retains within herself the source of all powers, male and female. It is also she who gives life, but she brings death into the universe as well.

She cuts off her brother's penis because it is too long, and copulates with him for the first time. She thus causes sexuality to appear by forcing her brother into an incestuous act subsequently forbidden to humans. She shapes men's bodies, she adorns them, decorates them and propels them into the cycle of initiations. With the "Old Man," she inaugurates the first form of "commercial" exchange. Finally, she dies and bequeaths her bones, lasting realities which will continue to protect the inhabitants of the region as long as they worship her. She will therefore always be with them, even though the Oksapmin know that, after her death, she went elsewhere, traveling across other regions and performing other feats. Before leaving, however, she entrusted them with the secret of a rite they were to perform in the event of a catastrophe: when the taro stopped growing, when the land fell barren, when famine threatened mankind with extinction.

Paradoxically, then – but the whole meaning of the myth resides in this paradox – the myth begins at the very beginning with a primal situation in which it is the woman who harbors both female and male characteristics, who is a being who does not accept reality as it stands but transforms it, civilizes it, a woman who is superior to man and encompasses him within herself before shaping him and cutting him loose. At the end of the story, the myth "rejoins" reality, since, when Afek disappeared, she left behind a new humankind, the same as today's humanity, where men hunt, initiate boys, do not raise pigs, do not cook, and so on, and are the only ones to have access to Afek, through her cult. At the end of the tale, men are in possession of all the powers, men's and women's. This time maleness encompasses femaleness. Reality is presented as the reverse of the myth, yet this reality is at the same time inhabited, permeated by the myth, because men know they owe their powers to Afek, but cannot at any cost divulge this secret to women, who must be "kept ignorant." The reality is therefore not quite the converse of the myth, since the men who claim to represent the whole of society by themselves and to govern it, live out this position of "strength" in the awareness of its precariousness, with the sentiment of its fragility.

For they know that all the powers they now exercise in society, over society, were not theirs originally. Afek gave them to men who had not asked for them. And if today they must "work" hard hunting wild animals and felling forests in order to plant the taro that feeds them (something they did until fifty years ago using stone tools), this is all because Olmoin, Afek's brother, was unable to resist the temptation to discover his sister's secrets. He followed her and spied on her and, ever since, animals do not give themselves to men and taro does not grow by itself; one must be hunted and the other must be planted. In short, because of their desire to find out more about women and to appropriate their powers, men caused the original abundance and easy living to disappear and now we must live in a world where one has to toil and struggle in order to survive. Clearly, as Marilyn Strathern writes, to recognize the qualities of "womanness" does not necessarily mean to acknowledge that women have these qualities. And yet what can be done so that the "Great Afek" is not in some way standing behind every woman?

Last of all, let us note that Afek acted single-handedly, without the help of other "gods." She asked permission from no one, and we see no one above her. We are dealing here with a religion without a "pantheon." This raises two questions. First question: why did she do everything she did? To make present-day humans and to civilize them? No one, in any case, seems to have "asked" her to do this. Her civilizing acts are presented as a free gift which puts those who received it without asking under a permanent obligation. Not only did she impose this order on the world, she also left instructions, commandments, which must not be disobeyed. Second question: how could humans ever "give back" what they received? This is obviously impossible. From the outset mankind is therefore indebted to the powers that fashioned man and bequeathed him the world he lives in, and this debt is ineffaceable. No counter-gift can measure up, be its equivalent, there is none that can efface it.

However humans are not in the same position with regard to the powers which created or shaped the universe and continue to control it, as with regard to the minor powers, forest spirits, for instance, with which they feel much more at ease. These can be entrapped, made fun of, tricked, or, on the contrary, one can make friends with them, associate with them and exchange presents and gestures of affection, as between humans. But with Afek or Yahweh, this is not possible. In the Bible, it is Eve, the woman, who eats the forbidden fruit, the apple containing all divine powers. It is woman who is unable to resist the desire to know more and, by taking of the forbidden fruit, causes mankind to be expelled from the Garden of Eden. In Telefolip it is Afek who contains all of the powers and gives them to humans, and it is man who brings death and work into the world when he seeks to appropriate the powers he was not given.

One is forced to conclude that, in the case of the "great powers" – gods, goddesses, all manner of supernatural beings – humankind finds itself confronted with beings with whom no equivalent exchange is possible; and there are at least three reasons for this. Because these powers originally gave men what they wished to give without the latter having asked. Because what the powers gave – the world, life, death – is such that men have no equivalent to give in return. And last, because the gods give even when they receive. They are "gracious" enough, "good" enough to accept. But just as they were not obliged to give, so the gods are not obliged to accept, or to give in return. The gods are not bound by the three obligations which are bound up together in the human world and which bind men. But the question still stands: why did they do what they did. Out of love for mankind? To persuade themselves of their own power? Something incomprehensible, obscure subsists for man whenever he attempts to understand divine actions.

The great powers of the invisible world to whom humans address their prayers, offerings, or sacrifices are therefore by definition recipients of gifts who are superior to the donors. And it is because men know that they might not be heard, and that their wishes and desires might not be answered, that they are often very strict about the performance of their rites. If beings in the invisible world are to consent to interrupt what they are doing and lend an ear to the pleas of men, these must be formulated in a language and according to procedures that are understandable and appropriate. It is for these reasons that, in my view, there can be no real question of true "contracts" between the great gods and men, and that, unlike Mauss, I do not think that, deep down, sacrifice is a contract between men and the gods. I am even less convinced that, by its form, sacrifice can be said to resemble potlatch on the pretext that "those gods who give and return gifts are there to give a considerable thing in the place of a small one."[12] Men could not engage in potlatch with Afek, who gave them everything and one day could take it all back. Of course to make a sacrifice is to give a life, to give a gift which is more likely than a simple prayer to create a greater obligation for the recipient to give in return. But a sacrifice is never really a business deal.

We now understand why, throughout history, religion has been the area that men could draw on for ready-made models of power, when some individuals began to rise well above the rest and to want to assert and legitimize their different position in society by their different origin. To them fell the right to wield power because they descended directly from the gods, as the great Polynesian chiefs claimed, or because they were themselves gods dwelling among men, as was said of Pharaoh. I do not mean that religion is the source of the caste or class relations which have emerged and developed in many parts of the world since Neolithic times. But it seems to me that religion might well have provided models for beings more powerful than men, sources of life and fertility, or sources of misfortune and catastrophe, to whom men were constantly compelled to make gifts and demonstrate their love, gratitude, and obedience, with fear and trembling. Religion also showed that these sources of life and wealth were not accessible to all men, and that, because of this, the few who did have access would serve society by performing the rites and sacrifices, by communicating directly with the gods for the benefit of all.

We are going to look at an example of this association which has often been established, over the course of history, between the religious monopoly of the imaginary means of access to the life-controlling powers and the political monopoly of the means of materially producing wealth, land, and labor: for this we will analyze a "prayer to the sacred tree and stone," which the Meto, a mountain people of southwest Timor, used to make to a supreme deity, the god of the Sky and the Earth, during a ritual in which they besought their god to send rain. In the 1960s, this region saw massive conversions to Christianity. In 1965, the Movement of the Spirit, backed by the Evangelical Church of Timor, swept through all of the communities and put formidable pressure on the new converts to abandon their traditional beliefs and practices, and to destroy all the sacred and cult objects associated with them.[13] At this time, an anthropologist, Andrew MacWilliam,[14] collected from already elderly men and women some of the invocations made in these rites. We have retained the prayer analyzed below.

For the Meto, the universe was dominated by a supreme deity invoked by the name of "Uis Nemo, Uis Pah," Lord of the Sky, Lord of the Earth. The Earth is the mother of creatures and man, the Sky is their father; this supreme god unites in him/herself all of the complementary and opposing aspects of the universe. Depending on the context, heat is more powerful than cold, the interior more powerful than the exterior, or the converse. In the area of kinship, givers of wives are always superior to the takers, but exchanges between the two are not symmetrical: the takers do not give women to their donors. They remain in their debt.

The Meto also believed in a number of supernatural beings – the master of the bees, and others – whose powers flowed from the primary divinity. They also worshipped the clan ancestors and the ancestors of the "houses," the local households. These ancestors were supposed to inhabit a world midway between the communities of the living and the sphere of the Supreme Being. Finally, they believed in evil spirits, spirits of women who died in childbirth or of people who died a violent death, doomed to wander the forest and the thickets along the river banks. Each household, each clan, each hamlet had its altar, made of a forked wooden post on which was placed a flat round stone. Hence the idea among the Meto that religion is "talking" to the sacred tree and to the sacred stone. Each family and each clan performed its own rites at its own altar. But these families and clans were grouped into political-religious communities, and it was at this level that they celebrated the collective rites meant to ensure the prosperity of all as members of the same community, the prosperity of the community as a whole.

Here it is indispensable to say a word about the political-religious structures of what I will call the "centralized chiefdoms," rather than "micro-states," which could still be found in southern Timor in the nineteenth century. These states were divided into five "domains," four of which were paired into opposite functions and grouped around a fifth, sacred domain, which stood at the center and where the tributes levied by the central power on the harvests of the clans and families living in the territory of that state were deposited.

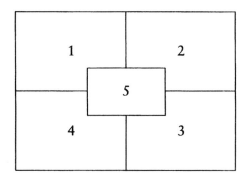

The land "belonged" in principle to this central power, which ceded to families the right to clear tracts in the forest and to cultivate them for a period of five years, in exchange for a tax of one silver coin and a red coral bead. At the end of the five years, the field was to be relinquished and returned to the care of the *a na'amnes*, a man charged by the central power with performing the collective agrarian rituals supposed to ensure the prosperity of each "territory," a territory being a political-religious space containing a dozen local communities and covering some 50 square kilometers.

The agriculture of this region is based on rice-growing in unirrigated fields and on the production of maize. As the climate is marked by a great fluctuation in the monsoon rains, and especially by their unpredictability, the ritual "management" of rain is of the utmost importance both for guaranteeing family subsistence and in order for families to pay their tribute to the authorities, to the masters at the center.

The rituals marking the beginning, the unfolding and the end of the agricultural cycle were decided by the *a na'amnes*, and were carried out under his supervision. He would go from community to community, from altar to altar, encircling, as it were, the territory in his rites. The prayers and sacrifices were held on mountain tops or near underground springs, at the transition points between the world of men and the world of the supreme deity and the spirits. The *a na'amnes* was also responsible for protecting the exploitation of certain types of trees, and particularly the sandalwood, which many peoples of southeast Asia and China imported from Timor. He saw to it that all tracts turned back to fallow were replanted with bamboo on all steep slopes and wherever water might erode the soil. He was also the first recourse in arbitrating land disputes. In short, the *a na'amnes* controlled both the material and the ritual processes of agricultural production. He combined in his person both the religious and the political aspects of power, which were united at the center of the "state." And he himself was appointed, or confirmed – if his father had been *a na'amnes* – in his charge by the central power.

Here then is the text of a prayer addressed to the supreme deity by one of these *a na'amnes*, who was the ritual guardian of the territory of a domain in southern Timor, custodian of the land and its resources – sandalwood and even the wild honey and the wax that was harvested twice a year for making candles and above all for export to Java, where, in the nineteenth century, there had been a thriving batik industry which consumed great quantities of wax:

At this moment I am standing before this stone, this, my ancestor's stone. This is why, my Lord of the Earth below, my Lord of the Sky above.

At this moment I am standing before this stone, placed here by my ancestor. I bring these animals to pray at the sacred stone, at the sacred tree of Polo, Esliu [here he goes on to name six other communities].

This stone, this tree, I bow my head in prayer, Earth below, Sky above. I beseech you for rain, Sky above, to wash the Earth below, so that I and the people of Polo … may eat and drink, to wash the whole

earth so that there may be maize, so that we may eat and drink our
fill.

That is why we bring these animals, we bow our heads in prayer to
the origin, the Earth below, that we may receive rain from the Sky
above.

At this point a chicken is sacrificed, plucked, and placed on the
altar stone. Its blood is sprinkled on the sacrificial rice, and a second
invocation begins, addressed this time to the animal.

Oh, fattened animal lying there, I am not punishing you, I am not
chastising you. I want to give you to the Earth below and to the Sky
above so that rain may fall, so that people may eat and drink aplenty,
and so that the Earth below may also be pleased.

Do not be frightened by the heat of the fire or by the sharp edge of
the knife, we are offering you so that we may eat well, drink well.

Next the throat of a pig or a goat is slit, and its head, liver, heart,
entrails, and testicles are placed on the altar. The sacrificed animals
as well as the rice have been provided by the communities for which
the *a na'amnes* is performing the rites, and he consecrates them
himself. Meat and rice are the foods offered on all "formal" occasions, in all ceremonies associated with life-cycle rituals, birth and so
on, and in all those which conclude or confirm an alliance between
two clans, two families. Then the last invocation is sent up:

I place this pig in the center [of the altar] so that you may always be
in our memory, so that you may be happy in Polo ... May this
roasted and cooked food enable me to serve you and present this
offering to you so that, in our hearts, we may eat and drink our fill on
this earth.

The ceremony ends with a meal at which the members of the
community consume the rice and the cooked flesh of the sacrificed
animals.

In this instance we are no longer dealing with a spirit-woman who
contains the women's and the men's powers and who finally, after
having remodeled the world in which humans live, raises the men
above themselves and makes them greater than women.[15] Here in
Timor, among the Meto, relations with the powers of the invisible
are different, as is the social structure. The clans and families themselves celebrate the cult of their ancestors, showing their respect and
their attachment, beseeching their aid and protection, fearing their
anger or revenge. But these family and clan rites are not perceived as

having the power to ensure the well-being of all. The rites are performed by men, but the gender division, the opposition between the sexes is included and transcended in another hierarchy, which separates the majority of the clans and families from a minority which owns the land and controls the rituals necessary to the life and prosperity of all. In Timor, one part of society stands above the rest and closer to the gods, but this part is no longer all of the representatives of one gender, the men as opposed to the women, as is the case among the Baruya or the Oksapmin, but all members of a few clans and their representatives as opposed to all other clans. A threshold has been crossed: a sort of clan-based aristocracy wields a centralized power over the rest of a population, also divided and organized into clans and other kin groups.

But this "twin monopoly" exercised by a few clans over the (for us) imaginary and real means of reproduction of life – sacred objects and ritual formulas, on the one hand, and land, labor and its products, on the other – is negligible compared with the formidable example of Egypt at the time of the Pharaohs, an example which is unique, even if it has been compared with those of the centralized states of pre-Columbian America, the Inca empire, also governed by a "Son of the Sun," the Aztec empire, and so on. It is unique because the person of Pharaoh concentrated all of the functions, all of the powers which, at other times and in other places, have been separated or shared; but also because this extreme concentration of powers took place in the first state to appear on the face of the earth, 3,000 years before Jesus Christ. Pharaoh was not a man who was closer to the gods, as was a Timor chief. He was not a man among the gods, as was the rajah of ancient India. He was a god who dwelled among men. He was the god closest to men, since he constantly lived among them and supported them in their existence, a god who had brought them everything – life, justice, prosperity, the arts, the sciences, in short a god who had civilized them.[16]

Pharaoh was god, the god Horus, born of incest between a brother and a sister, Osiris, his father, and Isis, his mother. He himself used to marry his sister, and upon dying (actually the term is improper since Pharaoh does not "die"), he would again become Osiris, his father. The names of successive Pharaohs, then, were nothing more than successive incarnations of the god Horus. Pharaoh's divine essence resides in his *kâ*, his breath, which is also his duplicate self. Pharaoh's *kâ* is the life-breath which animates all living creatures, so that their breath and their life all belong to him. In this sense, Pharaoh is "the father and the mother of all humans." He is the Only One. He has no equal, and before him, all humans, even those he charges with the highest functions, are equal, since all authority proceeds from him.

It is by him that opposites are balanced, that cosmic life is reproduced, that justice reigns among men, and it is with regard to him that each finds his place and function in society. He rules Egypt as the Sun rules the cosmos. He is the eternal fixed point, the pivot around which everything revolves. But Pharaoh is not the Sun. He descends from the Sun. In the beginning there was the Sun (Atum), uncreated creator. Atum brought forth from himself Air and Water, and from this couple were born the Earth and the Sky, who gave birth to the last four gods of the Ennead, among them Osiris and Isis, the father and mother of Horus, and of Pharaoh. The latter carries on the fecundating work of the primordial gods. Each year he takes his sacred boat to the headwaters of the Nile, to Silsileh, where the water is too shallow for navigation, and he performs the rite "which makes the Nile flow forth from its source," in which he throws into the water the papyrus on which are inscribed the prayers to the great river, which is none other than his father, Osiris. It is to Pharaoh that the peasants owe the fertile silt, it is he who "fattens the land." He is also the "mighty bull," the master of the beasts of the earth, and so on.

We are a very long way from Afek, who, having accomplished her task, disappeared, leaving behind her bones, which she entrusted to the Telefolmin initiation masters. We are also far from the Meto's supreme deity, from their masters of the earth and their priests. We have before us a god who constantly lives among men and constantly supports them in their existence. Men owe him everything because they owe everything to the gods, and Pharaoh is their representative among men. Pharaoh is perhaps the first human to have become a god in his lifetime, a man become god, but who thinks of himself (and is thought of by all) as a god become man. Not a "minor" god, a nature spirit, but a power, like Afek, one much greater still for being backed by the entire pantheon, the whole Egyptian cosmology, all the temples, all the rites celebrated by the priestly caste.

The divine essence of Pharaoh confronts us with two fundamental facts. On the one hand, it becomes understandable that those who owe everything, even their very existence and that of their progeny, to such a power, willingly *consent* to its authority, that their consent outweighs the violence they undergo in the exercise of this authority, in the exercise of power. Repressive violence existed in Egypt and was a constant threat, but over the thousands of years of its existence, the Egyptian empire experienced very few uprisings on the part of peasants and craftsmen resisting the forced labor and payment of tribute to which they were subjected. And the second basic fact, which also sheds light on the first, is that this consent was the expression of a *primordial debt* that humans owed the gods and in particular the god who dwelled among them, Pharaoh, a debt which all the counter-gifts of their labor, their harvest, and even their person could not counterbalance, and even less obliterate if Pharaoh were to demand their life.

Contrary to what many think and to what I myself have written,[17] there is something in this relationship between a god-king and his subjects which goes beyond the logic of exchange. For in response to the gifts made by the great gods, the powers of the invisible world – and Afek was one such power – there can be no true counter-gift. Nothing equivalent can be given and, of course, no better counter-gift; there can be no potlatch because the great gods are masters of every kind of wealth.

To be sure, Pharaoh "gave" everything, and not everything about his gifts was "imaginary." But these gifts drew on a power that was identical with himself, with his divine essence and with the sacred objects and formulas he held. Starting from there, from this point situated beyond any possibility of exchange, exchange became possible, between Pharaoh and his subjects and between the subjects themselves, whose relations always went through Pharaoh, were always conducted with reference to him. But let us return to the fact that not everything was imaginary about the "services" that Pharaoh rendered. The earliest dynasties appeared at the end of the Neolithic era, before the founding of Memphis, the capital of unified Egypt, at a time of great cultural and technical advances in writing, metal tools, monumental art. But it was not until the era of the kings and the unification of the kingdoms of Upper and Lower Egypt that men were able to dam the Nile and regulate its flow, which every year brought the fertile "black" soil that was surrounded on all sides by the "red" soil of the desert. And did not the Inca undertake a large-scale program of terracing which made the mountainside fit for growing corn? And did he not periodically open his grain-stores – which held the maize tributes paid by his subjects – to the poor or to communities deprived of the means of survival by natural catastrophes?

It was therefore necessary that some exercise a monopoly over the imaginary conditions for the reproduction of life in order for the castes and the classes to emerge and the institution which made it possible to govern these divided societies: the state in its various forms. It is not that religion somehow spawned castes and classes along the way; but it did provide the paradigm, the idea of beings infinitely more powerful than humans and to whom men are bound by an original debt which no counter-gift on their part can ever efface, beings to whom men owe respect, obedience, and gratitude, expressed by their prayers, offerings, and sacrifice. Religion provided the idea of hierarchical, asymmetrical relations, which were the source of both reciprocal obligations and a relationship of obedience situated beyond any possible reciprocity.

The castes and classes of antiquity could not have emerged had not these groups and these men appeared to have advanced further than other men into the space which from the outset separates man from the gods. But perhaps setting oneself apart from the rest of humanity, which then becomes a mass of "common men," approaching the gods and winning their ear are but two aspects of the process by which societies are divided and rebuilt upon real inequalities which it then becomes necessary to repress, keep silent about, or disguise as the best of all possible worlds.

Therefore sacrifices to God or to the gods are not fundamentally a business deal. It may look that way at one moment or another in history, as was the case in China, with the bundles of money burned in offering, or in the Christian Middle Ages with the traffic in "indulgences." But no religion can be reduced to a mercantile commerce between men and the gods. To men's original debt with regard to their gods corresponds a mental and bodily feeling, an attitude, that of the believer. That believers combat each other, that the believers of one religion accuse those of other religions of worshipping false gods, that they attempt by words or by violence to convert them to their own "true" gods, is a fact which has weighed and continues to weigh heavily in the history of mankind. But these struggles always imply the same act of faith: that there are indeed "true" gods.

I will conclude with three allusions. The first is to Yahweh, god of the Jews, and to the commandments contained in the book of Leviticus; the second is to Christ, who is not only a man, but the son of God made flesh, who came among men to die for them, redeem their sins and promise those who followed his word eternal life with God, his father; and the last is, the Rig Veda, one of the basic scriptures of the Hindu religion, a text which, unlike Leviticus, does not claim to be the word of a god, but a text with no origin, no author, a text which "appeared" bit by bit to a number of great "visionaries" of the past, who wrote down the fragments. It outlines a society in which the Brahmins were the only ones allowed to perform the major sacrifices, thereby setting them above the king, the rajah who, at the head of his warriors, could spill another blood, that of the enemies of the kingdom without or within. In the Rig Veda, debt is presented as constituent of human nature. It explains everything about our fate without being associated with a notion of original sin, as in Judaism or Christianity. The believer's path is clear. He must pay his debts to the gods, to the *rsi* (great seers), and to the fathers, and free himself from the cycle of lives, from successive reincarnations. This path will lead him there where there are neither gods, nor great seers, nor fathers. He will attain nirvana, there where the life-debt is expunged, and he will find himself in a state of beatific fusion, beyond even the cosmos, because it too is made up of differences and because, beyond that, differences no longer exist.[18] In Vedic India, faith is not belief in the gods but the certainty that the Veda is the Truth, an uncreated truth, without origin or author.[19]

The true man is the one who recognizes that he himself is a debt and does all that is required to discharge this debt by offering sacrifices.[20] Life is a deposit (*kurida*) for which we are indebted, but the debt of being born and living can never be completely obliterated, except for a few who have obtained absolute deliverance (*moksa*) and have become one with the Supreme Brahman, in the Absolute, which is a world without debt. In order to achieve this, some choose the ascetic life, forsaking all rites (by internalizing them), but at the same time giving up life in society. These are the "renouncers."[21]

But let us come back to Yahweh, and through him to Christ. Why Yahweh? For two reasons. Because he is the god of a tribe, or rather of a set of tribes, who recognize only one god for themselves, which is extremely rare. The God of the Israelites thus paved the way for the idea that there is only one God,[22] and consequently the idea that all other gods are false gods. That is the first reason. The second is that the text of the Bible, and particularly the book of Leviticus, clearly shows that men's sacrifices to the gods should be seen not as contracts concluded between men and the gods, but as obligations imposed by the gods on men, who will be rewarded if they obey. Let us listen to the opening verses of Leviticus:

> Yahweh called Moses, and from the Tent of Meeting addressed him, saying, "Speak to the sons of Israel; say to them, 'When any of you brings an offering to Yahweh, he can offer an animal from either herd or flock. If his offering is a holocaust of an animal out of the herd, he is to offer a male without blemish; it is to be offered at the entrance to the Tent of Meeting, so that it may be accepted before Yahweh. He is to lay his hand on the victim's head, and it shall be accepted as effectual for his atonement. Then he must immolate the bull before

Yahweh, and the sons of Aaron, the priests, shall offer the blood. They will pour it out on the borders of the altar which stands at the entrance to the Tent of Meeting. Then he must skin the victim and quarter it. The sons of Aaron, the priests, must put fire on the altar and arrange wood on this fire. Then the sons of Aaron, the priests, are to put the pieces, the head and the fat on the wood on the altar fire. He is to wash the entrails and legs in water, and the priest is to burn all of it on the altar. This holocaust will be a burnt offering and the fragrance of it will appease Yahweh.'" (Leviticus 1: 1–9)

Again we see a god explaining how to approach him if one wants to be heard, how to perform the rites, the sacrifices. It is he who promises to absolve the faults that men commit, intentionally or unintentionally – with the exception of a few, which are so abominable that no sacrifice can cleanse them away or make atonement. In this case men will have to put the guilty parties to death, cut them off from their people.[23]

In this text, God himself promises to hear men's prayers and to cleanse them of their sins by setting out the manner in which they are to come before him and present their offerings and sacrifices. He is the one who sets the "price" as it were, and fixes the rites. The exact observation of these rites becomes the condition for the granting of the petitions that the faithful address to God, since it was God himself who laid down the terms of the alliance and the exchanges, not men.

Abraham was about to sacrifice his son Isaac to God, but Yahweh stayed his hand. Yahweh did not sacrifice himself for mankind. Christ did. He consented to take on a human body, to live and to be crucified in order to save men from their sins, to redeem mankind in the eyes of God, his father, and to ensure that those who obeyed his word would be saved and have eternal life after the resurrection of the dead.

The Christian God, one God in three persons, bears a family resemblance to the great tribal gods we have encountered hitherto. He created everything. He is omnipresent, omniscient, omnipotent. But for the most part, the New Testament talks about the Son of God and does not dwell on the beginning, on the time when the world was created. The emphasis is on man, on his sins, on the evil that resides in him and flows out of him, which is attested by the insults and the hatred heaped on Christ at his trial and his crucifixion. But it was God himself who wanted this crucifixion, in order to give men one last chance to escape eternal damnation.

I would like to read the first Christian "manifesto," the creed drawn up at the first council of Nicea, June 19, 325, a few months after the Emperor Constantine's conversion to Christianity (which strengthened the ties between the empire and the state), but also in the midst of the crisis provoked by the heresy of Arius, a priest from Alexandria. Arius denied that the second person of the Holy Trinity, Christ, was equal to and one in Being with the Father, since Christ had been *begotten.* Let us look at the Church's response:

> We believe in God, Father almighty, maker of all that is seen and unseen;
> and in one Lord Jesus Christ, the Son of God, the only begotten of the father, in other words of the same substance as the father, God from God, light from light, true God from true God, begotten, not made, one in Being with the father, through whom all was made, that which is in heaven and that which is on earth; who for us men, and for our salvation, came down, took flesh, became man, suffered, rose again on the third day, ascended into heaven and will come to judge the living and the dead;
> and in the Holy Spirit.
> For those who say: "There was a time when he was not," and: "Before he was born he was not," and: "He was made from nothing," or who claim that the Son of God is of a different substance or a different essence, or that he is subject to change or alteration, the catholic and apostolic Church declares them anathema.[24]

Christ is therefore God and the Son of God. He came to live for thirty-three years among the inhabitants of Israel only in order to save all men from the evil that is in them and which threatens to damn them. This God shared his body with his followers by the miracle of the transubstantiation of the bread and the wine, which became his flesh and his blood; this miracle is repeated every time the priest celebrates holy mass and raises the chalice and the ciborium up to God.[25] The emphasis is no longer on the cosmos and its order, except for the allusion to the end of time and the end of the world. The emphasis is no longer, as in the case of Afek, on having given man a world refashioned by his care and rules to obey in order to build a society that is good. The stress is first and foremost on evil, on the disorder caused by man alone, not only by his faults, as in the case of Afek, but as a consequence of wanting to become God, wanting to steal from God the forbidden fruit, knowledge.

The emphasis is on evil and on man. For, in Christian monotheism, unlike polytheistic religions, evil is no longer as much the result of the gods' actions as of those of humans, gods, and humans sharing responsibility for the existence of evil. Here the scene tends to be reduced to a confrontation between one god, the Only God, and man, his creature, who has sinned. When the rest of the gods disappear, all of the evil they were causing is transferred to man, and of course to Satan, this double who, like man, was tempted to rise above his condition and to reign in God's stead. But there is little talk of Satan today, except in sects. Men's debt to a God who died on a cross to save them from the consequences of their own acts, from eternal damnation, is therefore even greater in Christianity than in any other religion.

Religion, St Thomas Aquinas wrote, is the debt men owe to God, and in the Christian religion, this debt is twofold, for God created man twice, the first time when he created the world, and again when Christ died on the cross to redeem man's sins, to atone for the original sin which caused Adam and Eve to be expelled from the earthly paradise. Religion is a debt, but it is better to read Thomas Aquinas: "In the first place, whatever man renders to God is due, yet it cannot be equal, as though man rendered to God as much as he owes Him."[26]

The Christian aspires to love God and to be forgiven and invited to sit at his right hand. In India, the believer respects the gods and discharges his debts to them, but he aspires to a world without debt in which there is no more God or Father.

These are some of the types of debt that men acknowledge owing the gods, to gods who are but imaginary duplicates of themselves and to whom they bind themselves in the (illusory) hope of being heard.

Concerning the critical function of the social sciences

Man produces duplicate selves but cannot and/or will not recognize himself in their replicas. Hence the importance of the social sciences (without singling out any particular one). All of them are necessary. All must work together, each taking a critical view of itself, its principles, its reductionism and its limits.

Their task is precisely to put man in his place, where he was and where he is, at the origin of himself and, from there to compare and explain the diversity of the forms of society and culture and the particularities of their histories. Their task is to construct the history and the sociology of ideas, institutions, techniques, tools, cultivated plants, and so on. But to put man in his place, to account for his real existence, to reconstruct his historical development, not the imaginary version but the effective development of his practices, his institutions, his representations, is to undertake a task which, objectively, in other words regardless of the philosophical or religious opinions of those who engage in this undertaking, runs counter to the intentions and the demonstrations of every discourse, of every system of representation which does not grant man this place, his place.

With respect to *all* of these systems, whether they are expressed as myths, religious dogmas, or philosophical principles, the social sciences, by putting man in his place (which is not only that of a being who lives in society but a being who produces society in order to live) *exercise a critical function*. Everything that has been produced by man, everything which has sprung from his practices and therefore from his mind, his psyche, must be returned to man, everything which comes out of man but which comes to stand before him as an alien reality must go back *into* him.

But is such a return really possible? This would mean that not only have men to let go of their illusions by recognizing their illusory character, but above all that they no longer need illusions in order to live, to make the societies in which they live. We already "know" we cannot "believe" this, and that we must not believe it. And yet mankind is continually changing, and the critical findings of the social sciences can help man choose concretely to be otherwise. There is therefore no reason to forsake the field of scientific research, to decree the vanity of the task of finding the humans who were and are behind the customs, rites, laws and systems that the social sciences study, and the task of explaining how and why, every time, man sees but does not recognize himself in his customs and his laws.[27]

It is a twin task, with twin levels of theoretical analysis, and to pass from one to the other we cannot do without the new knowledge that has been accumulated on the conscious and unconscious workings of the human mind. That is why the social sciences must, if not cooperate, at least maintain an ongoing dialogue with psychoanalysis, re-examining the postulates and the findings produced in this field from the standpoint of what is known of social systems very different from our own, which shape individuals according to their own principles and exert their control over all of the domains in which these humans interact, form ties, serve as ties, are social subjects. Such a dialogue should by all means be based on an acknowledgement of Jacques Lacan's advances with respect to Freud, but also of the negative effects of the premise, become dogma, that the symbolic dominates the imaginary.

4

The Dis-enchanted Gift

Our journey is drawing to a close. The enchanted land of sacred objects and gift-objects is receding into the distance. The objects are still there, to be sure; however the answers we have found to Mauss' questions about them have broken the spell.[1]

More to the point, our analyses lead us to the conclusion that there can be no human society without two domains: the domain of exchanges, whatever is exchanged and whatever the form of this exchange – from gift to potlatch, from sacrifice to sale, purchase or trade; and the domain in which individuals and groups carefully keep for themselves, then transmit to their descendants or fellow-believers, things, narratives, names, forms of thinking. For the things that are kept are always "realities" which transport an individual or group back to another time, which place them once again before their origins, before the origin.

It is beginning with these fixed, still points, these realities "anchored in the nature of things" that individual and collective identities are constructed and can develop. These are what give time its duration. One appreciates the forces able to destroy such anchor points, either bit by bit, nibbling away at them, or all at once, cutting them through in one stroke. And it is not indifferent for a society's future whether the forces that destroyed these anchor points arose from within the very modes of life and thought they had anchored, or whether they came from without, imposed by the conscious or involuntary pressures and aggressions from societies anchored elsewhere.

Concerning the necessary anchor points for fixing the identities
of societies and individuals in time

The following is a description of the life of the mikado, the Japanese
emperor, written nearly three centuries ago by a Dutch traveler,
Kaempfer, who set down a *History of Japan*, after having lived in
the country as it was in the process of opening its doors to the West.
The description is reproduced by James Frazer in *The Golden
Bough*:[2]

> The Mikado thinks that it would be very prejudicial to his dignity and
> holiness to touch the ground with his feet; for this reason, when he
> intends to go anywhere, he must be carried thither on men's shoul-
> ders. Much less will they suffer that he should expose his sacred
> person to the open air, and the sun is not worthy to shine on his head.
> There is such a holiness ascribed to all the parts of his body that he
> dares to cut off neither his hair nor his beard, nor his nails. However,
> lest he should grow too dirty, they may clean him in the night when
> he is asleep; because, they say, that which is taken from his body at
> that time, hath been stolen from him, and that such a theft does not
> prejudice his holiness or dignity. In ancient times, he was obliged to
> sit on the throne for some hours every morning, with the imperial
> crown on his head, but to sit altogether like a statue, without stirring
> either hands or feet, head or eyes, nor indeed any part of his body,
> because by this means, it was thought that he could preserve peace
> and tranquillity in his empire; for if, unfortunately, he turned himself
> on one side or the other, or, if he looked a good while towards any
> part of his dominions, it was apprehended that war, famine, fire, or
> some other great misfortune was near at hand to desolate the country.
> But it having been afterwards discovered, that the imperial crown was
> the palladium, which by its immobility could preserve peace in the
> empire, it was thought expedient to deliver his imperial person, conse-
> crated only to idleness and pleasures, from this burthensome duty,
> and therefore the crown is at present placed on the throne for some
> hours every morning.[3]

The mikado, or emperor, is truly the still point, in this case, the
point which anchors society in the cosmic order. Although he was a
god, some human trait prevented him from achieving perfect physical immobility, the complete stillness which would have forever
ensured the well-being of his subjects. Unfortunately for them, the
mikado could not help an occasional twitch, consequently occasion-
ing disturbances and misfortunes in some corner of his kingdom. An
object was therefore placed in his stead which partook of his divinity but which could remain totally immobile: his "crown."

Frazer makes two comments on this, one analytical, the other ideological:

> [The monarch] is the point of support on which hangs the balance of the world, and the slightest irregularity on his part may overthrow the delicate equipoise. The greatest care must, therefore, be taken both by and of him; and his whole life, down to its minutest details, must be so regulated that no act of his, voluntary or involuntary, may disarrange or upset the established order of nature. Of this class of monarchs the Mikado or Dairi, the spiritual emperor of Japan, is or rather used to be a typical example. He is an incarnation of the sun goddess, the deity who rules the universe, gods and men included; once a year all the gods wait upon him and spend a month at his court. During that month, the name of which means "without gods", no one frequents the temples, for they are believed to be deserted. The Mikado receives from his people and assumes in his official proclamations and decrees the title of "manifest or incarnate deity" [*akitsu kami*], and he claims a general authority over the gods of Japan. For example, in an official decree of the year 646 the emperor is described as "the incarnate god who governs the universe".[4]

Frazer's remarks[5] correctly identify the existence and importance of these anchor points fixed in time and necessary for grounding and legitimizing the way a society is organized, its structure and order. His observations converge with my own. But he adds, in a note, this judgement, which is that of a Westerner convinced of the superiority of the philosophies and sciences developed in his own culture:

> No doubt it is very difficult for the Western mind to put itself at the point of view of the Oriental and to seize the precise point (if it can be said to exist) where the divine fades into the human or the human brightens into the divine. In translating, as we must do, the vague thought of a crude theology into the comparatively exact language of civilised Europe we must allow for a considerable want of correspondence between the two: we must leave between them, as it were, a margin of cloudland to which in the last resort the deity may retreat from the too searching light of philosophy and science.[6]

Frazer was surely one of the European figures who was the least unaware that such figures, such institutions, such societies were found the world over, including in Europe, and at very different periods. But he was persuaded that, in the West, beliefs in divine kings and the process of divinizing humans belonged to a bygone era, were a phase that had been superseded by the progress realized over the course of civilization. By the early twentieth century, when

Frazer was writing his *Golden Bough*, the European monarchies had become "constitutional" ones, and the princely families as a rule contented themselves with non-speaking roles on the stages left them by the now "sovereign" peoples.

Did not history confirm Frazer's theses when Japan surrendered at the end of the Second World War. Emperor Hirohito had done nothing to keep his people from entering the war on the side of Nazi Germany, quite the contrary. After Japan's surrender, there was much discussion among the Allies over which of two positions to adopt. Some advocated eliminating the monarchy and entirely dismantling the former imperial system. Others, afraid of offending deep-seated Japanese sensibilities and thus causing civil strife, argued in favor of keeping the emperor but turning the divine-right monarchy into a European-style constitutional monarchy.[7] The latter prevailed. And for the first time in history, a living god was forced to confess that he was not god. Such was the content of the rescript that Emperor Hirohito was compelled to draw up on January 1, 1946 and which he addressed (in English) to General MacArthur, chief of the occupying forces: "The ties between Us and Our people have always stood upon mutual trust and affection. They do not depend upon mere legends and myths. They are not predicated on the *false* conception that the Emperor is divine and that the Japanese people are superior to other races and fated to rule the world."[8]

A new monarchy, a symbol-monarchy came into force on May 3, 1947. On the other side of the world, a Western people, heir to Christianity and the Holy German Empire, had also attempted to govern the world, this time in the name of the superiority of the Aryan race. Their *Führer* did not renounce his superhuman status; he committed suicide in his bunker. The Allies then undertook the process of denazifying the people who had waged war on them and of instructing them anew in democracy. Western-style democracy became the future of the free world. In 1989, with the fall of the Berlin Wall, it became the future of the whole world. This is why some entertained the idea that history might be coming to its end.

The "end" of history thus began in 1989, when "mankind" – confronted with the sudden and generalized collapse of communism, in other words of a form of society which had grown out of the union between a state-run economy and a dictatorship disguised as popular democracy – was obliged to admit that its only future lay in generalizing to all human societies the marriage between capitalism and democracy, two systems that arose in the West in different periods, but which gradually converged between the end of the eighteenth and the beginning of the twentieth century, depending on the country,[9] as the old-regime societies disappeared.

What, in this form of society which imagines itself to be eternal, is the place of exchange, and is there anything else beyond exchange? Apparently everything, or nearly, is for sale: means of consumption, means of production (including the land), means of destruction, means of communication, individuals' manual and/or intellectual labor, the use of their bodies. Ordinary things and precious things, works of art. And as everything which is bought and sold is bought and sold in exchange for money, the possession of money has become the necessary condition for a physical and social existence.

Money stands at the heart of all that is "alienable." It is continually entering and leaving the market and, as it circulates, it sweeps along thousands of other material and immaterial realities for which it is exchanged and into which it is changed – for a time. It does whatever it is made to do by the market relations contracted between individuals and between groups. Money is neither moral nor immoral. It is neutral. Let us say it is useful. It covers everything that is covered by the market. And it is always extending its range, driven by the necessity for capitalist production and trade to encompass more and more ground.

Money and profit therefore stand at the very heart of the system. They are inseparable from it and should therefore not be used as scapegoats when criticizing the negative consequences of the system's workings. For such a system, which is presented as the least bad of all possible systems, regularly and necessarily excludes from production – and therefore from the "job market" – hundreds of thousands of individuals whose life comes to depend on state aid or individual generosity, and therefore on an economy of state-managed redistribution or on an economy based on private giving.

We are therefore dealing with a society divided into groups whose interests and status are not the same, and which are even to a large extent opposed and contradictory. The division and opposition are structural, but this is not incompatible with the fact that a certain number of wage-earners can become capitalists and that a certain number of capitalists can lose their capital and begin another life. In sum, at the heart of capitalism there is undeniably a permanent source of social inequalities, which means that, in this system, as in all others, there are things to be repressed, things which "must" be passed over in silence or disguised as being in the "common interest."

But with this type of economy, at least in the West, goes a political system based on the principle that all people are free and equal before the law; free to do and think as they wish as long as their acts do not infringe on the rights of others or endanger the general interest, which it is the role of the state to represent and to defend. People who are unequal because of their place in the economy thus enjoy, on the political level in the framework of a democratic state, equal status before the law.

Concerning that which stands beyond the market in a market society

What room is left for gift-giving and sacred objects in this type of political and economic system? Clearly the possession of sacred objects endowed with the presence and the powers of the gods or of God does not give their owners access to political power. Religion or religions have become a "private matter," and sacred objects have no public power. They are kept and transmitted within the individual communities corresponding to the various religious denominations recognized and protected by the state.

But wealth, and money, which is the general form of wealth, do not give *direct* access to political power or state governance either. Of course political parties need money to conduct their campaigns and to persuade the citizens to vote for their candidates. Of course money can be used to "buy" votes, just as it can be used, in the form of discreet gifts on the part of companies and interest groups, to buy influence with the parties and individuals in power on both local and national levels.

There are therefore juridical and constitutional limits on the uses to which money can be put. In a society where almost everything can be bought or sold, the *individual*, the person, may not be bought or sold by a third party. Of course one may sell parts of oneself, one's blood, labor, or skills. A woman can rent her uterus to a childless couple and become a surrogate mother. And this process of dissociating and commercializing parts of the human being threatens to gain ground. But an individual's body remains their own property; this is guaranteed by law, and this property can never be turned into a commodity. Not everything, then, is "negotiable" in our profit-oriented society. Individuals, as persons, as corporeal and spiritual singularities, cannot be put on the market as commodities, whereas every day they deal in the market as economic agents. One can deprive a person of their freedom by putting them in prison for debt, but they cannot be sold in order to reimburse the same debt.

In ancient Greece, on the other hand, and in particular in Athens at the time of Solon, a free man could be sold into slavery to pay his debts and so become the property of another. Following Solon's reforms, all Athenian slaves came from outside; they were sometimes Greek, but most often "barbarians" taken prisoner of war or sold by their clan or their chief to slave traders. In the eighteenth century, the slaves in the American South were Blacks bought in Africa or born in the South. But in Missouri as in Greece, it was the person of the slave that was bought as a whole and not the use of his or her labor. This purchase was in no way a contract between master and slave; it was an agreement between two owners, one with money who needed slaves, the other with slaves and needing money. Market relations in ancient Greece and Rome thus had a very different extension from those in today's capitalist societies. Even if a lack of private income forces individuals to work for others, they retain their freedom with respect to their employer.

But if, in Western countries, the individual as a person cannot be transformed into a commodity or a gift-object, it is because the constitution in which the legal system is rooted does not belong to the sphere of market relations. It founds them, it limits them, but it is not a part of these relations. The constitution is the property of no one person as such; it is the common, inalienable property of all those who respect it because they have chosen it, "voted it in." The constitution of a republic is a common, public good. It presupposes the existence of a collective body of citizens who have voted for it. But for this to have come about, they had to behave as citizens – and not as obedient subjects of an Eastern or a Western divine-right king.

Just as individuals, as persons, are inalienable, present at once inside and outside the sphere of market relations, so the constitution is a social reality, a common good which, by its essence, cannot be the product of commercial exchange. The constituent "body" that underpins the French constitution is made up of all citizens, dead and alive, who have ever lived on the territory of France since the "people" first resolved themselves into the sovereign body, the source of the laws. This body emerged at the time of the French Revolution, with the first Constituent Assembly, and since then, in a certain manner, has never ceased to exist. Over the past two centuries, the constitution has changed, the state has adopted a number of forms – constitutional monarchy or republic – before settling into the republican form. But behind these changes, the same body persists. The constituent body is therefore a collective, indivisible reality, both immaterial and material, caught up in time and timeless, which would disappear only if democracy were to be lastingly abolished. This is no longer the body of Pharaoh, the body of a god;

it is the body of a sovereign people, provisionally represented and embodied by the president of the republic; elected by a majority of the French citizenry – of those who cast their vote – the president becomes the president of all the French. For the space of a few years he is the custodian of the constitution, the symbol of the republic. His function places him above political parties and factional divisions. For a time he embodies the unity and identity of a whole, the nation, of which the state is merely an instrument and not the embodiment. He becomes the fixed point.

The code of law which founds the rights of *individuals* is therefore collective in its essence. It is the *common* property of all those who live under one constitution and recognize it as theirs, their inalienable property which lies beyond the sphere of commercial relations. It is a gift which free men and women bestow upon themselves and which founds, not their intimate, private relations, but their public social relationships. Here we see how, in our societies, the political sphere has taken the place of religion, and how the constitutions with which peoples endow themselves are, in a certain manner, equivalents of the sacred objects men believed they had received from the gods as a means of helping them to live together and to live well. However, if the political has taken the place once occupied by religion, it henceforth and continually runs the risk of becoming sacralized.

The return of the gift and the displacement of the enigma

So what room is there left for gift-giving in our Western societies? It obviously cannot play the role it still fulfills in many parts of the world, and not only in Melanesia. In our societies, is no longer necessary to exchange gifts in order to produce and reproduce the basic social structures. For instance, a man does not have to "give" his sister, a woman does not have to "give" her brother in order to marry. Nor does one have to compete in exchanges of gifts and wealth in order to gain access to political power. Gift-exchange exists, but it is now free from the burden of having to produce and reproduce the fundamental social relationships common to *all* members of society.

The giving of gifts has become above all a subjective, personal and individual matter. It is the expression and the instrument of personal relationships located beyond the spheres of the market and the state. In France it of course continues to be practiced as it has for centuries, in relations between kin and between friends. Between close friends and close relatives, it is still an obligation. It testifies to this proximity by the absence of calculation, by the refusal to treat close friends and relatives as a means to one's own ends. In our culture, gift-giving thus continues to partake of an ethic and a logic which are not those of the market and of profit, which are even opposed to them and resist them.

There are several adages in French to the effect that, talking about money with a member of the family is the best way to make trouble. It is as though money were fatal to feelings, as though it killed all affection. In reality, money is not the guilty party, it is merely the admission, the Trojan horse of personal interests that are different if not conflicting, which are usually repressed, contained in order to preserve the appearance or the reality of a united community. To be sure, the subjective gift is the opposite of market relations, but it still bears their stigmata. For, in the imaginary of individuals and groups, it appears a bit as the dreamed-of other side, as the *rêve inversé*, the "inverted dream"[10] of the relations of power, interest, manipulation, and submission involved in commercial relations and the quest for profit, on the one hand, and in political relations and the conquest and exercise of power, on the other. When idealized, the "uncalculating" gift operates in the imaginary as the last refuge of a solidarity, of an open-handedness which is supposed to have characterized other eras in the evolution of humankind. Gift-giving becomes the bearer of a utopia (a utopia which can be projected into the past as well as into the future).

Mauss harbored this dream and, at the end of the First World War, he called upon the state and the generosity of the wealthy to enable our Western societies to get back on the path of social progress and not become imprisoned, in his terms, in the "cold reasoning of the merchant, the banker, and the capitalist."[11] Mauss dreamed of a world where the well-off would be generous and the state resolved to build a more just society. He was fighting two enemies: Bolshevism and unfettered capitalism, liberalism.

Today circumstances have changed. Bolshevism, which gave birth to both Russian- and Chinese-style socialism, and to the "popular democracies," has collapsed and died. It seems, however, that it took with it to the grave two ideas that it ultimately betrayed, after having momentarily appeared to be their vehicle: the idea that democracy can really be exercised by all and the idea that it can even extend beyond the political framework into the economic sphere. These ideas seem to have gone to the heaven of utopias, and the old myth of economic liberalism, of faith in the virtues of the marketplace and of competition as the only institutions capable of solving the essential problems of society, has resurfaced.

But however efficient capitalism may be, it still accumulates exclusions – of individuals and nations – and exacerbates social fractures and gulfs between nations. The state is supposed to represent all sections of society; it has a mandate to govern society in such a way that the conflicts of interests and the contradictions which develop between certain parts do not prevent it reproducing itself as a whole, still less expel any one part from the whole. Yet today the state has taken upon itself to withdraw not only from the economic sphere, but also from health care and from education, or it is ever more eager to do so. It is in this *fin-de-siècle* context that generous giving, the "unreturned" gift is once again solicited: but this time the mission is to help resolve problems of *society*. The number of charitable organizations is on the rise, whereas, at the beginning of the century Mauss saw charity as "still wounding for him who has accepted it."[12] But today's charity makes use of today's means. It utilizes the media, it has spawned a bureaucracy and, in the West, it feeds on the televised images of the misfortunes and ills, conjunctural or permanent, that beset the four corners of the earth.

Gift-giving, in the Western world, has thus once again begun to spread beyond the sphere of private life and personal relationships to which it had been progressively relegated as the market tightened its grip on production and exchange, and the state took an ever greater hand in managing inequalities. Before the magnitude of society's problems and the manifest incapacity of the market and the state to find solutions, gift-giving looks as though it may once again become an objective and socially necessary condition for the reproduction of society. This time round, however, it will not be the reciprocal giving of equivalent things. Nor will it be potlatch-giving, since the recipients would be hard put to "reciprocate," and even harder put to give more in turn.

The institution of charitable giving thus looks set for a comeback. But charity is not the Promised Land. It can give the recipient time to turn around. But it cannot give him everything, for only the gods give everything or have given everything, but that was because they were not men.[13] Gifts will buy time, but time for what?

We live in a society which, by the very way it functions, separates individuals from each other, isolates them within their own family, and affords them advancement only by opposing them to one another. We live in a society which liberates, as no other has ever done, all of the forces, all of the potentials slumbering within the individual, but which also encourages people to make their own way by using others. Our society lives and prospers only at the cost of a permanent deficit of solidarity. The only new solidarities it can imagine are in the form of negotiated contracts. But not everything can be negotiated: there remains all that goes into the bonds between individuals, all that comprises their relationships – public and private, social and intimate – all that means that human beings live in society but that they must also produce society in order to live.

The boundaries of social negotiation are nevertheless clear. Can one imagine a child making a contract with its parents to be born? The idea is absurd. And its absurdity shows that the first bond between humans, that of birth, is not negotiated between the parties involved. And yet it is just such inescapable facts that our society tends to pass over in silence.

Bibliography

~

Appadurai, Arjun (ed.), *The Social Life of Things: Commodities in a Cultural Perspective*, Cambridge, Cambridge University Press, 1986.

Aristotle, *Aristotle's Politics*, translated by Benjamin Jowett, New York, The Modern Library, 1943.

Aristotle, *The Ethics of Aristotle*, edited by John Burnett, New York, Arno Press, 1973.

Asies, "Donner et recevoir," Special issue, edited by Flora Blanchon, *Revue du Centre de Recherche sur l'Extrême-Orient*, Paris, Presses de l'Université de Paris-Sorbonne, 1 (1992).

Assoun, Paul-Laurent, *Le Fétichisme*, Paris, Presses Universitaires de France, 1994.

Augé, Marc, *Le Dieu objet*, Paris, Flammarion, 1988.

Barnett, Homer G., "The Nature of the Potlatch," *American Anthropologist*, 40 (1938), pp. 349–58.

Barraud, Cécile, "Des relations et des morts: analyse de quatre sociétés vues sous l'angle des échanges," in Jean-Claude Galey (ed.), *Différences, valeurs et hiérarchie. Textes offerts à Louis Dumont*, Paris, Éditions de l'École des Hautes Études en Sciences Sociales, 1984, pp. 421–520.

Bataille, Georges, *La Part maudite*, Paris, Éditions de Minuit, 1964, and *Œuvres complètes*, Paris, Gallimard, 1976, vol. 7.

Battaglia, Deborah, "Projecting Personhood in Melanesia: The Dialectics of Artefact Symbolism on Sabarl Island," *Man*, 18 (1993), pp. 289–304.

Bayley, Frederick George (ed.), *Gifts and Poisons: The Politics of Reputation*, Oxford, Basil Blackwell, 1971.

Benedict, Ruth, *The Chrysanthemum and the Sword: Patterns of Japanese Culture*, Boston, Houghton Mifflin, 1946; French translation: *Le Chrysanthème et le sabre*, with a preface by Jane Cobbi, Paris, Picquier Poche, 1996.

Bensa, Alban, "Des ancêtres et des hommes," in R. Boulay (ed.), *De nacre et de jade. Art canaque*, Paris, Réunion des Musées de France, 1990, pp. 130–60.

Bensa, Alban, "Présentation de Bernhard, Laum," *Genèses*, 8 (1992), pp. 60–4.

Benveniste, Émile, *Le Vocabulaire des institutions indo-européennes*, Paris, Éditions de Minuit, 1968; English translation: *Indo-European Language and Society*, translated by Elizabeth Palmer, London, Faber, 1973.

Berndt, Robert, *Excess and Restraint: Social Control among a New Guinea Mountain People*, Chicago, University of Chicago Press, 1962.

Best, Eldon, *Forest Lore of the Maori* (1909), Wellington, E. C. Keating, Government Printer, 1977.

Bloch, Maurice and Johathan Parry, *Money and the Morality of Exchange*, Cambridge, Cambridge University Press, 1989.

Boas, Franz, *The Social Organization and the Secret Societies of the Kwakiutl Indians*, Washington, DC, 1897.

Boas, Franz and George Hunt, *Ethnology of the Kwakiutl*, 35th Annual Report of the American Bureau of Ethnology (1913–14), Washington, 1921, 2 vols.

Bohannan, Paul, "The Impact of Money on an African Subsistence Economy," *Journal of Economic History*, 19, 4 (1959), pp. 491–503.

Bohannan, Paul and Laura, *Tiv Economy*, Evanston, Northwestern University Press, 1968.

Bonheux, Marie-Ange and Annie Fargeau, *Pharaon. Les Secrets du pouvoir*, Paris, Armand Colin, 1988.

Bottéro, Jean, *La Naissance de Dieu. La Bible et l'historien*, Paris, Gallimard, 1986.

Bottéro, Jean, *Babylone et La Bible*, Paris, Les Belles Lettres, 1994.

Bourdillon, Michael and Meyer Fortes (eds), *Sacrifice*, New York, Academic Press, 1980.

Boyd, David, "The Commercialization of Ritual in the Eastern Highlands of Papua New Guinea," *Man*, 20, 2 (1985), pp. 325–40.

Brumbaugh, Robert, "Afek Sang: The Old Woman's Legacy to the Mountain-Ok," in Barry Craig and David Hyndman (eds), *Children of Afek: Tradition and Change among the Mountain-Ok of Central New Guinea*, Sydney, Oceania Monograph, 1990, pp. 54–87.

Burke, Edmond, *The Sublime and the Beautiful*, New York, Lupton, 1900.

Carrier, James, "The Gift in Theory and Practice in Melanesia: A Note on the Centrality of Gift Exchange," *Ethnology*, 31, 2 (1992), pp. 185–93.

Clarck, Jeffrey, "Pearl-Shell Symbolism in Highlands Papua New Guinea, with Particular References to the Wiru People of Southern Highlands Province," *Oceania*, 61 (1991), pp. 309–39.

Cobbi, Jane, "Don et contre-don. Une tradition à l'épreuve de la modernité," in A. Berque (ed.), *Le Japon et son double*, Paris, Masson, 1987, pp. 159–68.

Cobbi, Jane, "L'Obligation du cadeau au Japon," in Charles Malamoud (ed.), *Lien de vie, nœud mortel. Les Représentations de la dette en Chine, au Japon et dans le monde entier*, Paris, Éditions de l'École des Hautes Études en Sciences Sociales, 1988, pp. 113–65.

Cobbi, Jane, *Pratiques et représentations sociales des Japonais*, Paris, L'Harmattan, 1993.

Codere, Helen, *Fighting with Property*, New York, J. J. Augustin, 1950.

Codere, Helen (ed.), *Kwakiutl Ethnography*, Chicago and London, University of Chicago Press, 1966.

Craig, Barry and David Hyndman (eds), *Children of Afek: Tradition and Change among the Mountain-Ok of Central New Guinea*, Sydney, Oceania Monograph, 1990.

Dalton, George, "Primitive Money," *American Anthropologist*, 1 (1965), pp. 44–65.

Damon, Frederick, "The Kula and Generalized Exchange: Considering some Unconsidered Aspects of the Elementary Structures of Kinship," *Man*, 15 (1980), pp. 267–92.

Damon, Frederick, "Representation and Experience in Kula and Western Exchange Spheres (Or, Billy)," *Research in Economic Anthropology*, 14 (1993), pp. 235–54.

Damon, Frederick, "The Problem of the Kula on Woodlark Island: Expansion, Accumulation, and Over Production," *Ethnos*, 3–4 (1995), pp. 176–201.

Deacon, Arthur Barnard, *Malekula: A Vanishing People in the New Hebrides*, London, Routledge, 1934.

de Coppet, Daniel, "La Monnaie, présence des morts et mesure des temps," *L'Homme*, 10, 1 (1979), pp. 2–39.

Derlon, Brigitte, "Droits de reproduction des objets de culte, tenure foncière et filiation en Nouvelle-Irlande," *L'Homme*, 34, 2 (1994), pp. 31–58.

Derlon, Brigitte, *De mémoire et d'oubli. Anthropologie des objets* malanggan *de Nouvelle-Irlande*, Paris, Éditions du Centre National de la Recherche Scientifique and Éditions de la Maison des Sciences de l'Homme, 1997.

Derrida, Jacques, *Donner le temps*, Paris, Gallilée, 1991; English translation: *Given Time, I: Counterfeit Money*, translated by Peggy Kamuf, Chicago, University of Chicago Press, 1992.

Descombes, Vincent, "L'Équivoque du symbolique," *Confrontations*, 3 (1980).

Descombes, Vincent, *Grammaire des objets en tous genres*, Paris, Éditions de Minuit, 1983.

Détienne, Marcel (ed.), *Tracés de fondation*, Leuwen, Peeters, 1990.

Détienne, Marcel and Jean-Pierre Vernant, *La Cuisine du sacrifice en pays grec*, Paris, Gallimard, 1979.

Dillon, Wilton, *Gifts and Nations: The Obligation to Give, Receive and Repay*, The Hague and Paris, Mouton, 1968.

Dournes, Jacques, *Coordonnées-structures joraï familiales et sociales*, Paris, Institut d'Ethnologie, 1972.

Drucker, Philip and Robert F. Heizer, *To Make My Name Good: A Reexamination of the Southern Kwakiutl Potlatch*, Berkeley, University of California Press, 1967.

Dumeige, Gervais, *La Foi catholique*, Paris, Éditions de l'Orante, 1993.

Durand, Jean-Louis, *Sacrifice et labour en Grèce ancienne. Essai d'anthropologie religieuse*, Paris and Rome, La Découverte and École Française de Rome, 1986.

Einzig, Paul, *Primitive Money in its Ethnological, Historical and Economic Aspects*, London, Eyre and Spottiswoode, 1948.

Epstein, Arnold Leonard, "Tambu, the Shell-Money of the Tolai," in Robert Hook (ed.), *Fantasy and Symbol*, London, Academic Press, 1979, pp. 144–205.

Erman, Adolf, *La Religion égyptienne*, Paris, Payot, 1952.

Errington, Frederick and Deborah Gewertz, *Articulating Change in the "Last Unknown,"* San Francisco, Westview Press, 1991.

L'Éthique du don. Jacques Derrida et la pensée du don, Colloque de Royaumont, ed. J.-M. Rabaté and M. Wetzel, Paris, Métaillié-Transition, 1992.

L'Ethnographie, XCL, 117 (1995), special issue, "Regards actuels sur Durkheim et sur Mauss," ed. Marcel Fournier and Luc Racine.

Feil, Daryl Keith, "The Bride in Bridewealth: A Case from the New Guinea Highlands," *Ethnology*, 20 (1981), pp. 63–75.

Feil, Daryl Keith, *Ways of Exchange: The Enga Tee of Papua New Guinea*, St Lucia, University of Queensland Press, 1984.

Fenichel, Otto, *Collected Papers*, New York, Norton, 1954.

Finley, Moses I., "La Servitude pour dettes," *Revue historique de droit français et étranger*, 43, 11 (1965), pp. 159–84.

Firth, Raymond, *Primitive Economics of the New Zealand Maori*, London, Routledge, 1929.

Firth, Raymond, *Elements of Social Organization*, London, Watts and Co., 1951.

Fournier, Marcel, "Bolchevisme et socialisme selon Marcel Mauss," *Liber*, 1992, pp. 9–15.

Fournier, Marcel, *Marcel Mauss*, Paris, Fayard, 1994.

Fournier, Marcel, "Marcel Mauss, l'ethnologue et la politique: le don," *Anthropologie et sociétés*, 19, 1–2 (1995), pp. 57–69.

Fox, James, "The Movement of the Spirit in the Timor Area: Christian Traditions and Ethnic Identities," in James Fox (ed.), *Indonesia: The Making of a Culture*, Canberra, The Australian National University, 1980, pp. 235–46.

Francillon, Georges, "Un profitable échange de frères chez les Tetum du Sud-Timor central," *L'Homme*, 29, 1 (1989), pp. 26–43.

Frankfort, Henri, *Kingship and the Gods: A Study of Ancient Near East Religion as the Integration of Society and Nature*, Chicago, University of Chicago Press, 1948.

Frankfort, Henri (ed.), *Before Philosophy*, Chicago, Pelican, 1949.

Frazer, James, *The Golden Bough: A Study in Magic and Religion*, abridged edn, London, Macmillan, 1963; complete edn: *The Golden Bough: A Study in Magic and Religion.*, New York: St Martin's Press, 1990, 3rd edn.

Freud, Sigmund, *The Standard Edition of the Complete Psychological Works of Sigmund Freud*, translated under the general editorship of James Strachey, in collaboration with Anna Freud, assisted by Alix Strachey and Alan Tyson, vol. 13: *Totem and Taboo and Other Works*, London, Hogarth Press and the Institute of Psychoanalysis, 1964.

Freud, Sigmund, *Nouvelles conférences d'introduction à la psychanalyse*, translated by Rose-Marie Zeitlin, Paris, Gallimard, 1984.

Galey, Jean-Claude (ed.), *Différences, valeurs et hiérarchie. Textes offerts à Louis Dumont*, Paris, Éditions de l'École des Hautes Études en Sciences Sociales, 1984.

Gathercole, Peter, "Hau, Mauri and Utu: A Re-examination," *Mankind*, 11 (1978), pp. 334–40.

Gernet, Jacques, "La Notion mythique de la valeur en Grèce," *Journal de psychologie normale et pathologique*, 41, 4 (October–December 1948), pp. 415–62.

Godelier, Maurice, "La Monnaie de sel des Baruya de Nouvelle-Guinée," *L'Homme*, 9, 2 (1969), pp. 5–37.

Godelier, Maurice, "Économie marchande, fétichisme, magie et science selon Marx dans *Le Capital*," *La Nouvelle Revue de psychanalyse*, special issue, "Objets du fétichisme," 2 (Autumn 1970), pp. 197–213.

Godelier, Maurice, *Rationalité et irrationalité en économie*, Paris, Maspero, 1966; English translation: *Rationality and Irrationality in Economics*, translated by Brian Pearce, New York and London, Monthly Review Press, 1972.

Godelier, Maurice, *Horizon, trajets marxistes en anthropologie*, Paris, Maspero, 1973; English translation: *Perspectives in Marxist Anthropology*, translated by Robert Brain, Cambridge, Cambridge University Press, 1977.

Godelier, Maurice, "L'État: les processus de sa formation, la diversité de ses formes et de ses bases," *Revue internationale des sciences sociales*, 37, 4 (1980), pp. 657–71.

Godelier, Maurice, *La Production des Grands Hommes*, Paris, Fayard, 1982; new edn 1996; English translation: *The Making of Great Men: Male Domi-*

nation and Power among the New Guinea Baruya, translated by Rupert Swyer, Cambridge, Cambridge University Press, 1986.

Godelier, Maurice, *L'Idéel et le matériel*, Paris, Fayard, 1984; English translation: *The Mental and the Material: Thought, Economy and Society*, translated by Martin Thom, London and New York, Verso, 1986.

Godelier, Maurice, "L'Occident – mirroir brisé," *Annales ESC*, 5 (September–October 1993), pp. 1183–1207.

Godelier, Maurice, "Monnaies et richesses dans divers types de société et leur rencontre à la périphérie du capitalisme," *Actuel Marx*, special issue, "L'Inconscient du social," 15 (April 1994), pp. 77–97.

Godelier, Maurice, "Du quadruple rapport entre les catégories du masculin et du féminin," in *La Place des femmes. Les Enjeux de l'identité et de l'égalité au regard des sciences sociales*, Paris, La Découverte, 1995, pp. 439–42.

Godelier, Maurice and Marilyn Strathern (eds), *Big Men and Great Men: Personifications of Power in Melanesia*, Cambridge, Cambridge University Press, and Paris, Éditions de la Maison des Sciences de l'Homme, 1991.

Goldman, Irving, *Ancient Polynesian Society*, Chicago, University of Chicago Press, 1970.

Goody, Jack, "Icônes et iconoclasme en Afrique," *Annales ESC*, 6 (1991), pp. 1235–51.

Goody, Jack and Stanley Teyaraja Tambiah (eds), *Bridewealth and Dowry*, Cambridge, Cambridge University Press, 1973.

Goux, Jean-Joseph, "Catégories de l'échange: idéalité, symbolicité, réalité," in *Encyclopédie philosophique*, Paris, Presses Universitaires de France, 1989, pp. 227–33.

Goux, Jean-Joseph, "A propos des trois ronds," in *Lacan avec les philosophes*, Paris, Albin Michel, 1991, pp. 173–8.

Goux, Jean-Joseph, "Les Médiateurs de l'échange," unpublished contribution to the seminar *Psychanalyse et sciences sociales*, Paris, 1994.

Gregory, Christopher, "Gifts to Men and Gifts to God: Gift Exchange and Capital Accumulation in Contemporary Papua New Guinea," *Man*, 15, 4 (1980), pp. 626–52.

Gregory, Christopher, "A Conceptual Analysis of a Non-capitalist Gift-Economy with Particular Reference to Papua New Guinea," *Cambridge Journal of Economics*, 5 (1981), pp. 119–35.

Gregory, Christopher, *Gifts and Commodities*, London and New York, Academic Press, 1982.

Guery, Patrick, "Sacred Commodities: The Circulation of Medieval Relics," in Arjun Appadurai (ed.), *The Social Life of Things: Commodities in a Cultural Perspective*, Cambridge, Cambridge University Press, 1986, pp. 169–94.

Hegel, G. W. F., *Philosophy of Fine Arts*, translated by F. P. B. Omaston, London, Bell, 1920, 4 vols.

Hiatt, Les R., "Secret Pseudo-procreation Rites among the Australian Aborigenes," in L. R. Hiatt and C. Jayawardena (eds), *Anthropology in Oceania*, Sydney, Angus and Robertson, 1971, pp. 77–88.

Hou, Chin-Lang, *Monnaies d'offrande et la notion de trésorerie dans la religion chinoise*, Paris, Presses Universitaires de France and Maisonneuve, 1975.

Hughes, Ian, "Traditional Trade," in E. Ford (ed.), *Papua New Guinea Resource Atlas*, Sydney, Jacaranda Press, 1973.

Hughes, Ian, *New Guinea Stone Age Trade: The Geography and Ecology of Traffic in the Interior*, Canberra, Australian National University, 1977.

Irvin, Thomas T., "The Northwest Coast Potlatch since Boas, 1897–1972," *Anthropology*, 1, 1 (1977), pp. 65–77.

Jonaitis, Aldona, *Chiefly Feasts: The Enduring Kwakiutl Potlatch*, Seattle, University of Washington Press, 1991.

Jorgensen, Dan, "Taro and Arrows: Order, Entropy and Religion among the Telefomin," doctoral dissertation, University of British Columbia, 1981.

Kan, Sergueï, *Symbolic Immortality: The Tlingit Potlatch of the Nineteenth Century*, Washington, Smithsonian Institution Press, 1989.

Kan, Sergueï, "The Nineteenth Century Tlingit-Potlatch: A New Perspective," *American Ethnologist*, 13, 2 (1986), pp. 191–212.

Kant, Immanuel, *Critique of Judgment*, Oxford, Clarendon Press, 1952.

Kant, Immanuel, *Observations on the Feeling of the Beautiful and Sublime*, Berkeley, University of California Press, 1960.

Kasaipwalova, John and Ulli Beier, *Yaulabuta: An Historical Poem from the Trobriand Islands*, Port Moresby, Institute of Papua New Guinea Studies, 1978.

Keesing, Roger, "Rethinking Mana," *Journal of Anthropological Research*, 40, 1 (1984), pp. 137–56.

Kirch, Patrick V., *The Evolution of the Polynesian Chiefdoms*, Cambridge, Cambridge University Press, 1984.

Kirchoff, Paul, "The Principle of Clanship in Human Society," in Morton Fried (ed.), *Readings in Anthropology*, vol. 2, New York, Thomas E. Cromwell Co., 1955, pp. 259–70.

Kramer, Samuel Noah, *Le Mariage sacré à Sumer et à Babylone*, London, Berg International, 1983.

Lacan, Jacques, *Écrits*, Paris, Éditions du Seuil, 1960.

Lacan, Jacques, *Séminaire II: Le Moi dans la théorie de Freud*, Paris, Éditions du Seuil, 1978.

Laum, Bernhard, *Heiliges Geld – eine historishche Untersuchung über den sakralen Ursprung des Geldes*, Tübingen, Mohr, 1924.

Leach, Jerry and Edmund (eds), *The Kula: New Perspectives on Massim Exchange*, Cambridge, Cambridge University Press, 1983.

Ledermann, Rena, *What Gifts Engender: Social Relations and Politics in Mendi, Highlands Papua New Guinea*, New York, Cambridge University Press, 1986.

Leenhardt, Maurice, *Notes d'ethnologie néo-calédonienne*, Paris, Institut d'Ethnologie, 1930.

Lemonnier, Pierre, *Guerre et Festins*, Paris, Éditions de la Maison des Sciences de l'Homme, 1990.

Lemonnier, Pierre, "Le Porc comme substitut de vie: formes de compensation et échanges en Nouvelle-Guinée," *Social Anthropology*, 1 (1993), pp. 33–55.

Lévi-Strauss, Claude, *Les Structures élémentaires de la parenté*, Paris, Presses Universitaires de France, 1949; English translation: *The Elementary Structures of Kinship*, translated by James Harle Bell, John Richard von Sturmer, and Rodney Needham, Boston, Beacon Press, 1969.

Lévi-Strauss, Claude, "Introduction à l'œuvre de Mauss," in *Sociologie et anthropologie*, Paris, Presses Universitaires de France, 1950, pp. i–lii; English translation: *Introduction to the Work of Marcel Mauss*, translated by Felicity Baker, London, Routledge and Kegan Paul, 1987.

Lévi-Strauss, Claude, *La Pensée sauvage*, Paris, Plon, 1962; English translation: *The Savage Mind*, Chicago, University of Chicago Press, 1969.

Lévi-Strauss, Claude, *Le Cru et le cuit*, Paris, Plon, 1964; English translation:

The Raw and the Cooked: Introduction to a Science of Mythology, translated by John and Doreen Weightman, Harmondsworth, Penguin, 1986.

Lévi-Strauss, Claude, *Du miel aux cendres*, Paris, Plon, 1964; English translation: *From Honey to Ashes: Introduction to a Science of Mythology*, vol. 2, translated by John and Doreen Weightman, Chicago, University of Chicago Press, 1983.

Linnekin, Jocelyn, "Fine Mats and Money: Contending Exchange Paradigms in Colonial Samoa," *Anthropological Quarterly*, 64, 1 (1991), pp. 1–14.

Lojkine, Jean, "Mauss et 'l'Essai sur le don'," *Cahiers internationaux de sociologie*, 86, 1 (1989), pp. 141–58.

Lojkine, Jean, "Valeur, valeur d'usage et valeur symbolique," *Cahiers internationaux de sociologie*, 90 (1991), pp. 225–8.

Longinus, *On the Sublime*, Cambridge, Cambridge University Press, 1899.

MacCall, Grant, "Association and Power in Reciprocity and Requital: More on Mauss and the Maori," *Oceania*, 52, 4 (1982), pp. 303–19.

MacCormack, Geoffrey, "Mauss and the 'Spirit' of the Gift," *Oceania*, 52, 4 (1982), pp. 286–93.

MacWilliam, Andrew, "Prayers of the Sacred Stone and Tree: Aspects of Invocation in West Timor," in *Canberra Anthropology*, 14, 2 (1991), pp. 49–59.

Malamoud, Charles, "Théologie de la dette dans les Brahmana," in *La Dette*, special issue of *Purusartha*, Paris, Éditions de l'École des Hautes Études en Sciences Sociales, 1990, pp. 39–62.

Malamoud, Charles, "La Dette au texte: remarques sur la dette constitutive de l'homme dans la pensée de l'Inde ancienne," in *De l'argent à la dette*, special issue of *Cliniques méditerranéennes*, 33–4 (1992), pp. 37–47.

Malamoud, Charles, "La Scène sacrificielle: observations sur la rivalité du mythe et du rite dans l'Inde védique," *Psychanalystes*, 41 (1992), pp. 19–33.

Malamoud, Charles et Madeleine Biardeau, *Le Sacrifice dans l'Inde ancienne*, Paris, Presses Universitaires de France, 1976.

Malinowski, Bronislaw, "Baloma: The Spirits of the Dead in the Trobriand Islands," *Journal of the Royal Anthropological Institute*, 45 (1917).

Malinowski, Bronislaw, "The Primitive Economy of the Trobriand Islanders," *Economic Journal*, 31, 121 (March 1921), pp. 1–16.

Malinowski, Bronislaw, *Argonauts of the Western Pacific*, London, Routledge, 1922.

Malinowski, Bronislaw, *Crime and Custom in Savage Society*, London, Routledge and Kegan Paul, 1926 (8th printing, 1966).

Maranda, Pierre and Elli Köngäs, "Le Crâne et l'utérus. Deux théorèmes nordmalaitais," in *Échanges et communications. Mélanges offerts à Lévi-Strauss à l'occasion de son soixantième anniversaire*, Leiden, Mouton, 1970, vol. 2, pp. 829–81.

Marsaudon, Françoise, "Nourritures et richesses. Les Objets cérémoniels comme signes d'identité à Tonga et à Wallis (Polynésie occidentale)," unpublished manuscript, 1995.

Martin, Jean-Marie, *Le Shintoïsme, religion nationale*, Hong-Kong, Imprimerie de Nazareth, 1924.

Marx, Karl, *A Contribution to the Critique of Political Economy*, ed. with an Introduction by Maurice Dobb, New York, International Publishers, 1970.

Marx, Karl, *Capital: A Critique of Political Economy*, vol. 1, translated by Ben Fowkes; vol. 3, translated by David Fernbach, Harmondsworth, Penguin Books in association with New Left Review, 1976 and 1981.

Maunier, René, "Recherches sur les échanges rituels en Afrique du Nord," *L'Année sociologique* (1927), pp. 12–87.

Mauss, Marcel, "Esquisse d'une théorie générale de la magie," in collaboration with Henri Hubert, *L'Année sociologique* (1902–3); reprinted in *Sociologie et anthropologie* (see below).

Mauss, Marcel, "Origine de la notion de la monnaie," *Anthropologie* (Institut Français d'Anthropologie), 3, 1 (1914), pp. 14–20.

Mauss, Marcel, "Essai sur le don. Forme et raison de l'échange dans les sociétés archaïques," *L'Année sociologique*, new series, 1 (1925); English translation: *The Gift: The Form and Reason for Exchange in Archaic Societies*, translated by W. D. Halls, Foreword by Mary Douglas, New York and London, W. W. Norton, 1990.

Mauss, Marcel, *Manuel d'ethnographie*, Paris, Payot, 1947.

Mauss, Marcel, *Sociologie et anthropologie*, Paris, Presses Universitaires de France, 1950.

Mauss, Marcel and Henri Hubert, "Essai sur la nature et la fonction du sacrifice," *L'Année Sociologique*, 2 (1899). Reprinted in Mauss, *Œuvres*, Paris, Éditions de Minuit, vol. 1, pp. 193–324.

Mauzé, Marie, "La Loi anti-potlatch chez les Kwagul," *Bulletin de l'Amérique indienne*, 29 (1983), pp. 3–5, 9–11, 30–1.

Mauzé, Marie, "Boas, les Kwakiutl et le potlatch: éléments pour une réévaluation," *L'Homme*, 26, 4 (October–December, 1986), pp. 21–63.

Meillassoux, Claude, "Potlatch," *Encyclopaedia universalis*, Paris, 1980, vol. 13, p. 424.

Meillassoux, Claude, "Commentaire à l'article de Marie Mauzé," *L'Homme*, 26, 4 (1986), pp. 54–5.

Moisseeff, Marika, "Les Objets cultuels aborigènes ou comment représenter l'irreprésentable," *Genèse*, 17 (September 1994), pp. 8–32.

Moisseeff, Marika, *Un long chemin semé d'objets cultuels*, Paris, Éditions de l'École des Hautes Études en Sciences Sociales, 1995.

Morris, Ian, "Gift and Commodity in Archaic Greece," *Man*, 21 (1986), pp. 1–17.

Munn, Nancy, "The Transformation of Subjects into Objects in Walpiri and Pitjandjara Myth," in Robert Berndt (ed.), *Australian Aboriginal Anthropology*, Wedlands, University of Western Australia Press, 1970, pp. 141–63.

Murra, John, "On Inca Political Structure," in Ray Vern (ed.), *Systems of Political Control and Bureaucracy in Human Societies*, Seattle, University of Washington Press, 1958, pp. 30–41.

Murra, John, "Cloth and its Function in the Inca State," *American Anthropologist*, 64, 4 (1962), pp. 710–28.

Otto, Rudolf, *Le Sacré. L'Élément irrationnel dans l'idée du divin et son rapport avec le rationnel*, Paris, Payot, 1949.

Panoff, Michel, "Marcel Mauss: The Gift Revisited," *Man*, 5 (1970), pp. 60–70.

Panoff, Michel, "Objets précieux et moyens de paiement chez les Maenge de Nouvelle-Bretagne," *L'Homme*, 20, 2 (1980), pp. 6–37.

Panoff, Michel, "Une figure de l'abjection en Nouvelle-Bretagne: le *rubbish man*," *L'Homme*, 94 (January–February 1985), pp. 57–72.

Petitat, André, "Le Don: espace imaginaire, normatif et secret des acteurs," *Anthropologie et sociétés*, 19, 1–2 (1995), pp. 17–44.

Petrequin, Pierre and Anne-Marie, *Écologie d'un outil. La Hache de pierre en Irian Jaya*, Paris, Éditions du Centre National de la Recherche Scientifique, 1993.

Pitt-Rivers, Julian, *Mana*, London, London School of Economics, 1974.

Polanyi, Karl, *Primitive, Archaic and Modern Economies*, New York, Anchor Books and Doubleday and Co., 1968.

Quiggin, Hingston A., *A Survey of Primitive Money: The Beginning of Currency*, London, Methuen, 1963.

Racine, Luc, "L'Obligation de rendre les présents et l'esprit de la chose donnée: de Marcel Mauss à René Maunier," *Diogène*, 154 (1991), pp. 69–94.

Ray, Vern (ed.), *Systems of Political Control and Bureaucracy in Human Societies*, Seattle, University of Washington Press, 1958, pp. 30–41.

Roheim, Geza, "Heiligies Geld in Melanesien," *Internationale Zeitschrift für Psychyoanalyse*, 9 (1923), pp. 384–401.

Rospabé, Philippe, *La Dette de vie. Aux origines de la monnaie*, preface by Alain Caillé, Paris, La Découverte and MAUSS, 1995.

Rothkrug, Lionel, "Popular Religion and Holy Shrines," in J. Obelkevitch (ed.), *Religion and People*, Chapel Hill, University of North Carolina Press, 1987.

Rubel, Paula and Abraham Rosman, *Feasting with My Enemy*, New York, Columbia University Press, 1971.

Rubel, Paula and Abraham Rosman, "Potlatch and Hakari: An Analysis of Maori Society in Terms of the Potlatch Model," *Man*, 6 (1971), pp. 660–73.

"Le Sacrifice," in *Systèmes de pensée en Afrique noire*, publication of the Fifth Section of the École Pratique des Hautes Études, cahiers nos. 2, 3, 4, 5, 6, 1976, 1978, 1979, 1981, 1983.

Sahlins, Marshall, "Poor Man, Rich Man, Big Man, Chief," *Comparative Studies in Society and History*, 5 (1963), pp. 285–303.

Sahlins, Marshall, "On the Sociology of Primitive Exchange," in Michael Banton (ed.), *The Relevance of Models for Social Anthropology*, London, Tavistock Publication, 1965, pp. 139–236.

Sahlins, Marshall, "Philosophie politique de l' 'Essai sur le don'," *L'Homme*, 8, 4 (1968), pp. 5–17.

Sahlins, Marshall, "*The Spirit of the Gift*: une explication de texte," in *Échanges et communications. Mélanges offerts à Claude Lévi-Strauss à l'occasion de son soixantième anniversaire*, Leiden, Mouton, 1970, vol. 2, pp. 998–1012.

Sahlins, Marshall, "The Spirit of the Gift," in *Stone Age Economics*, New York, Aldine and De Gruyter, 1972, pp. 149–83.

Schulte-Tenckhoff, Isabelle, *Potlatch, conquête et invention*, Lausanne, Éditions d'en bas, 1986.

Schwimmer, Eric, "Le Don en Mélanésie et chez nous: les contradictions irréductibles," *Anthropologie et sociétés*, 19, 1–2 (1995), pp. 71–94.

Seizelet, Eric, *Monarchie et démocratie dans le Japon d'après-guerre*, Paris, Maisonneuve & Larose, 1990.

Servet, Jean-Michel, *Essai sur les origines des monnaies*, Lyon, Université de Lyon-III, 1974.

Servet, Jean-Michel, *Numismata, État et origines de la monnaie*, Lyon, Presses Universitaires de Lyon, 1984.

Shannon, Claude Elwood and Warren Weaver, *The Mathematical Theory of Communication*, Urbana, University of Illinois Press, 1949.

Silber, Ilana, "Gift-Giving in the Great Traditions: The Case of Donations to Monasteries in the Medieval West," *Archives européennes de sociologie*, 36 (1995), pp. 209–43 (lecture given in Princeton, 1995).

Sillitoe, Paul, *Give and Take: Exchange in Wola Society*, Canberra, Australian National University Press, 1979.

Sinclair, James, *Behind the Ranges: Patrolling in New Guinea*, Victoria, Melbourne University Press, 1966.

Snyder, Sally, "Quest for the Sacred in Northern Puget Sound: An Interpretation of Potlatch," *Ethnology*, 14 (1975), pp. 149–61.

Specht, Jim and Peter White (eds), "Trade and Exchange in Oceania and Australia," special issue of *Mankind*, 11 (1978).

Sraffa, Pietro, *Production of Commodities by Means of Commodities: Prelude to a Critique of Economic Theory*, Cambridge, Cambridge University Press, 1960.

Strathern, Andrew, "Finance and Production: Two Strategies in New Guinea Highlands Exchange Systems," *Oceania*, 40 (1969), pp. 42–67.

Strathern, Andrew, *The Rope of Moka: Big Men and Ceremonial Exchange in Mount Hagen, New Guinea*, Cambridge, Cambridge University Press, 1971.

Strathern, Andrew, "By Toil or by Guile? The Use of Toils and Crescents by Tolai and Hagen Men," *Journal de la Société des Océanistes*, 31, 49 (1975), pp. 363–78.

Strathern, Andrew, "Transactional Continuity in Mount Hagen," in B. Kapferer (ed.), *Transaction and Meaning*, Philadelphia, Institute for the Study of Human Issues, 1976, pp. 217–87.

Strathern, Andrew, "Finance and Production Revisited," in G. Dalton (ed.), *Research in Economic Anthropology*, Greenwich, CT, JAI Press, 1978.

Strathern, Andrew, "*Tambu* and *Kina*: 'Profit', Exploitation and Reciprocity in Two New Guinea Exchange Systems," *Mankind*, 11 (1978), pp. 253–64.

Strathern, Andrew, "The Central and the Contingent: Bridewealth among the Melpa and the Wiru," in J. L. Komaroff (ed.), *The Meaning of Marriage Payments*, London, Academic Press, 1980, pp. 49–66.

Strathern, Andrew, "Alienating the Inalienable," *Man*, 17 (1982), pp. 548–51.

Strathern, Andrew, "The Kula in Comparative Perspective," in Jerry and Edmund Leach, *The Kula*, Cambridge, Cambridge University Press, 1983, ch. 2.

Strathern, Marilyn, "Culture in a Netbag," *Man*, 16 (1981), pp. 665–88.

Strathern, Marilyn, "Subject or Object? Women and the Circulation of Valuables in Highlands New Guinea," in R. Hirschon (ed.), *Women and Property, Women as Property*, London, Croom Helm, 1984, pp. 158–75.

Strathern, Marilyn, "Marriage Exchanges: A Melanesian Context," *Annual Review of Anthropology*, 13 (1984), pp. 41–73.

Strathern, Marilyn, *The Gender of the Gift*, Berkeley, University of California Press, 1988.

Suttles, Wayne, "Affinal Ties, Subsistence and Prestige among the Coast Salish," *American Anthropologist*, 62 (1960), pp. 296–305.

Tcherkézoff, Serge, "La Question du 'genre' à Samoa. De l'illusion dualiste à la hiérarchie des niveaux," *Anthropologie et sociétés*, 16, 2 (1992), pp. 91–117.

Testart, Alain, *Les Chasseurs-cueilleurs ou l'origine des inégalités*, Paris, Société d'Ethnographie, 1982.

Testart, Alain, *De la nécessité d'être initié*, Nanterre, Société d'Ethnologie, 1992.

Testart, Alain, *Des dons et des dieux*, Paris, Armand Colin, 1993.

Testart, Alain, "Des rhombes et des tjurunga: la question des objets sacrés en Australie," *L'Homme*, 125 (1993), pp. 31–65.

Thomas, Yan, "L'Institution de l'origine: *Sacra Principiorum Populi Romani*," in Marcel Détienne (ed.), *Tracés de fondation*, Leuven and Paris, Peeters, 1990, pp. 143–70.

Thomas Aquinas, *Summa Theologica*, Complete English edition in 5 volumes, translated by the Fathers of the English Dominican Province, Westminster, MD, Christian Classics, 1981.

Titmus, Richard, *The Gift Relationship: From Human Blood to Social Policy*, London, George Allen and Unwin, 1971.

Toffin, Gérard, "Hiérarchie et idéologie du don dans le monde indien," *L'Homme*, 30 (2), 114 (1990), pp. 130–42.

Tort, Michel, "Le Différend," *Psychanalystes*, 33 (1989), pp. 9–17.

Trautmann, Thomas, "*The Gift* in India: Marcel Mauss as Indianist," lecture given at the 36th meeting of the Society of Asian Studies, 1986.

Turgot, Jacques, *Écrits économiques*, Paris, Calmann-Lévy, 1970.

Valeri, Valerio, *Kingship and Sacrifice: Ritual and Society in Ancient Hawaii*, Chicago, University of Chicago Press, 1985.

Vayda, Peter A., "A Reexamination of Northwest Coast Economic Systems," *Transactions of the New York Academy of Sciences*, 2, 23 (7), (1961), pp. 618–24.

Vilar, Pierre, *Or et monnaie dans l'histoire*, Paris, Flammarion, 1975.

Weiner, Annette, *Women of Value, Men of Renown: New Perspectives in Trobriand Exchange*, Austin, University of Texas Press, 1976.

Weiner, Annette, "Inalienable Wealth," *American Ethnologist*, 12, 2 (1985), pp. 210–27.

Weiner, Annette, *Inalienable Possessions: The Paradox of Keeping-while-Giving*, Berkeley, University of California Press, 1992.

Weiner, Annette, "Plus précieux que l'or: relations et échanges entre hommes et femmes dans les sociétés d'Océanie," *Annales ESC*, 2 (1992), pp. 222–45.

Weiner, Annette and Jane Schneider, *Cloth and Human Experience*, Washington, Smithsonian Institution, 1989.

Weiner, James, *The Heart of the Pearl-Shell*, Berkeley, University of California Press, 1988.

Wiener, Norbert, *Cybernetics*, New York, John Wiley, 1948.

Will, Eric, "De l'aspect éthique des origines grecques de la monnaie," *Revue historique*, (October–December, 1954), pp. 209–31.

Notes

~~~

Introduction

1 Marcel Mauss, "Essai sur le don. Forme et raison de l'échange dans les sociétés archaïques," *L'Année sociologique*, new series, 1 (1925), reprinted in *Sociologie et anthropologie* (Paris, Presses Universitaires de France 1950). Translated into English as *The Gift: The Form and Reason for exchange in Archaic Societies*, transl. by W. D. Halls, Foreword by Mary Douglas (New York and London, W. W. Norton, 1990), p. 65. The quotations are taken from the English edn, hereafter cited as *The Gift*. Some passages have been retranslated for this edition.

2 *The Gift*, p. 75.

3 *The Gift*, p. 3.

4 Claude Lévi-Strauss, "Introduction à l'œuvre de Mauss," in *Sociologie et anthropologie* (Paris, Presses Universitaires de France, 1950). English transl., *Introduction to the Work of Marcel Mauss*, transl. by Felicity Baker (London, Routledge and Kegan Paul, 1987), p. 47; all references are to the English edn.

5 Maurice Godelier, *La Production des Grands Hommes* (Paris, Fayard, 1982; new edn 1996). English transl., *The Making of Great Men: Male Domination and Power among the New Guinea Baruya*, transl. by Rupert Swyer (Cambridge, Cambridge University Press, 1986); all references are to the English edition.

6 Annette Weiner, *Inalienable Possessions: The Paradox of Keeping-while-Giving* (Berkeley, University of California Press, 1992).

Chapter 1   The Legacy of Mauss

1 Mauss, *The Gift*, p. 14.

2 *The Gift*, p. 7.

3 *The Gift*. pp. 11–13. The emphasis is ours. Elsdon Best spells the name of

his Maori informant "Tamati Ranapiri," while Mauss always writes "Ranaipiri." I have kept Mauss' spelling because it appears in so many of the quotations.

4 *The Gift*, p. 43.
5 *The Gift*, p. 45.
6 *The Gift*, p. 45.
7 Claude Lévi-Strauss, *Introduction to the Work of Marcel Mauss* (London, Routledge and Kegan Paul, 1987), p. 46.
8 *Introduction*, pp. 48–9.
9 *Introduction*, p. 47.
10 *Introduction*, p. 55.
11 *Introduction*, pp. 63 and 64.
12 *Introduction*, p. 64.
13 "In certain essential domains, such as that of kinship, the analogy with language, so strongly asserted by Mauss, could enable us to discover the precise rules by which, in any type of society, cycles of reciprocity are formed whose automatic laws are henceforth known, enabling the use of deductive reasoning in a domain which seemed subject to the most total arbitrariness" (Lévi-Strauss, *Introduction*, p. 43).
14 *Introduction*, pp. 43–4. Lévi-Strauss is referring to Norbert Wiener, who had just published his famous work, *Cybernetics* (New York, John Wiley, 1948) and to Claude E. Shannon and Warren Weaver's *The Mathematical Theory of Communication* (Urbana, University of Illinois Press, 1949).
15 *Introduction*, pp. 45–6.
16 *Introduction*, p. 47.
17 Vincent Descombes had already demonstrated this in "L'Équivoque du symbolique," *Confrontations*, 3 (1980), p. 93:

> By replacing the sacred, an admittedly unsettling notion, by the symbolic, a concept apparently cleansed of all mystery, French sociology thought it had moved a step closer to understanding its object. But it then asks this symbolism to perform services it is not equipped to render. It is supposed, at the same time, to partake of algebra, in other words of the manipulation of symbols, and of "symbolic efficacy," as Lévi-Strauss says, that is, of a sacrament. Sacrifices and sacraments have the effect of producing the social body, which spawns algebraists: and one catches oneself dreaming of a self-producing algebra which would make it possible to manipulate the social body. The theory of the symbolic always has a foot in both camps, then: it is half algebraic algebra and half religious algebra. It is therefore indispensable to forgo the "symbolic," however prestigious, in order to move beyond structuralism and once again envisage the enigmatic reality of the sacred.

I personally do not think that we either need to or can "forgo the symbolic." The problem is to establish its true place in the production of society, of our social being, and to determine whether this place dominates or is subordinate to the other components of reality.
18 Lévi-Strauss, *Introduction*, p. 48.
19 *Introduction*, pp. 57–8.
20 Karl Marx: "It is in reality much easier to discover by analysis the earthly kernel of the misty creations of religion than to do the opposite, i.e. to develop from the actual given relations of life their corresponding heavenly

forms" (*Capital: A Critique of Political Economy*, Harmondsworth Penguin Books in association with New Left Review, vol. 1, transl. by Ben Fowkes, 1976, p. 494; translation slightly modified):

> value is here the independently acting agent of a process in which, while constantly assuming the form in turn of money and commodities, changes its own magnitude, throws off surplus-value from itself considered as original value, and thus valorizes itself independently. ... By virtue of being a value, it has acquired the occult ability to add value to itself. It brings forth living offspring, or at least lays golden eggs. (ibid., p. 255)

It is the "personification of things and reification of the relations of production, this religion of everyday life" (ibid., vol. 3, transl. by David Fernbach, 1981, p. 969). Cf. Maurice Godelier, "Économie marchande, fétichisme, magie et science selon Marx dans *Le Capital*," *La Nouvelle Revue de psychanalyse*, special issue "Objets du fétichisme," 2 (Autumn 1970), pp. 197–213. It was one of Hegel's fundamental ideas that logic (knowledge of the essence) should be the basis of phenomenonology (knowledge of appearances).

21 Lévi-Strauss, *Introduction*, p. 30.
22 *Introduction*, p. 56.
23 *Introduction*, p. 53.
24 *Introduction*, p. 36.
25 *Introduction*, p. 35.
26 *Introduction*, pp. 55–6.
27 *Introduction*, p. 64.
28 *Introduction*, p. 63.
29 *Introduction*, pp. 62–3.
30 *Introduction*, p. 21.
31 *Introduction*, pp. 59–61.
32 *Introduction*, p. 37.
33 "Mauss still thinks it possible to develop a sociological theory of symbolism, whereas it is obvious that what we need to look for is a symbolic origin of society" (Lévi-Strauss, *Introduction*, p. 21; translation modified).
34 Jacques Lacan, *Écrits* (Paris, Éditions du Seuil, 1960), p. 810. Lacan, in his constant effort to "emphasize the autonomy of the symbolic," which Freud, as he rightly remarks, "never formulated," is much less circumspect than Lévi-Strauss when the latter posits a big-bang theory of the emergence of language. For Lacan, the symbolic order is "absolutely irreducible to what is commonly called human experience" (p. 368), "nor can it be deduced from any historical or psychic process of origination," somewhat like Descartes' idea of God which cannot be a product of the human mind because human intelligence is finite and, since the idea of God supposes the infinite, only God himself could have put the idea into people's heads. Furthermore, Lacan also, as Jean-Joseph Goux stresses, "multiplies the historical and anthropological references pointing to certain socially and historically privileged moments in which this symbolic order emerges ... the exchange of women, hieroglyphics, algebra, the name of the father, sacred writings, law codes, machines" ("Les Médiateurs de l'échange," contribution to the seminar *Psychanalyse et sciences sociales*, Paris, 1994).
35 *"I therefore claim to show, not how men think in myths, but how myths think themselves in men's minds without their being aware of the fact. And*

... *it would perhaps be better to go still further and, disregarding the thinking subject completely, proceed as if the myths were thinking among themselves or thinking each other*" (the italics are Lévi-Strauss') (Lévi-Strauss, *Le Cru et le cuit*, Paris, Plon, 1964). Quoted from the English translation, *The Raw and the Cooked: Introduction to a Science of Mythology*, transl. by John and Dorene Weightman (Harmondsworth, Penguin, 1986; translation modified), p. 12.

36 Freud: "If, assimilating as is customary, activity and masculinity, we want to call [the libido] male, we should nevertheless not forget that it also represents aspirations to passive goals ... the expression 'female libido' is totally unjustified" (*Nouvelles Conférences d'introduction à la psychanalyse*, transl. Rose-Marie Zeitlin, Paris, Gallimard, 1984, p. 176; Translated from the French version).

37 Cf. Michel Tort, "Le Différend," *Psychanalystes*, 33 (1989), pp. 9–17.

38 Jean-Joseph Goux, "A propos des trois ronds," in *Lacan avec les philosophes* (Paris, Albin Michel, 1991), pp. 173–8.

39 Karl Marx, *A Contribution to the Critique of Political Economy* (New York, International Publishers, 1970), p. 124.

40 This dogma is already found in the mid-nineteenth century and does not disappear until the early twentieth.

41 Marx, *Capital*, vol. 1, pp. 189–90: "Since the expression of the value of commodities is purely an ideal act, we may use purely imaginary or ideal gold to perform this operation."

42 *The Gift*, p. 14.

43 *The Gift*, p. 15.

44 Mauss compares to offerings and sacrifices the practice of giving alms, which resembles gift-giving to the extent that the latter contributes to the redistribution of wealth and that the wealthy are always in danger of displaying an excess of wealth intolerable to others. But alms are also a portion of the sacrifice that the gods willingly leave for humans. Mauss traces back to the Hebrew term *zedaqa* and the Arabic *sadaka* the origin of the doctrine of charity and alms, "which, with Christianity and Islam, spread around the world" (*The Gift*, p. 18.)

45 *The Gift*, p. 16. Mauss also writes:

> Contract sacrifice supposes institutions of the kind we have described [potlatch, kula, etc.] and, conversely, contract sacrifice realizes them to the full, because those gods who give and return gifts are there to give a considerable thing in the place of a small one. It is perhaps not a result of pure chance that the two solemn formulas of the contract – in Latin *do ut des*, in Sanskrit, *dadami se, dehi me* – also have been preserved in religious texts. (*The Gift*, p. 17.)

46 *The Gift*, p. 16.

47 *The Gift*, p. 14.

48 *The Gift*, pp. 16–17.

49 *The Gift*, pp. 43–4.

50 *The Gift*, p. 134, n. 245.

51 "It would seem that among the Kwakiutl there were two kinds of copper objects: the more important ones that do not go out of the family ... and certain others that circulate intact, that are of less value, and that seem to serve as satellites for the first kind" (*The Gift*, p. 134, n. 245). And

concerning the Trobrianders' valuables: "the two kinds of *vaygu'a*, those of the *kula* and those that Malinowski for the first time calls 'permanent' *vayg'ua*, those which do not enter into obligatory exchanges" (*The Gift*, pp. 16–17).

52 *The Gift*, pp. 9–10. Cf. Annette Weiner, "Plus précieux que l'or: relations et échanges entre hommes et femmes dans les sociétés d'Océanie," *Annales ESC*, 2 (1992), pp. 222–45.

53 Maurice Godelier, "L'Occident – miroir brisé," *Annales ESC*, 5 (September–October 1993), pp. 1183–1207.

54 Cf. Georges Francillon, "Un profitable échange de frères chez les Tetum du Sud-Timor central," *L'Homme*, 29, 1 (1989), pp. 26–43.

55 Jacques Dournes, *Coordonnées-structures joraï familiales et sociales* (Paris, Institut d'Ethnologie, 1972).

56 *Sumbola*, in other words, contracts, treaties. Quoted by Vincent Descombes, "L'Équivoque du symbolique," p. 92.

57 *The Gift*, p. 6.

58 *The Gift*, p. 36.

59 *Manuel d'ethnographie* (Paris, Payot, 1947), p. 185. W. D. Halls has translated *prestation* as "service." However the French term covers much more, not only the exchange of services, but of material wealth, women, rituals, spells, etc. We have therefore adopted the French term.

60 *The Gift*, pp. 4–5.

61 *The Gift*, p. 6.

62 *Manuel*, p. 188.

63 *Manuel*, p. 185.

64 *The Gift*, p. 5.

65 *The Gift*, p. 5.

66 *The Gift*, p. 5.

67 *The Gift*, pp. 6.

68 *The Gift*, p. 7

69 *The Gift*, p. 8.

70 Christopher Gregory, *Gifts and Commodities* (London and New York, Academic Press, 1982).

71 *The Gift*, p. 3.

72 *The Gift*, p. 54.

73 *The Gift*, p. 134, n. 245.

74 *The Gift*, p. 153, n. 125.

75 On this point, the reader may consult: Peter Gathercole, "Hau, Mauri and Utu: A Re-examination," *Mankind*, 11 (1978), pp. 334–40; Grant MacCall, "Association and Power in Reciprocity and Requital: More on Mauss and the Maori," *Oceania*, 52, 4 (1982), pp. 303–19; Geoffry Mac-Cormack, "Mauss and the 'Spirit' of the Gift," *Oceania*, 52, 4 (1982), pp. 286–93; Luc Racine, "L'Obligation de rendre les présents et l'esprit de la chose donnée: de Marcel Mauss à René Maunier," *Diogène*, 154 (1991), pp. 69–94; Michel Panoff, "Marcel Mauss: The Gift Revisited," *Man*, 5 (1970), pp. 60–70.

76 Marcel Mauss, *Manuel*, p. 177.

77 *Manuel*, p. 177.

78 *Manuel*, p. 179; our emphasis.

79 (London, Routledge, 1929).

80 Firth, *Primitive Economics of the New Zealand Maori*, p. 420.

81 *Échanges et communications* (Leiden, Mouton, 1970), 2 vols, pp.

998–1012. Reprinted in Marshall Sahlins, *Stone Age Economics* (New York, Aldine and De Gruyter, 1972), pp. 149–83.

82 For the English translation, see *The Gift*, p. 11.

83 Quoted from Sahlins, *Stone Age Economics*, p. 152. Paradoxically, like Mauss, Bruce Biggs omitted from the first sentence the phrase in which Ranaipiri refers to the *whangai hau* rite, which we have reintroduced. In passing I would point out that Mauss, following Best, clearly states that *taonga* are "personal property"; this is not mentioned in the Maori text.

84 Elsdon Best, "Maori Forest Lore..." Part III, *Transactions of the New Zealand Institute*, 42: pp. 433–81 (p. 439), quoted in Sahlins, *Stone Age Economics*, p. 158. After this passage, Best quoted Ranaipiri, who explained that there were two fires, one for the priests and the other for the sister of the clan chief who owned these hunting grounds, her presence attesting to these rights. Annette Weiner criticized Marshall Sahlins for having cut this passage, thus erasing this woman from the scene and the political and minimizing the religious importance of women in this society. Cf. A. Weiner, "Inalienable Wealth," *American Ethnologist*, 12, 2 (1985), pp. 210–27.

85 Elsdon Best, *Forest Lore of the Maori* (1909) (Wellington, E. C. Keating, Government Printer, 1977), pp. 7, 8, 9.

86 *Forest Lore of the Maori*, p. 198.

87 Sahlins, *Stone Age Economics*, p. 160.

88 *Stone Age Economics*, pp. 160–1.

89 *Stone Age Economics*, p. 160.

90 *The Gift*, pp. 11–12.

91 *The Gift*, pp. 11–12.

92 *The Gift*, p. 91, n. 32.

93 It should be remembered that Mauss' disciples, including those who worked most closely with him, did not unanimously accept their master's hypothesis of the existence of a spirit in the object which made it want to return to its point of departure. For example, René Maunier, who on Mauss' advice studied the Kabyle *taoussa*, i.e. the competitive gift-giving at critical moments in the life-cycle (birth, circumcision, betrothal, marriage, funeral, etc.), did not follow his master on this point. See "Recherches sur les échanges rituels en Afrique du Nord," *L'Année sociologique* (1972), pp. 12–87.

94 Marcel Mauss was familiar with the nineteenth-century authors Krause and Jacobsen, and with the work of Boas' contemporaries, Sapir, Hill Tont, etc.

95 *The Gift*, p. 6.

96 *The Gift*, p. 6.

97 *The Gift*, p. 6.

98 *The Gift*, p. 37.

99 *The Gift*, p. 40.

100 *The Gift*, p. 37.

101 *The Gift*, p. 115, n. 148.

102 *The Gift*, p. 39.

103 *The Gift*, pp. 41–2.

104 *The Gift*, p. 74.

105 *The Gift*, p. 122, n. 201.

106 *The Gift*, p. 43.

107 *The Gift*, p. 44 and p. 132, n. 240.

108 *The Gift*, p. 134, n. 245.

109 *The Gift*, p. 44.
110 *The Gift*, p. 44.
111 *The Gift*, p. 43.
112 *The Gift*, p. 43.
113 *The Gift*, p. 45.
114 *The Gift*, p. 45.
115 *The Gift*, p. 131, n. 237.
116 *The Gift*, p. 44.
117 *The Gift*, p. 45.
118 *The Gift*, pp. 45–6.
119 Claude Meillassoux, "Potlatch," *Encyclopaedia universalis* (Paris, 1980), vol. 13, p. 424.
120 Marie Mauzé, "Boas, les Kwakiutl et le potlatch: éléments pour une réévaluation," *L'Homme*, 26, 4 (October–November 1986), pp. 21–63. Since the publication of this article, a new book has come out which has added to our knowledge about the potlatch: Serguei Kan, *Symbolic Immortality: The Tlingit Potlatch of the Nineteenth Century* (Washington, Smithsonian Institution Press, 1989).
121 Claude Meillassoux, "Commentaire à l'article de Marie Mauzé," *L'Homme*, 26, 4 (1986), pp. 54–5.
122 It is simply the money invested in financial operations that gives the illusion that money creates money. Elsewhere it is necessary to exchange money for means of production, means of consumption, labor, or services *before* money begins to flow in.
123 *The Gift*, p. 69.
124 Marcel Fournier, *Marcel Mauss* (Paris, Fayard, 1994), pp. 417ff.
125 *The Gift*, p. 154, n. 7.
126 *The Gift*, p. 76.
127 *The Gift*, p. 66.
128 *The Gift*, p. 67.
129 *The Gift*, p. 109, n. 123; our emphasis. Elsewhere Mauss adds that "even the work of older professional ethnographers (Krause, Jacobsen) or more recent ones (Sapir, Hill Tont, etc.) tend in the same direction."
130 *The Gift*, p. 109, n. 123.
131 *The Gift*, p. 109, n. 123.
132 "Essai sur le don," p. 208, n. 3. Nevertheless he compares Kwakiutl chiefs with their Celtic, Germanic, etc. counterparts as they must have been *before* the development of feudalism in Western Europe. "Germanic civilization ... remained an essentially feudal and peasant society, and the notions and even the terms 'buying price' and 'selling price' seem to be of recent origin. In earlier times it had developed to the extreme the entire system of potlatches, but in particular, the complete system of gifts [nonagonistic prestations]" (*The Gift*, p. 60). Mauss cites Tacitus, an obligatory reference in Europe since Grimm.
133 *The Gift*, p. 136, n. 256.
134 *The Gift*, p. 122, n. 209.
135 *The Gift*, p. 114, n. 144.
136 *The Gift*, p. 110, n. 131.
137 *The Gift*, p. 110, n. 131; our emphasis. To my knowledge, Jean Lojkine, in his article, "Mauss et l'‘Essai sur le don’: portée contemporaine d'une étude anthropologique sur une économie non marchande" (*Cahiers internationaux de sociologie*, 86, 1 [1989], pp. 141–58), is one of the few to have

highlighted the effort Mauss put into decentering and recentering his theory with respect to political economic concepts. A Marxist himself, Lojkine considers Meillassoux's criticism of Mauss to be unfounded and out of place (p. 143).

138 *The Gift*, p. 72; our emphasis. Mauss is referring to Malinowski's article entitled "The Primitive Economy of the Trobriand Islanders," *Economic Journal*, 31, 121 (March 1921), pp. 1–16.

139 *The Gift*, p. 72.

140 *The Gift*, pp. 72–3; our emphasis.

141 *The Gift*, p. 33; our emphasis.

142 *The Gift*, p. 76; our emphasis. For the idea of total social phenomena, see also pp. 30, 35, and 46.

143 *The Gift*, p. 79.

144 *The Gift*, p. 80.

145 Pietro Sraffa, *Production of Commodities by Means of Commodities: Prelude to a Critique of Economic Theory* (Cambridge, Cambridge University Press, 1960).

146 Unlike Marilyn Strathern (*The Gender of the Gift*, Berkeley, University of California Press, 1988), I think that commercial relations have existed for centuries alongside gift-exchanges in the societies Mauss analyzed, and, conversely, that gift-exchange is still a widespread practise in market economies. I see no "essential" opposition between Melanesian societies as "gift-based" societies and Western society as a "commodity-based" society.

147 Maurice Godelier, *L'Idéel et le matériel. Pensée, économies, sociétés* (Paris, Fayard, 1984). English translation, *The Mental and the Material. Thought, Economy and Society*, transl. by Martin Thom (London and New York, Verso, 1986).

148 Jean Lojkine ("Mauss et 'L'Essai sur le don'," pp. 153–4) is also one of the few to have emphasized that "non-commercial" reciprocity does not mean transparencey, and that there is such a thing as "non-commercial fetishism," of which the potlatch is a perfect example. Lojkine makes it clear that Marx did not see this when he wrote: "but every serf knows, without having to consult Adam Smith, that what he expends in the service of his lord is a specific quantity of his own personal labour-power. The tithe owed to the priest is more clearly apparent than his benediction." And he goes on to ask how the force of religion is to be explained, or the sacred character of royal power.

149 In a certain manner, money is a substitute both for sacred and for precious objects, which were themselves originally substitutes: the former for gods, the latter for humans. The interplay of substitutes can be carried further still. A striking example is provided by the money the Chinese use for offerings; these are pieces of paper printed like money which are burned in ritual dishes in the home as an offering to the house gods. This money is divided into gold money (burned for the heavenly gods) and silver money (burned for the evil spirits and the shades that inhabit the nether world). These monies are used by the faithful on their own initiative. In addition there are "treasury monies" and "monies for resolving crises." These require a specialist. These monies have been analyzed in a remarkable study by Hou Chin-Lang, *Monnaies d'offrande et la notion de trésorerie dans la religion chinoise* (Paris, Presses Universitaires de France and Maisonneuve, 1975). Behind these practices lies the idea that there exists a capital of life and happiness; when an individual is born, he incurs a debt *vis-à-vis* the

treasury, a sort of bank with two accounting systems, one celestial, the other infernal, which manages the relations humans entertain with the spirits and the gods. I will come back to this theme at the close of this book, when I refer to the Rig Veda and to the notion of life-debt in India.

150 *The Gift*, p. 48.
151 *The Gift*, p. 47.
152 *The Gift*, p. 60.
153 *The Gift*, p. 55.
154 *The Gift*, p. 74.
155 "L'Essai sur le don", p. 208, n. 3.
156 *The Gift*, p. 133, n. 243.
157 *The Gift*, p. 16.
158 *The Gift*, p. 118, n. 167.
159 E.g. Alain Testart, *Les Chasseurs-cueilleurs ou l'origine des inégalités* (Paris, Société d'Ethnographie, 1982).
160 *The Gift*, p. 81.
161 *The Gift*, p. 68; emphasis in Mauss.
162 *The Gift*, p. 75.
163 *The Gift*, p. 77.
164 *The Gift*, p. 69.
165 Homer G. Barnett, "The Nature of the Potlatch," *American Anthropologist*, 40 (1938), pp. 349–58.
166 Indeed, Kirchoff had already outlined a model of this type of social organization and had compared it to the kin groups found in the Polynesian kingdoms, the *kainga*. Marie Mauzé's article, "Boas, Les Kwakiutl et le potlatch: éléments pour une réévaluation" (*L'Homme*, 26, 4, October–December 1986) gives a clear summary of what we know about their social organization.
167 Georges Bataille, *La Part maudite* (Paris, Éditions de Minuit, 1967).
168 Marie Mauzé, "La Loi anti-potlatch chez les Kwagul," *Bulletin de l'Amérique indienne*, 29 (1983), pp. 3–5, 9–11, 30–1.
169 *The Gift*, p. 133, n. 243. "Boas has studied closely the way in which each copper object increases in value with the series of potlatches: the value of the Lesaxalayo copper objects in about 1906–1910 was 50 boats, 6000 buttoned blankets, 260 silver bracelets, 60 gold bracelets, 70 gold earrings, 40 sewing machines, 25 gramophones, 50 masks."
170 "Even after long contact with Europeans – since the eighteenth century with the Russians, and since the beginning of the nineteenth century, with French Canadian trappers – apparently none of the considerable transfers of wealth constantly taking place among them is carried out save in the solemn form of the potlatch" (*The Gift*, pp. 33 and 108, n. 119).
171 "At least in lands such as those of the Haida and the Tlingit, where phratries exist, there still remain considerable traces of the one-time total prestations. Presents are exchanged for any and every reason, for every 'service' and every thing is given back later, or even at once, and is immediately given out again. ... Older writers describe the potlatch no differently, so much so that one may wonder whether it constitutes a distinct institution" (*The Gift*, p. 42).
172 *The Gift*, p. 21.
173 *The Gift*, p. 21.
174 *The Gift*, p. 21.
175 *The Gift*, p. 26.

176 *The Gift*, p. 105, n. 63. Mauss pays the same tribute to Turnwald, who studied the Banaro in New Guinea and the Buin in the Solomon Islands.

177 *The Gift*, p. 72.

178 *The Gift*, p. 99, n. 18.

179 *The Gift*, p. 21.

180 *The Gift*, p. 21.

181 *The Gift*, p. 22.

182 *The Gift*, p. 22.

183 *The Gift*, p. 27.

184 *The Gift*, p. 22.

185 *The Gift*, p. 23.

186 At least so it seemed in Malinowski's day; today the directions are reversed, without it being clear when and why this switch took place.

187 *The Gift*, p. 24.

188 *The Gift*, p. 26. Mauss also cites Malinowski, who refers to Dobuan comments on the kula, comparing armshells and necklaces to dogs "playfully nuzzling one another" (*The Gift*, p. 25).

189 *The Gift*, p. 24.

190 *The Gift*, p. 24.

191 *The Gift*, p. 102, n. 32.

192 *The Gift*, p. 28.

193 *The Gift*, p. 28.

194 *The Gift*, p. 23.

195 *The Gift*, pp. 23–4.

196 *The Gift*, p. 26.

197 *The Gift*, pp. 30–1.

198 *The Gift*, p. 32.

199 To sum up, the whole area of the islands, and probably part of the world of Southern Asia that is related to it, possess the same [?] legal and economic system. The conception one should have regarding these Melanesian tribes, even richer and more committed to trade than the Polynesians, is therefore very different from usual. These people possess an extra domestic economy and a very developed system of exchange that throbs with life more intensely and more precipitantly perhaps than the one that our peasants or the fishing villages along our coasts were familiar with maybe not even a hundred years ago. They have an extensive economic life, going beyond the confines of their islands and their dialects, which represents a considerable trade. With their gifts made and reciprocated, they have a rigorous system which takes the place of the system of buying and selling. (*The Gift*, p. 32)

It is interesting to see how Mauss advances the idea that gift-exchanges in these societies have greater economic importance and are more dynamic than commercial relations, which also exist.

200 *The Gift*, p. 32.

201 *The Gift*, p. 32.

202 *The Gift*, p. 16.

203 *The Gift*, pp. 16–17. Mauss is referring to Malinowski's article published in 1917 in the *Journal of the Royal Anthropological Institute*, no. 45: "Baloma, the Spirits of the Dead in the Trobriand Islands."

204 *The Gift*, p. 100, n. 22.

205 Mauss cites a kula spell from the island of Sinaketa, which emphasizes this rivalry: "I am going to rob my *kula*, I am going to pillage my *kula*. I am going to *kula* until my boat sinks ... My fame is a clap of thunder. My tread, an earthquake" (*The Gift*, p. 104, n. 48). And he adds: "The conclusion of the formula is also interesting, but again, only from the viewpoint of the potlatch ... The concluding line is strangely American in its outward form" (ibid.).

206 Mauss highlights Malinowski's famous passage on which Lévi-Strauss also comments: "The whole of tribal life is nothing more than a constant 'giving and receiving'; every ceremony, every legal or customary act is carried out only with a material gift and a gift in return accompanying them. Wealth given and received is one of the principal instruments of social organization, of the chief's power, of the bonds of kinship through blood or marriage" (*Argonauts of the Western Pacific*, London, Routledge, 1922, p. 167; Mauss, *The Gift*, p. 106, n. 85).

207 "To possess one is 'exhilarating, strengthening, and calming in itself'. Their owners fondle and look at them for hours. Mere contact with them passes on their virtues. *Vaygu'a* are placed on the forehead, on the chest of a dying person ... They are his supreme comfort" (*The Gift*, p. 24).

208 *The Gift*, pp. 100–2, n. 29.

209 Mauss mentions, but does not dwell on the existence of paid labor in the Trobriand Islands, where the Europeans hired pearl-fishers. But these laborers still had to fulfill their obligations to their tribes and to take part in fishing in order to exchange their catch for agricultural goods produced by inland groups. Malinowski notes: "The obligation still holds good today, in spite of the disadvantages and losses that the pearl fishermen suffer, obliged to carry on fishing and to lose considerable sums in wages to fulfil a purely social obligation" (*The Gift*, p. 106, n. 87).

210 Annette Weiner, *Women of Value, Men of Renown: New Perspectives in Trobriand Exchange* (Austin, University of Texas Press, 1976).

211 For an overview, see Jerry and Edmund Leach (eds), *The Kula: New Perspectives on Massim Exchange* (Cambridge, Cambridge University Press, 1983).

212 As women cannot take to sea for several weeks on end, they usually entrust their kula to their brothers.

213 *Mapula* is the gift that Malinowski, in the *Argonauts*, had listed under "pure gifts," a notion he later abandoned in *Crime and Custom in Savage Society*, explaining that he had not looked closely enough at the context of these gifts and that they were also part of a long chain of interested transactions between affines. Upon reading the *Argonauts*, Mauss immediately took exception to Malinowski's expression "pure gift" (*The Gift*, p. 32), saying that it "was really inapplicable"; likewise Firth, in *Elements of Social Organization* (London, Watts and Co., 1951). Nevertheless, Sahlins was to return to the notion under another label, that of "generalized reciprocity." Cf. Marshall Sahlins, *Stone Age Economics*, ch. 5.

214 Cf. Annette Weiner, *Inalienable Possessions*, chs 3 and 4, and "Plus précieux que l'or", pp. 222–45.

215 Frederick Damon, "The Kula and Generalized Exchange: Considering Some Unconsidered Aspects of the Elementary Structure of Kinship," *Man*, 15 (1980), p. 284.

216 John Kasaipwalova and Ulli Beier, *Yaulabuta: An Historical Poem from the Trobriand Islands* (Port Moresby, Institute of Papua New Guinea Studies, 1978).

217 Andrew Strathern, "The Kula in Comparative Perspective," in Jerry and Edmund Leach (eds), *The Kula*, pp. 84–5.

218 Frederick Damon, "The Problem of the Kula on Woodlark Island: Expansion, Accumulation, and Over-Production," *Ethnos*, 3–4 (1995), pp. 176–201.

219 *The Gift*, p. 24.

220 *The Gift*, p. 23–4.

221 Frederick Damon, "Representation and Experience in Kula and Western Exchange Spheres (Or, Billy)," *Research in Economic Anthropology*, 14 (1993), pp. 235–54.

222 Andrew Strathern, *The Rope of Moka: Big Men and Ceremonial Exchange in Mount Hagen, New Guinea* (Cambridge, Cambridge University Press, 1971), ch. 5.

223 Andrew Strathern, "Finance and Production: Two Strategies in New Guinea Highlands Exchange Systems," *Oceania*, 40 (1969), pp. 42–67; "Finance and Production Revisited," in G. Dalton (ed.), *Research in Economic Anthropology* (Greenwich, CT, JAI Press, 1978).

224 Andrew Strathern, "*Tambu* and *Kina*: 'Profit', Exploitation and Reciprocity in Two New Guinea Exchange Systems," *Mankind*, 11 (1978), pp. 253–64.

225 Andrew Strathern, "By Toil or by Guile? The Use of Coils and Crescents by Tolai and Hagen Big Men," *Journal de la Société des Océanistes*, 31, 49 (1975), pp. 363–78.

226 Andrew Strathern, "Alienating the Inalienable", *Man*, 17 (1982), pp. 548–51.

227 Andrew Strathern, "Transactional Continuity in Mount Hagen", in B. Kapferer (ed.), *Transaction and Meaning* (Philadelphia, Institute for the Study of Human Issues, 1976), pp. 217–87.

228 Other systems of exchange exist in Melanesia. We have not talked about the Tolai exchanges in New Britain, analyzed by R. Salisbury and A. Epstein, or the Kapauku exchanges in Irian Jaya, analyzed by Pospisil. All should be compared, like a series of vast transformations of the logics of gift exchange.

229 Godelier, *L'Idéel et le matériel*, p. 169.

Chapter 2   Substitute Objects for Humans and for the Gods

1 See the article by Patrick Guery, "Sacred Commodities: The Circulation of Medieval Relics," in Arjun Appadurai (ed.), *The Social Life of Things; Commodities in a Cultural Perspective* (Cambridge, Cambridge University Press, 1986), pp. 169–94. See also Ilana Silber, "Gift-Giving in the Great Traditions: The Case of Donations to Monasteries in the Medieval West," lecture given at Princeton University in 1995. I am grateful to I. Silber for allowing me to consult this text before its publication.

2 The notion of the fire lighted by Father-Sun and the sexual organs pierced at one go by the bursting flint stones strongly resembles Lévi-Strauss' big-bang theory of language or Lacan's theory of symbolic order. Before, nothing was possible, afterwards everything was.

3 M. Godelier, *The Making of Great Men* (Cambridge, Cambridge University Press, 1996), pp. 95–6.

4 Yan Thomas, "L'Institution de l'origine: *Sacra Principiorum Populi Romani*," in Marcel Détienne, *Tracés de fondation* (Leuven and Paris, Peeters, 1990), pp. 143–70. I am most grateful to Yan Thomas for his generous permission to use his archives and thus enabling me to search out the objects held sacred by the Romans in the many fragmentary sources he has gathered and on which he commented for me.

5 Thomas, "L'Institution de l'origine," pp. 143 and 162.

6 Dionysius of Halicarnassus, *Roman Antiquities* I. 68–9.

7 Our position follows that of Annette Weiner in her article "Inalienable Wealth," *American Ethnologist*, 12, 2 (May 1988), pp. 210–27.

8 While stressing the fact that sacred objects are those objects which are kept, and which tend to be kept out of gift- and commercial exchanges, I do not pretend to be unaware of the evidence of the buying and selling of objects, rites, and secret spells observed and described in numerous societies throughout the world and at different epochs. There are even examples in New Guinea of the "purchase" of rites and sacred objects associated with the cult of a female spirit of fertility among the Enga and other cultures. The donation of relics of the holy apostles by the popes of the Middle Ages, who disposed of the vast catacomb treasure, the trade in relics by such professionals as Deusdona, who had obtained the right to sell relics of the martyrs buried in Rome to Abbot Hilduin of Soissons, ensured the circulation throughout Europe of slivers of bone or other vestiges, which were embedded in the altars of newly constructed churches and convents and conserved there. These sacred relics, whether given or sold, were regularly coveted, stolen, or pillaged, or became the object of pilgrimages which drew thousands of worshippers and provided a source of income for the abbeys and churches that held the objects. But all this circulation, all this traffic made sense only in reference to "sacred realities" which could not be sold or traded and which resided in Rome and Jerusalem. See Guery, "Sacred Commodities," pp. 169–94. See also Lionel Rothkrug, "Popular Religion and Holy Shrines," in J. Obelkevitch (ed.), *Religion and People* (Chapel Hill, University of North Carolina Press, 1987).

9 Mauss, *The Gift*, p. 134, n. 245.

10 Godelier, *The Making of Great Men*, pp. 156–7.

11 Godelier, *The Making of Great Men*, pp. 124–5.

12 Godelier, *The Making of Great Men*, p. 70.

13 Godelier, *The Making of Great Men*, p. 70. Once the young initiates – the boys of nine or ten – have been separated from their mother and have had their septum pierced, they receive a new set of clothes which shows that they now belong to the category of first-stage initiates. These clothes are half male and half female, in accordance with this transitional stage halfway between the world of women and that of men. They wear on their buttocks a thin strip of bark which is called, precisely, "the tadpole's tail."

14 We will encounter the same theme later, when we analyze the figure of old Afek, a spirit-woman who is the main focus of worship for the tribes of the Oksapmin region in New Guinea. She is supposed to be responsible for the existence of game and cultivated plants, of hunting and agriculture, but also for life, death, and marriage.

15 Godelier, *The Making of Great Men*, p. 71.

16 Cf. M. Godelier, "Du quadruple rapport entre les catégories du masculin et du féminin," in *La Place des femmes. Les Enjeux de l'identité et de l'égalité au regard des sciences sociales* (Paris, La Découverte, 1995), pp. 439–42.

17 That is also why the Baruya language has a specific term for menstrual blood which distinguishes it from the blood that circulates in the bodies not only of men and women but also of animals.

18 An imaginary magnification of men legitimized by their exclusive access to sacred objects that have come down from the Dreamtime and which contain the power to reproduce life, not only human life, as in the case of the Baruya *kwaimatnie*, but the life of all animal and plant species. This power originally belonged to women and was stolen from them by men, as in the Australian Aboriginal myth of the Dhanggawul, three characters from the Dreamtime, a brother and two sisters. In this myth the brother steals his sisters' sacred baskets (uterus) and the phallic sticks they contain. These sacred objects are used at the moment in the initiations when the young boys' bodies are marked (circumcision, subincision), and they are shown the sacred objects and/or taught the founding myths as the original events described in them are re-enacted. It would be interesting and no doubt highly rewarding to compare the institutions and thought systems found in Australian Aboriginal and Baruya (and other New Guinea) societies.

Above and beyond the resemblances, however, large differences remain. In Australia, bull-roarers are male and female, in Baruya culture they are male. Baruya men claim only to re-engender and promote the growth of boys outside their mother's womb, whereas Aboriginal men are temporarily invested, in the course of their *intichiuma* ceremonies, with the capacity enjoyed by the Dreamtime beings, to reproduce, to multiply all living species, not only humans. We are indebted to Alain Testart for several remarkable analyses of Australian Aboriginal initiation rites, and particularly for analyses of the nature of their bull-roarers or of their *tjuringa*. Testart has analyzed the nature of the most sacred object present at the most important point in the rites performed during the last stage of the initiations, the *ambilia-ekura*, an object which must be raised and lowered by the master of the ceremony throughout the night, a gesture which determines women's fertility. This *ambilia-ekura* is made up of two *tjuringa* held together by woven hair strings; the *ambilia* is said to be the child and the *ekura*, the pocket, the uterus. This in some respects recalls the Baruya's vagina-flute, or their most powerful *kwaimatnie*, the woman-*kwaimatnie*. See Alain Testart, "Des rhombes et des tjurunga, la question des objets sacrés en Australie," *L'Homme*, 125 (1993), pp. 31–65, and esp. pp. 32–5 and 58–60; *De la nécessité d'être initié* (Nanterre, Société d'Ethnologie, 1992), esp. the chapter concerning the *engwura*, pp. 147–90; *Des dons et des dieux* (Paris, Armand Colin, 1993), chs 3 and 12. Nevertheless, I do not agree with Alain Testart when he asserts, in *Des dons et des dieux*, that "the act of revealing during the initiation is a demystification, or to put it bluntly a profession of atheism ... what the young men learn as soon as they have gone through the initiation ordeals [is that] this whole business is only a bunch of old wives' tales, cunningly orchestrated by initiated men to mislead them, [that] there is nothing supernatural to fear, no such thing exists, there are merely the male human protagonists of the ritual" (p. 37). This is a reductive view, as I will show below when I analyze what is called the "sacred."

Having briefly mentioned Testart's work, I cannot pass over the equally remarkable studies of Marika Moisseeff, whose work on the "Aranda initiation cycle," a few copies of which have been circulating informally since 1978, is finally available: *Un long chemin semé d'objets cultuels* (Paris, Éditions de l'École des Hautes Études en Sciences Sociales, 1995). See, too, her article, "Les Objets cultuels aborigènes ou comment représenter l'ir-représentable," *Genèses*, 17 (September 1994), pp. 8–32, devoted to the *tjuringa*, which Marika Moisseeff calls: "self-referring concept-artefacts." I do not conclude, as she does, that *tjuringa* are "signifiers in their pure state" (p. 32). In fact, her entire analysis proves the contrary and obviates this reference to a concept advanced by Lévi-Strauss to describe the "spirit" that dwells in things, the Maori *hau*. All these studies, those of Testart and Moisseeff, as well as my own, cannot fail to take account of Nancy Munn's now famous article, "The Transformation of Subjects into Objects in Walbiri and Pitjanjara Myth," in Robert Berndt (ed.), *Australian Aboriginal Anthropology* (Wedlands, University of Western Australia Press, 1970), pp. 141–63. See also Les R. Hiatt, "Secret Pseudo-procreative Rites among the Australian Aborigines," in L. R. Hiatt and C. Jayawardena (eds), *Anthropology in Oceania* (Sydney, Angus and Robertson, 1971), pp. 77–88.

19 My analysis does not deal with the "esthetic" or "artistic" character of sacred objects, but with the emotion inspired by the sacred character of these things. The separation between sacred and precious object is manifest in the case of the monstrance, where the sacred object – a piece of the body or the clothing of a saint – is displayed in the center, behind a plate of glass. The monstrance may be made of gold or heavily ornamented, a true work of art symbolizing the wealth of the Church and intended to glorify God and his saints. But the sacred object in its center has no character other than that of having been a piece of the body of a "friend of Christ." It is not set apart by anything particularly "beautiful." The sublime with which we are concerned has nothing to do with art, and I have used this term only for want of a better one. Perhaps "numinous" would be more fitting, but it would need a discussion which goes beyond our present scope. Cf. Rudolf Otto, *Le Sacré* (Paris, Payot, 1949).

20 C. Lévi-Strauss, *Introduction to the Work of Marcel Mauss* (London, Routledge and Kegan Paul, 1987) p. 56.

21 Lévi-Strauss, *Introduction*, p. 64.

22 Lévi-Strauss, *Introduction*, p. 53. Lévi-Strauss' book, *La Pensée sauvage* (Paris, Plon, 1962) shows clearly that the "the science of concrete things" in "primitive" societies is perfectly consistent with the construction of magical-religious systems. Such concrete knowledge provides mythic thought processes with materials, images and patterns of relations drawn from observation of the animal and plant kingdoms.

23 The imaginary, I repeat, is comprised at the same time of everything people add mentally to their real capacities and of everything they subtract from them.

24 Hence the profanatory character of the selling of masks and other sacred objects once carefully preserved in the clan to outsiders, to tourists or collectors. But there is often one individual willing to steal them from his own clan and secretly sell them for a few francs or a fistful of dollars. Hence, too, the missionaries' relentless efforts to destroy these objects, often down to the last one, in order to root out every vestige of idolatry. Public destruction is another type of profanation intended to demonstrate the superiority of the missionaries' god.

25 Brigitte Derlon, *De mémoire et d'oubli. Anthropologie des objets* malanggan *de Nouvelle-Irelande* (Paris, Éditions du Centre National de la Recherche Scientifique and Éditions de la Maison des Sciences de l'Homme, 1997);

"Droits de reproduction des objets de culte, tenure foncière et filiation en Nouvelle-Irlande," *L'Homme*, 34, 2 (1994), pp. 31–58.

26 *Coix gigantea, Konig, ex Rob.* A plant that originally came from southeast Asia. See Maurice Godelier, "La Monnaie de sel des Baruya de Nouvelle-Guinée," *L'Homme*, 9, 2 (1969), pp. 5–37; "Monnaies et richesses dans diverses types de société et leur rencontre à la périphérie du capitalisme," *Actuel Marx*, 15 (April 1994), pp. 77–97.

27 This point had already been raised by Jean-Michel Servet in 1974, in his *Essai sur les origines des monnaies* (Lyon, Université de Lyon-III), pp. 74–9. In this work, Servet criticized my sense of the term "currency" as I had used it in my first publication on Baruya salt. I concede the point all the more willingly as what I presently have to say about objects as substitutes for people and gods converges with his ideas on the origins of money being not commercial but political and religious.

28 The Baruya did not know where they came from, since the first shells came from the sea, and, until the arrival of the Europeans, they did not know of its existence. And yet their myths told of a great expanse of water, a sort of immense lake.

29 Cf. Andrew Strathern, "Finance and Production: Two Strategies in New Guinea Highlands Exchange Systems," *Oceania*, 40 (1969), pp. 42–67; *The Rope of Moka* (Cambridge, Cambridge University Press, 1971); James Weiner, *The Heart of the Pearl-Shell* (Berkeley, University of California Press, 1988).

30 Once more I would like to emphasize that, in this system, no one is interested in returning the equivalent of what he has received. This is not the goal. The goal is to place the recipient of the gift in a situation of permanent inferiority, to substitute more or less stable hierarchical relations for unstable reciprocal relations. Here, too, but in an entirely different way from non-antagonistic gifts or counter-gifts, to give in turn is not the same thing as to give back.

31 See Jack Goody and Stanley Jeyarada Tambiah (eds), *Bridewealth and Dowry* (Cambridge, Cambridge University Press, 1973), a work which gave rise to a good deal of discussion.

32 Andrew Strathern, "The Central and the Contingent: Bridewealth among the Melpa and the Wiru," in J. L. Komaroff (ed.), *The Meaning of Marriage Payments* (London, Academic Press, 1980), pp. 49–66. On the Enga *tee*, another type of ceremonial exchange, see Daryl Keith Feil, "The Bride in Bridewealth: A Case from the New Guinea Highlands," *Ethnology*, 20 (1981), pp. 63–75, and his book, *Ways of Exchange: The Enga Tee of Papua New Guinea* (St Lucia, University of Queensland Press, 1984).

33 As among the Mendi in Highlands New Guinea, who forbid direct exchange of women because it prevents affines from vying with them in competitive gift-exchange. Cf. Rena Lederman, *What Gifts Engender: Social Relations and Politics in Mendi, Highlands Papua New Guinea* (New York, Cambridge University Press, 1986). See too our analysis of this example in *Big Men and Great Men: Personifications of Power in Melanesia* (Cambridge, Cambridge University Press, and Paris, Éditions de la Maison des Sciences de l'Homme, 1991), p. 284.

34 In 1981, I witnessed an attempt on the part of a number of representatives of Baruya lineages to substitute a system of marriage payments for the traditional system of direct exchange of women, *ginamare*. This gave rise to some sharp debates, collective public discussions, in which the bulk of the young

unmarried men voiced their attachment to the tradition in order to avoid the "rich men" among them being the only ones able to marry and "have all the women." Some publicly accused their elders of wanting to "sell" their daughters whereas they had not had to "buy" their wives. The matter stopped there, but some years later a number of these young men who had left to work on plantations returned with wives they had "bought" with their money from the tribes around these plantations or from the Chimbu and other Highland groups where payment of *bridewealth* is traditional and who are always short of money because it all goes into *ceremonial exchanges.*

35 Mauss, *The Gift,* p. 37: "One not only promotes oneself, but also one's family, up the social scale." The collapse of the Indian populations on the northwest coast of the United States created an unnatural situation characterized by the fact that more and more titles fell vacant while there were fewer and fewer men with more and more European money and goods.

36 *The Gift,* pp. 37–8: "As may be seen, the notion of honour, which expresses itself violently in Polynesia and is always present in Melanesia, is, in this case [in North America], really destructive ... The Polynesian word *mana* itself symbolizes not only the magical force in every creature, but also his honour, and one of the best translations of the word is 'authority', 'wealth'."

37 *The Gift,* p. 37: "Everything is based upon the principles of antagonism and rivalry. The political status of individuals in the brotherhoods and clans, and ranks of all kinds, are gained in a 'war of prosperity', just as they are in real war, or through chance, inheritance, alliance and marriage. Yet everything is conceived of as if it were a 'struggle of wealth'." See also p. 113, n. 141: "The potlatch is a war. Among the Tlingit it bears the name of 'War Dance'."

38 To have never existed or to no longer exist.

39 *The Gift,* p. 69.

40 *The Gift,* p. 75; see also p. 77: "In our view, however, it is not in the calculation of individual needs that the method for an optimum economy is to be found."

41 James Sinclair, *Behind the Ranges: Patrolling in New Guinea* (Victoria, Melbourne University Press, 1966). In ch. 3 of this work, Sinclair tells of the arrival of his patrol, the first, among the Batiya (Baruya), the salt-makers, one July morning in 1951 (pp. 24–75).

42 *The Gift,* p. 46.

43 *The Gift,* p. 76.

44 "This ethics and this economy still function in our own societies, constantly and, so to speak, hidden below the surface" (*The Gift,* p. 4). Mauss' method was first to examine the legal systems in search of economic and moral forms of gift-giving. All he found in the ancient codes of the Greeks, Romans and Jews were vestiges, but he discovered a vigorous presence in the Old Germanic system which he believed could be explained, in accordance with nineteenth-century *idées reçues,* by the fact that "Germanic civilisation was itself a long time without markets" (*The Gift,* p. 60). This did not mean for him that the Germanic peoples lived in a "natural economy" (p. 5)

45 Mauss says: "In that separate existence that constitutes our social life" (*The Gift,* p. 65) and goes on to invoke pell-mell rules of hospitality, popular attitudes, and customs, etc.

46 Georges Bataille, *La Part maudite* (Paris, Éditions de Minuit, 1964). In this

work, Bataille declares his desire to uncover "the fundamental movement which strives to restore wealth to its true function, to gift-giving, to squandering without any counterpart" (*Œuvres complètes*, Paris, Gallimard, 1976, vol. 7, p. 44). For him, Aztec society with its bloody sacrifices is the very model of a consumption society (pp. 52–4).

47 See David Boyd, "The Commercialization of Ritual in the Eastern Highlands of Papua New Guinea," *Man*, 20, 2 (1985), pp. 325–40.

48 Robert Berndt, *Excess and Restraint: Social Control among a New Guinea Mountain People* (Chicago, University of Chicago Press, 1962), p. 84.

49 Jane Cobbi, "Don et contre-don. Une tradition à l'épreuve de la modernité," in A. Berque (ed.), *Le Japon et son double* (Paris, Masson, 1987), pp. 159–68; "L'Obligation du cadeau au Japon," in Charles Malamoud (ed.), *Lien de vie, nœud mortel. Les Représentations de la dette en Chine, au Japon et dans le monde entier* (Paris, Éditions de l'École des Hautes Études en Sciences Sociales, 1988), pp. 113–65; *Pratiques et représentations sociales des Japonais* (Paris, L'Harmattan, 1993), "L'Échange des cadeaux au Japon," pp. 103–16, and "Le Marché du cadeau," pp. 151–63.

50 *The Gift*, p. 18.

51 *The Gift*, p. 97, n. 79; italics added.

52 Valerio Valeri, *Kingship and Sacrifice: Ritual and Society in Ancient Hawaii* (Chicago, University of Chicago Press, 1985); Irving Goldman, *Ancient Polynesian Society* (Chicago, University of Chicago Press, 1970).

53 John Murra, "On Inca Political Structure," in Ray Vern (ed.), *Systems of Political Control and Bureaucracy in Human Societies* (Seattle, University of Washington Press, 1958), pp. 30–41.

54 Patrick V. Kirch, *The Evolution of the Polynesian Chiefdoms* (Cambridge, Cambridge University Press, 1984).

55 Cf. Mauss on Kwakiutl dishes and Haida spoons: "The dishes and spoons used solemnly for eating, and decorated, carved and emblazoned with the clan's totem of rank, are animate things. They are the replicas of the *inexhaustible instruments, the creators of food, that the spirits gave to one's ancestors* ... The dishes of the Kwakiutl and the spoons of the Haida are essential items that circulate according to very strict rules and are meticulously shared out among the clans and the families of the chiefs" (*The Gift*, p. 44; italics added). Concerning stone axes in New Guinea, see the study by Pierre and Anne-Marie Petrequin, *Écologie d'un outil. La Hache de pierre en Irian Jaya* (Paris, Éditions du Centre National de la Recherche Scientifique, 1993).

56 Cf. Michel Panoff, "Une figure de l'abjection en Nouvelle-Bretagne: le *rubbish man*," *L'Homme*, 94 (January–February 1985), pp. 57–72.

57 Marcel Mauss, *The Gift*, p. 128, n. 226.

58 Arthur Barnard Deacon, *Malekula: A Vanishing People in the New Hebrides* (London, Routledge, 1934), pp. 196–7.

59 As early as 1923, Geza Roheim had already advanced a psychoanalytic interpretation of Melanesian currencies in an article whose title he borrowed from Laum, the proponent of the sacred-origin theory of struck coins: "Heiliges Geld in Melanesien," *Internationale Zeitschrift für Psychoanalyse*, 9 (1923), pp. 384–401. More recently, A. Epstein, a remarkable connoisseur of the New Britain Tolai, a tribe which amasses huge quantities of shell-money for the purpose of seeing it redistributed at funeral ceremonies, attempted a psychoanalytic analysis of the symbolism of this money, which he associates with anal eroticism: "Tambu, the Shell Money of the Tolai," in

Robert Hook (ed.), *Fantasy and Symbol* (London, Academic Press, 1979), pp. 144–205. He finds his references in Freud, Abraham and Otto Fenichel (1938), "The Drive to Amass Wealth," in *Collected Papers* (Norton, New York, 1954), pp. 89–108. The case of the Tolai is exceptional in Oceania insofar as they were quick to adopt and develop a capitalist market economy and are one of the richest groups in New Guinea. At the same time, they went on importing and using their shell-money in all of their funeral and other rites because they considered it to be "heavier," more "moral" than the national currency, the *kina*, based on the dollar, which they did not find "moral" enough. They even started the first bank in the world to keep in reserve and to change traditional shell-money. Cf. Frederick Errington and Deborah Gewertz, *Articulating Change in the "Last Unknown"* (San Francisco, Westview Press, 1991), ch. 2: "Dueling Currencies in East New Britain: The Construction of Shell Money as National Cultural Property," pp. 49–76.

60 Jeffrey Clarck, "Pearl-Shell Symbolism in Highlands Papua New Guinea, with Particular References to the Wiru People of Southern Highlands Province," *Oceania*, 61 (1991), pp. 309–39. We can also cite Deborah Battaglia's study: "Projecting Personhood in Melanesia: The Dialectics of Artefact Symbolism on Sabarl Island," *Man*, 18 (1983), pp. 289–304.

61 Marilyn Strathern observed some time ago that "the value put on womanness is not necessarily to be equated with value put on women," in "Culture in a Netbag," *Man*, 16 (1981), p. 676. See also, by the same author, "Subject or Object? Women and the Circulation of Valuables in Highlands New Guinea," in R. Hirschon (ed.), *Women and Property, Women as Property* (London, Croom Helm), pp. 158–75. And of course her most important book, *The Gender of the Gift* (Berkeley, University of California Press, 1988).

62 Malinowsky explains how long it took him to understand why "ugly, useless objects" were for Trobriand Islanders "the vehicle of important sentimental associations" which "inspire with life" and "prepare for death" (*Argonauts of the Western Pacific*, London, Routledge, 1922, pp. 89, 513–14). See also Annette Weiner's comments in *Inalienable Possessions: The Paradox of Keeping-while-Giving* (Berkeley, University of California Press, 1992).

63 Paul Bohannan, "The Impact of Money on an African Subsistence Economy," *Journal of Economic History*, 19, 4 (1959), pp. 491–503. And especially, Paul Bohannan and Laura Bohannan, *Tiv Economy* (Evanston, Northwestern University Press, 1968).

64 Cf. Christopher Gregory, *Gifts and Commodities* (London and New York, Academic Press, 1982).

65 The importance of textiles, of the mats used to wrap statues of the gods and sacred objects, is attested in other parts of the world, in Polynesia, for example, among the Maori (A. Weiner) and on Tonga (F. Marsaudon). Archeology and ethnohistory tell us that this was true as well in the Inca empire and in the earlier great Andean civilizations. See Annette Weiner and Jane Schneider, *Cloth and Human Experience* (Washington, Smithsonian Institution, 1989); John Murra, "Cloth and its Function in the Inca State," *American Anthropologist*, 64, 4 (1962), pp. 710–28; Françoise Marsaudon, "Nourriture et richesse. Les Objets cérémoniels comme signes d'identité à Tonga et à Wallis," unpublished manuscript, 1995.

66 See Pierre Maranda and Elli Köngäs Maranda, "Le Crâne et l'utérus. Deux

théorèmes nord-malaitais," in *Échanges et communications*, vol. 2, pp. 829–61. I thank P. Maranda for this information, which is still in part unpublished, and for his suggestion that I compare these sacred objects with those of the Catholic religion: the tabernacle containing the consecrated ciborium, the communion wafers for distribution, and the altar which, in principle, contains a relic.

67 Maurice Leenhardt, *Notes d'ethnologie néo-calédonienne* (Paris, Institut d'Ethnologie, 1930), ch. 4, pp. 47–55. It should be remembered that the value of Tlingit coppers varied according to their height and was reckoned in numbers of slaves. Cf. *The Gift*, pp. 45 and 133, nn. 242, 243, with references to Boas and to Swanton.

68 Serge Tcherkézoff drew my attention to a Samoan custom which is based on the interplay of certain oppositions I have mentioned here: that of divisible and indivisible, of profane and sacred. In Samoa, when a murderer comes to pay the price of his murder, he presents himself in a squatting position, holding in his hands stones of the kind that are heated to cook the food in the earth ovens. He presents himself as a pig that has been given to be killed, cooked, divided up, and eaten. He is wrapped in a thin mat which contains soul, *mana*, representing the divine light which, as it envelops things also gives them life. The mat is indivisible. But the pig, when it is cooked, is divided and shared out. Each part of its body has a name and goes to a given person according to rank. The pig belongs to the category of *oloa*, the mat to the category of *tonga*. Cf. S. Tcherkézoff, "La Question du 'genre' à Samoa. De l'illustration dualiste à la hiérarchie des niveaux," *Anthropologie et sociétés*, 16, 2 (1992), pp. 91–117, esp. p. 101. See also Daniel de Coppet, "La Monnaie, présence des mots et mesure du temps," *L'Homme*, 10, 1 (1979), pp. 2–39; Cécile Barraud, "Des relations et des morts. Analyse de quatre sociétés vues sous l'angle des échanges," in J. C. Galey (ed.), *Différences, valeurs et hiérarchie. Textes offerts à Louis Dumont* (Paris, École des Hautes Études en Sciences Sociales), pp. 421–521.

69 James Carrier, "The Gift in Theory and Practice in Melanesia: A Note on the Centrality of Gift Exchange," *Ethnology*, 31, 2 (1992), pp. 185–93. In New Caledonia today, the black and white shell "moneys" are worth between 1,500 and 8,000 Pacific francs (in 1997, 1 Pacific franc equaled approximately $0.98). In Samoa, the finest mats are worth thousands of dollars and their value can only increase with their age. In many Pacific Islands societies, people had little difficulty understanding what could be done with European money, with the exception of alienating ancestral land, selling it for money. To obtain white men's money, they had to sell (at a very low price) their labor – which they had not previously done among themselves – or sell products that the Europeans wanted to buy from them (copra) and which the Europeans themselves had often introduced, such as coffee or tea.

70 Malinowski, *Argonauts*, p. 211.

71 Malinowski, *Argonauts*, pp. 187–8.

72 Bernhard Laum, in his major work, *Heiliges Geld – eine historische Untersuchung über den sakralen Ursprung des Geldes* (Tübingen, Mohr, 1924), cites Jeremias' work on the ancient Orient (1913). A. Jeremias showed how, in Babylonia, metals symbolized the gods: gold stood for the Sun, silver for the Moon, copper for Venus, etc. (*Handbuch der altorientalischen Geisteskultur*, Leipzig, J. C. Hinrichs, 1913, p. 86) Laum's theses did not fail to arouse a number of reservations and readjustments, for a coin stamped with

a state seal cannot be explained uniquely by reference to religious beliefs as the principal origin. There had already to be a developed city-state, and economic and, above all, political relations which forced religion into a new place in society, centered on the political sphere and the law, in order for the first coins bearing a state seal to appear in Western society. Cf. Eric Will, "De l'aspect éthique des origines grecques de la monnaie," *Revue historique*, (October–December 1954), pp. 209–31: "Although Laum exaggerated in turning his back on the demands of economic life, however rudimentary, it is certain that the rationalism of modern economists is unable to account for the most original features of Greek civilization" (p. 214). See Alban Bensa, "Présentation de Bernhard Laum," *Genèses*, 8 (1992), pp. 60–4. Émile Benveniste, in *Le Vocabulaire des institutions indo-européennes* (Paris, Éditions de Minuit, 1968), vol. 1, pp. 132–3, showed that the English verb "to sell" comes from the Gothic *saljan*, which meant "to sacrifice an offering to a deity," and that the verb "to buy" came from the Gothic *bugjan*, "to redeem, to buy someone out of slavery." Thus in Europe, too, as in Melanesia, money was the equivalent of a life.

73 Marcel Mauss (*The Gift*, pp. 100–2, n. 29), replying to Malinowski and to Simiand, who had criticized him for his "lax" use of the notion of money, writes: "On this reasoning, there has only been economic value where there has been money, and there has only been money when precious things, themselves intrinsic forms of wealth and signs of riches, have been really made into currency, namely, have been inscribed and impersonalized, and detached from any relationship with any legal entity, whether collective or individual, other than the state that mints them. But the question posed in this way concerns only the arbitrary limit that must be placed on the use of the word. In my view, one only defines in this way a second type of money – our own" (p. 100, n. 29). See Mauss, "Origine de la notion de la monnaie," *Anthropologie* (Institut Français d'Anthropologie), 3, 1 (1914), pp. 14–20. In the same perspective, see Jean-Michel Servet, *Numismata. État et origines de la monnaie* (Lyon, Presses Universitaires de Lyon, 1984).

74 The original French version of this book was already finished before the publication of Philippe Rospabé's *La Dette de vie. Aux origines de la monnaie* (Paris, La Découverte and MAUSS, 1995). This is the book of a sociologist, very well documented particularly in the area of Melanesian ethnography and the ongoing debates among anthropologists. His conclusions converge with my own, but the book lacks an analysis of objects that are not given, of the sacred things that are the very source of the meaning of the precious objects which circulate as payment for a life or a death (bridewealth, compensations, etc.).

75 Michel Panoff, "Objets précieux et moyens de paiement chez les Maenge de Nouvelle-Bretagne," *L'Homme*, 20, 2 (1980), pp. 6–37.

76 In this respect, one cannot help being surprised that Mauss, who was acquainted with these phenomena, could write, concerning the Trobrianders' vocabulary of exchange, which he described as a "somewhat childish legal language" (*The Gift*, p. 30): "One cannot credit the extent to which all such vocabulary is complicated by a *curious incapacity to divide and define,* and by the strange refinements of the nomenclature" (p. 31). He even speaks of the inability of the legal systems in the "whole area of the islands" "to isolate and divide up their economic and juridical concepts," and he compares these systems with Germanic law, which he sees as demonstrating the same inability (p. 32). Curiously, as though to correct an overly Eurocentric

judgement, he adds: "But they had no need to do so [to isolate and divide]" (p. 32).

Chapter 3   The Sacred

1 C. Lévi-Strauss, *Introduction to the Work of Marcel Mauss* (London, Routledge and Kegan Paul, 1987), p. 56.
2 Marcel Mauss, "Esquisse d'une théorie générale de la magie," in collaboration with Henri Hubert, *L'Année sociologique* (1902–3); reprinted in *Sociologie et anthropologie* (Paris, Presses Universitaires de France, 1950), p. 119.
3 Mauss, "Esquisse d'une théorie générale de la magie," p. 123, and again: "Owing to the notion of *mana*, magic, the domain of desire, is replete with rationalism."
4 All of Lévi-Strauss' writings concerning the analysis of Amerindian myths and, more broadly, the study of the forms and processes of the "savage mind," i.e. thinking "in its savage state," have yielded fundamental findings, new perspectives which every one of us, not only the ethnologists, should incorporate into our own work if we want to go forward. But it is not hard to show that these studies and their results do not substantiate the famous theses proposed in *Introduction to the Work of Marcel Mauss*. On the contrary, they show that indigenous symbols and concepts are not signifiers in their pure state, that the way symbolic thinking proceeds, and its use of metaphor and metonymy are an attempt at an imaginary totalization and explanation of the order which reigns in the universe, or which should reign in society. My criticisms are therefore not directed at these analyses and will never bring us to neglect or underestimate their achievements. They are aimed at the philosophical formulas on which they are purportedly based.
5 Alain Testart adopts the same prudent attitude in the opening pages of his book *Des dons et des dieux* (Paris, Armand Colin, 1993), when he writes, "the worst definition of religion one can find is probably that which equates it with a belief in one or several gods" (p. 17).
6 Mauss, *The Gift*, p. 16.
7 Michael Bourdillon and Meyer Fortes (eds), *Sacrifice* (New York, Academic Press, 1980), p. 82.
8 Testart, *Des dons et des dieux*, pp. 27–9. Nevertheless, we do not agree with this author when he says he is "struck by the very obvious correlation between absence of sacrifice and the stateless character of a society." This is an overreduction. Likewise for the claim that "Melanesia has never practiced sacrifices" (p. 29).
9 See Marcel Détienne and Jean-Pierre Vernant, *La Cuisine du sacrifice en pays grec* (Paris, Gallimard, 1979), and on the myth of Prometheus, who stole the fire which separated men from the gods.
10 Many fine studies have been published on the societies in New Guinea which worship Afek. They are localized in the Star Mountains region, where the Sepik and Fly rivers rise. See in particular: Barry Craig and David Hyndman (eds), *Children of Afek: Tradition and Change among the Mountain-Ok of Central New Guinea* (Sydney, Oceania Monograph, 1990), especially ch. 5, written by Robert Brumbaugh: "Afek Sang: The Old Woman's Legacy to the

Mountain-Ok," pp. 54–87; Dan Jorgensen, "Taro and Arrows: Order, Entropy and Religion among the Telefomin" (doctoral dissertation, University of British Columbia, 1981).

11 We are most grateful to Lorenzo Brutti for this information, which was collected for the first time in August 1995. I give a succinct account here which does not do justice to the complexity of the material, but it already shows how important it is for our knowledge of these societies and, on a more general level, for reflection on the relationship between religion and society.

12 *The Gift*, p. 17. And, referring to his "Essai sur le sacrifice," Mauss adds: "It is perhaps not a result of pure chance that the two solemn formulas of the contract – in Latin, *do ut des*, in Sanskrit, *dadami se, dehi me* – also have been preserved in religious texts." But that contracts between humans are sacred, covered by the authority of a religion, does not mean that men's exchanges with the gods can be *reduced* to a contract.

13 James Fox, "The Movement of the Spirit in the Timor Area: Christian Traditions and Ethnic Identities," in James Fox (ed.), *Indonesia: The Making of a Culture* (Canberra, The Australian National University, 1980), pp. 235–46.

14 Andrew MacWilliam, "Prayers of the Sacred Stone and Tree: Aspects of Invocation in West Timor," *Canberra Anthropology*, 14, 2 (1991), pp. 49–59.

15 In the Afek rite we have just described, in which a man is sacrificed to restore the land's fertility, the children (the sons) of the victim used to be killed so that they might not later avenge their father's death.

16 The studies on ancient Egypt and on sacred kingship are countless. One of the most recent we consulted is that by Marie-Ange Bonheux and Annie Fargeau, *Pharaon. Les Secrets du pouvoir* (Paris, Armand Colin, 1988). But some of the earlier works are still useful and, for certain points, irreplaceable. Particularly, Henri Frankfort, *Kingship and the Gods* (Chicago, University of Chicago Press, 1948) and his edited volume, *Before Philosophy* (Chicago, Pelican, 1949). In *Kingship and the Gods*, Frankfort wrote:

> The ancient Near East considered kingship the very basis of civilization. Only savages could live without a king. ... But if we refer to kingship as a political institution, we assume a point of view which would have been incomprehensible to the ancients. We imply that the human polity can be considered by itself. The ancients, however, experienced human life as part of a widely spreading network of connections which reached beyond the local and the national communities into the hidden depths of nature and the powers that rule nature. ... Whatever was significant was imbedded in the life of the cosmos, and it was precisely the king's function to maintain the harmony of that integration. (p. 3)

17 Maurice Godelier, "L'État: les processus de sa formation, la diversité de ses formes et de ses bases," *Revue internationale des sciences sociales*, 37, 4 (1980), pp. 657–70; *The Mental and the Material* (London, Verso, 1986), pp. 179–207.

18 Charles Malamoud, "Théologie de la dette dans les Brahmana," *La Dette*, special issue of the journal *Purusartha* (Éditions de l'École des Hautes Études en Sciences Sociales), 1990, pp. 39–62; "La Dette au texte: remarques sur la dette constitutive de l'homme dans la pensée de l'Inde ancienne," in *De l'argent à la dette*, special issue of *Cliniques méditerranéennes*, 33–4

(1992), pp. 37–47; Gérard Toffin, "Hiérarchie et idéologie du don dans le monde indien", *L'Homme*, 114, 30 (2) (1990), pp. 130–42.

19 Charles Malamoud, "La Scène sacrificielle: observations sur la rivalité du mythe et du rite dans l'Inde védique," *Psychanalystes*, 41 (1992), pp. 19–33. All of Charles Malamoud's publications have been of most valuable help and leave me in a state of "perpetual debt" to this author. See also an earlier work published in collaboration with Madeleine Biardeau, *Le Sacrifice dans l'Inde ancienne* (Paris, Presses Universitaires de France, 1976).

20 The true man must also make gifts to the Brahmins, and, while the latter are obliged to accept these gifts, they may not reciprocate. The gift will be returned through the impersonal mechanism of *karma*, in which each person's fate is determined by all of his earlier lives, by all past actions. Cf. Thomas Trautmann, "*The Gift* in India: Marcel Mauss as Indianist," lecture given at the 36th meeting of the Society of Asian Studies, 1986. Trautmann shows that Mauss, who knew Sanskrit and was acquainted with the major sources, particularly the Mahabharata, recognized the full importance of the gift in ancient India, but had underrated the religious principles which codified the practice. Cf. *The Gift*, p. 147, n. 61: "Concerning the main subject of our analysis, the obligation to reciprocate, we must acknowledge that we have found few facts in Hindu law. Even so, the most apparent fact is the rule that forbids reciprocity. ... The cunning Brahmins in fact entrusted the gods and the shades with the task of returning gifts that had been made to themselves." A most "Voltarian" explanation.

21 Malamoud, "Théologie de la dette."

22 See on this subject, Jean Bottéro, in particular, *La Naissance de Dieu, La Bible et l'historien* (Paris, Gallimard, 1986) and *Babylone et La Bible* (Paris, Les Belles Lettres, 1994).

23 The translator has used the Jerusalem Bible, reader's edition (Garden City, Doubleday and Company, 1968).

> You must not lie with a man as with a woman. This is a hateful thing. You must not lie with any animal, you would thereby become unclean. A woman must not offer herself to an animal, to have intercourse with it. This would be a foul thing [in another translation "an abomination"]. Do not make yourselves unclean by any of these practices, for it was by such things that the nations that I have expelled to make way for you made themselves unclean. The land became unclean; I exacted the penalty for its fault and the land had to vomit out its inhabitants. But you must keep my laws and customs, you must not do any of these hateful things, neither native nor stranger living among you. For all these hateful things were done by the people who inhabited this land before you, and the land became unclean. If you make it unclean, will it not vomit you out as it vomited the nation that was here before you? Yes, anyone who does one of these hateful things, whatever it may be, any person doing so must be cut off from his people. (Leviticus 18: 22–9)

In the French edition, the author quotes from the Bible d'Alexandrie, with introduction and notes by Paul Harlé and Didier Pralon (Paris, Éditions du Cerf, 1988).

24 Translated from the text translated and commented by Gervais Dumeige, in *La Foi catholique* (Paris, Éditions de l'Orante, 1993), p. 6.

25 "As they were eating, Jesus took some bread, and when he had said the

blessing he broke it and gave it to the disciples. 'Take it and eat,' he said, 'this is my body.' Then he took a cup, and when he had returned thanks he gave it to them. 'Drink all of you from this,' he said, 'for this is my *blood*, the blood of the *covenant*, which is to be poured out for many for the forgiveness of sins. From now on, I tell you, I shall not drink wine until the day I drink the new wine with you in the kingdom of my Father' " (Matthew, 26: 26–9).

26 Thomas Aquinas, *Summa Theologica*, Complete English edition in 5 volumes, translated by the Fathers of the English Dominican Province (Westminster, MD, Christian Classics, 1981) vol. 3, p. 1521, Q.80 Pt.II.

27 Sigmund Freud: "We are thus prepared to find that primitive man transposed the structural condition of his own mind into the external world; and we may attempt to reverse the process and *put back* into the human mind what animism teaches as to the nature of things" (*The Standard Edition of the Complete Psychological Works of Sigmund Freud*, translated under the general editorship of James Strachey, in collaboration with Anna Freud, assisted by Alix Strachey and Alan Tyson, vol. 13: *Totem and Taboo and Other Works*, London, Hogarth Press and the Institute of Psychoanalysis, 1953, p. 91). Karl Marx: "It is, in reality, much easier to discover by analysis the earthly kernel of the misty creations of religion than to do the opposite, i.e. to develop from the actual given relations of life their corresponding heavenly forms" (*Capital*, vol. 1, Harmondsworth, Penguin Books in association with New Left Review, 1976, p. 494).

Chapter 4   The Dis-enchanted Gift

1 See p. 6.

2 In fact, in "Taboo and the Perils of the Soul" (1911), which is the second part of *The Golden Bough*, devoted to the "magician king in primitive society." This is an expanded version of the article "Taboo," which Frazer wrote at the behest of Robertson Smith for the *Encyclopaedia Britannica*, 9th edn (1886).

3 Kaempfer, *History of Japan*, cited by Frazer in *The Golden Bough: A Study in Magic and Religion*, abridged edn (London, Macmillan, 1963), pp. 222–3.

4 Frazer, *The Golden Bough*, abridged edn, p. 222.

5 In other societies, Africa for instance, the anchor point, the fulcrum from which to move the world, the king, is condemned to remain *totally invisible*. In the ancient kingdom of Abomey there were two kings: a visible one, who acted in broad daylight, was surrounded with respect, but was a false king, a stand-in for the true king, who remained invisible. As an Abomey saying goes, the true king "has no eyes, cannot see ... has no mouth, cannot speak ... all he perceives is 'good'." Commenting on this saying, Marc Augé adds: "Everything is done in order that the sovereign body, the physical manifestation of the king, be increasingly identified with this stone-like indifference" (*Le Dieu objet*, Paris, Flammarion, 1988, p. 131). Ultimately the true king might even not exist. But it would perhaps be asking too much to base a kingdom on the mere *idea* of kingship, without a king, true or false, for the people to see. Behind all of these cultural choices lies the universal problem

of how to represent the unrepresentable, the inexpressible. Unlike Christianity, which has chosen to represent God the Father as a majestic old man with a white beard, Islam has always rejected any such anthropomorphism. Cf. Jack Goody, "Icônes et iconoclasme en Afrique", *Annales ESC*, 6 (1991), pp. 1235–51.

6 Frazer, *The Golden Bough: A Study in Magic and Religion*, 3rd edn (New York: St Martin's Press, 1990), part II: "Taboo and the Perils of the Soul," ch. 1: "The Burden of Royalty," Part 1: "Royal and Priestly Taboos," pp. 2–3, n. 2.

7 With the support of a few anthropologists like Ruth Benedict, who had never been to Japan, but who had made a study, for the Office of War Information, of "Japanese Behavior Patterns" (report 25), which she carried out on Japanese living in the United States. The report was made into a book, *The Chrysanthemum and the Sword* (1946), which was immediately and has remained a huge success. See the new edition of the French translation (Paris, Picquier Poche, 1996) with a preface by Jane Cobbi, who recalls the context and assesses the impact of Benedict's theses.

8 Cited by Eric Seizelet, *Monarchie et démocratie dans le Japon d'après guerre* (Paris, Maisonneuve and Larose, 1990), pp. 143–217.

9 The young "United States of America" were the first to realize this marriage, at the end of the eighteenth century, when they ceased being a British Crown colony and became a "republic," unencumbered by the presence of ancient Western forms of ownership, production – feudal or other – as was the case in Europe. Before these "free," enterprising Westerners, lay an immense, untouched country that was empty, and empty because they were emptying it as they drove before them the former inhabitants, the Indians, who today have either vanished or are living on "reservations."

10 To use the happy expression of André Petitat in "Le Don: espace imaginaire, normatif et secret des acteurs," *Anthropologie et sociétés*, 19, 1–2 (1995), p. 18, special issue entitled "Retour sur le don." André Petitat unites his efforts with those of Alain Caillé and his colleagues at the journal *MAUSS* (efforts to which I would like to pay tribute here) to criticize utilitarianism and once more to make room in life for relationships, and non-commercial principles of thought and action.

11 Mauss, *The Gift*, p. 75.

12 *The Gift*, p. 65. Mauss is quoting a sura from the Koran: Sura II, 265.

13 It was perhaps this sublime desire that made Jacques Derrida write, in his book *Donner le temps* (Paris, Galilee, 1991): "Ultimately, the gift as gift should not appear as a gift to the receiver or to the giver" (p. 26). "In this sense, the gift is the impossible. Not impossible but the impossible. The very figure of the impossible" (p. 19). The true gift, then, would be the gift given by someone who, without reason, gives without knowing that he is giving to someone who would never owe him anything because he would not know that he had been given something. Even Christ had a reason for giving his life. He gave it out of love for mankind. It is understandable that, having analyzed gift-giving from this angle, Jacques Derrida considers that he has entirely parted company with tradition and especially with Mauss, of whom he writes: "One could even venture to say that Marcel Mauss' monumental book, *The Gift*, talks about everything but gift-giving: he deals with economy, exchange, contracts, one-upmanship, sacrifice, gift, *and* counter-gift, in short with everything in the object which drives one to give *and* to cancel the gift" (p. 39). "One is reduced to wondering, in sum, what and

who Mauss is talking about" (p. 41; translations made for this edn; italics in the original). The task of deconstructing an object in order to make it more intelligible before reconstructing it on the basis of new hypotheses is here carried to absurd lengths because, in the end, the deconstructed object has been entirely dissolved.

Index

~∞~

index by Timothy Penton